"*Going Public* is truly unique. It is embodied sexual
violence scholarship that brings 'the personal is political'
and 'the political is personal' to life. Macfarlane's critical
reflections on her own victimization, survival, resistance,
advocacy, and activism are central to her insight and legal
analysis. The result is simultaneously painful, inspiring,
challenging, demoralizing, empowering, and practical,
with recommendations for changes to civil and criminal
law and institutional approaches for dealing with sexual
violence. A must-read."

> CHARLENE Y. SENN, professor and Canada
> Research Chair in Sexual Violence, Department
> of Psychology, and Women's and Gender Studies,
> University of Windsor

"This is a memoir, manifesto, an honest *cri de coeur* all
wrapped in one of what sexual violence and abuse does to
women, and it must be read by all who seek justice, truth,
reforms of a distorted legal system, and accountability
for institutional cover-ups. *Going Public* is a page-turner
of truth, bravery, persistence, and morality by a leader
of reform in the justice system. How she sought, and
eventually gained, some small modicum of justice as she
moved from legal professional to activist litigant is an
extraordinary story."

> CARRIE MENKEL MEADOW, distinguished
> professor of law, University of California, Irvine and
> Georgetown University Law Center (Emerita)

"Professor Julie Macfarlane provides a fascinating and in-valuable insight into civil litigation involving sexual abuse claims and modern rape trials. Her openness and courage in disclosing her own experience of sexual abuse and her fight to improve institutional responses demonstrate a moral courage of awe-inspiring dimensions."

JENNIFER TEMKIN, professor of law, City University of London

"Few victims are brave enough to lay matters out in a comprehensive way, especially to strangers, no matter how genuine and interested those people are. I salute Dr. Macfarlane's understanding that a book written not from an academic perspective, but a personal one, will be incredibly illuminating and help other victims understand that they are not alone."

WAYNE BARKAUSKAS Q.C., family law lawyer, mediator, and parenting coordinator

"Julie Macfarlane dedicated her career to improving access to justice in Canada. After breaking her silence, Macfarlane's personal search for justice will inspire readers. *Going Public* is more than a #MeToo memoir; it is a call to action to fundamentally change institutional responses to sexual violence.

> MANDI GRAY, activist and subject of the documentary *Slut or Nut: Diary of a Rape Trial*

"This book resonated with me both personally and professionally. We have many examples of institutions failing survivors, but only now are we starting to formally document the stories of complainants who have experienced institutional betrayal after reporting and the acute effects it has on their lives. It is time that we speak frankly about these issues in all their complexities out in the open instead of behind closed doors. Dr. Macfarlane is helping us do just that."

> CONNOR SPENCER, national chair of Students for Consent Culture Canada

GOING
PUBLIC

Julie Macfarlane

GOING PUBLIC

A Survivor's Journey from Grief to Action

Between the Lines
Toronto

Going Public
© 2020 Julie Macfarlane

First published in 2020 by
Between the Lines
401 Richmond Street West
Studio 281
Toronto, Ontario M5V 3A8
Canada
1-800-718-7201
www.btlbooks.com

All rights reserved. No part of this publication may be photocopied,
reproduced, stored in a retrieval system, or transmitted in any form
or by any means, electronic, mechanical, recording, or otherwise,
without the written permission of Between the Lines, or (for
copying in Canada only) Access Copyright, 69 Yonge Street, Suite
1100, Toronto, ON M5E 1K3.

Every reasonable effort has been made to identify copyright
holders. Between the Lines would be pleased to have any errors or
omissions brought to its attention.

Cataloguing in Publication information available from
Library and Archives Canada
ISBN 9781771134750

Designed by DEEVE
Printed in Canada

We acknowledge for their financial support of our publishing
activities: the Government of Canada; the Canada Council for the
Arts; and the Government of Ontario through the Ontario Arts
Council, the Ontario Book Publishers Tax Credit program, and
Ontario Creates.

Dedicated to all the women and girls who are holding on to a secret about sexual violence. I hope this book affirms and strengthens you to step forward when you are ready.

If you ever feel lonely, just remember you are doing this for a whole community.

—Dr Jo-Anne Lewicki

It just amazes me that I can be part of the energy it takes to serve each other.

—Carole King, "One"

CONTENTS

PREFACE

I grew up in England in small rural communities during the 1960s and 70s, my early education in a two-room island schoolhouse. I am now a professor of law at a Canadian university and have worked all over the world. The stories told in this book take place in England and in Canada as well as Hong Kong and Australia.

For most of my academic career, I have focused on issues and topics that reflect my curiosity in people's experiences of the law and the legal system. I am especially drawn to understanding the experiences of individuals and groups who do not see their needs and interests met in the legal system, whether because of poor processes, dominant cultural assumptions, or the hostile use of power against them. Two such groups are North American Muslims and self-represented litigants. I have researched, written, and spoken all over the world about how conflict and injustice are addressed formally by the courts and informally inside communities and families. I have a longstanding interest as a legal educator in how lawyers can be effective in advocating and assisting people to have access to just processes and outcomes. My research over the past thirty-five years has focused on gathering data that fills a gap—how disputants experience mediation and other conflict resolution processes; what is important about religious, cultural, and legal processes in ending marriage; why people represent themselves in court with lawyers—and then disseminating that information to the public and raising public awareness. Some of these projects have had an impact on public consciousness, conversation, and policy.

As a teacher and researcher, I have always sought to connect personal experiences—those of my students and of my research subjects—to a better understanding of social phenomena. I am convinced that scholarly research and analysis can, and should, play a critical role in deepening public discourse over the issues we study. I have described this as "academic activism," and it has been a motivating theme throughout my life and work.

MY PERSONAL STORY AND A LEGAL ANALYSIS

This book is different from anything I have written before. While far from a traditional memoir, it places some of my formative personal experiences inside the frame of legal analysis. I have written a number of books in which others were the research subjects; in this book I am, in part, the research subject. My personal experiences of sexual violence and abuse as a child, teenager, and young woman are described in an effort to do what I have long done with materials external to myself—reflect, analyze, and gain insight about their meaning and consequences. If you are reading this and have your own experiences of sexual violence and abuse you should be aware that there are detailed descriptions of these experiences in this book. My goal is to affirm and inspire you but this book might also upset you. Please take care of yourself.

My personal disclosures in this book also carry more explicit activist motivations. I know how hard it is to talk openly about experiences of rape and sexual assault, and it has taken me four decades to reach this stage in my own story. I believe that acknowledging experiences like mine that are shared by vast numbers of silent others is an important step toward a more compassionate, nuanced, and realistic public discourse over sexual violence.

This book describes my journey from victim to change agent and the lessons I have learned along the way. It's a journey that covers decades—most of my life in fact—during which I have started my family, developed my career, moved around the world, and found many ways to do the work I love. It also reflects my belief that we do our best work when we bring all of ourselves to the job. That includes the ugly, nasty bits of our history as well as our skills and talents.

Written from the perspective of both a survivor of sexual violence and a legal scholar, this book offers an insider understanding of our flawed legal and workplace processes and the impulse to institutional protectionism. But it also explores how these can be challenged and changed. The changes that I believe are required for legal processes to enable access to justice for victims of sexual violence reflect my personal experiences as a conflict process specialist, survivor, an activist and advocate, and a legal expert. The worlds of activism and scholarship are often kept apart, but in this book my personal experiences, academic insights, and work as an advocate inform one other. My legal training has expanded my knowledge and confidence, and my experience as an activist has sharpened my ideas about change. We often try to separate the personal from the professional and the political from the academic. I have learned over and over that this is a false and disempowering dichotomy.

My goal is to develop the beginning of a blueprint for future activism on sexual violence, distilled from my own failures, successes, insights, frustrations, conversations with other survivors, and legal training. Changing societal attitudes toward sexual violence begins and ends with changing the entrenched culture of disbelief and denial. It is this culture that sets the context for every narrative in this book and that is finally being challenged by the #MeToo movement. For centuries, misogyny and prejudicial treatment toward women have been broadly tolerated, even celebrated. If you believe this is a bygone era, remember that the United States recently elected a president who openly bragged about sexually assaulting women. This book is about how we challenge each of these dimensions of sexual violence, and what change would mean for a society that is committed to respect and safety for women and girls.[1]

CHAPTER 1

PRIVATE GRIEF

I was born in 1958, and by the time I was twenty-four years old, I had four times experienced violent sexual assaults. First as a child, an older boy attacked me and tried to rape me in my woodland playground; then as a teenager, I was sexually abused for a year by my church minister; at college, I was date-raped and became pregnant; and then I had an eighteen-month-long violent domestic relationship. For decades, I buried my memories and my feelings about what had happened to me.

I carried on with my life, as if none of this had happened. As if it were normal. I dealt with none of the impacts. For most of my twenties, I pushed my memories of sexual and physical violence as firmly as I could manage to the back of my mind, focusing on building a career as an academic and a life among friends and colleagues, who were for the most part not connected to this past. If asked, I most likely would have expressed content with my life.

Then in 1986, my personal life went through a major upheaval. I found myself accidentally pregnant by a man I had been dating on and off for about eighteen months. Initially very anxious, the day I collected a positive pregnancy test I experienced an extraordinary rush of clarity. I would raise this child on my own. I was ready to be a single mother.

My baby daughter and I lived in a tiny flat along with our dog. It was a testing time in many ways. After paying the mortgage and for a nanny to take care of my daughter while I was at work, we had little left over from my pay cheque. I was always exhausted. But I was deeply, truly happy. I loved my little girl. I loved being a mother. I could do this—I had no real idea how, but I found that my instincts, with input from my girlfriends, usually more or less worked. I was fortunate that my daughter was extremely tolerant about being my parenting experiment, willing to sleep anywhere I took her and in constant good humour. Once she could speak, she was always happy to tell me what she needed and to give me advice on how to take care of her (she still does). I was a little slapdash in the hygiene department—one of my girlfriends used to come over each day and rewash the baby bottles and teats, finding my standards far too low—but my daughter survived and eventually developed a great immune system. The support and love of my friends, especially my women friends, was a gift beyond price in these years.

When my daughter was a little less than a year old, I started to work with a psychotherapist. I felt better able now to begin to face some of what had happened in the past. Gradually, as I shall describe in this book, I began to come to terms with the meaning and consequences of what happened.

MY STORY

My first terrifying encounter with sexual violence was as a child of four or five. I lived in a rural community on the Isle of Wight, a small island off the south coast of Britain. I loved to play in a small wooded copse about five minutes' walk away from my home. Sometimes I played there with other children; sometimes I was alone. I remember dragging a child-sized desk and chair all the way from my bedroom up to the copse one afternoon and setting up my first office in a small leaf-filled hollow in the ground in the middle of the woods.

One day I was playing there alone when a teenage boy I recognized from my village grabbed me, forced me down on the ground, pulled off my pants, and tried to vaginally penetrate me. As I write this, I can recall with clarity the pain of the branches and twigs on the forest floor pressing into my bare bottom and back. I can still feel his penis as he shoved it inside me.

It was sunny and had been a lovely day. I think it must have been the weekend because I remember my father was home. As I tried to tell my mother what happened, I sat on her lap. We sat looking out into the backyard of our house. I groped for the words to describe what had happened to me. What should I call this boy's "thing"? What was the name for my "thing"? Somehow, in what I am sure were heartbreakingly graphic, childish terms, I managed to describe what had happened. The freedom and adventure of my childhood had collapsed in an instant into terror.

About a decade later, as a teenager, I was a member of an Anglican church congregation in the town of Chichester, where we now lived. At thirteen and fourteen, looking for meaning, I got caught up in the Billy Graham evangelical excitement and become a Jesus person. I joined an Anglican church and continued to practise as a Christian. By sixteen, I began to have doubts about my faith. I went to my church minister for advice. He met with me in his private study, as his children (whom I sometimes babysat) played in an adjacent room. That day was the first of a series of repeated sexual assaults over the next year. The minister forced me to give him what I much later understood to be oral sex, telling me to get down on my knees in front of him in the study. He said that this was what God wanted and it would help me resolve my doubts. He then harassed and stalked me in my home town until I left to go to university, almost twelve months later. He showed up regularly at my home, offering to take me out for driving lessons. No matter how many excuses I came up with, my mother always insisted that I go with him ("so kind of the minister!"). He would expose himself to me and masturbate or force me to give him oral sex in the car, in remote country lanes, on isolated beaches, in hayfields. He would lie in wait for me as I walked home from my Saturday job as a dishwasher in a restaurant—the short cut home went through a dark alleyway—and grabbing me, he would roughly rub his body against me over my clothing.

I escaped, with inordinate relief, to attend university on the other side of the country in 1976. Eighteen months later, I was date-raped at a university event by a friend (I thought) who played on the men's basketball team (I played on the women's). I had helped him back to his dorm as he had been drinking heavily and I was worried he would not make it unassisted. I opened the door and pulled him inside the room. As soon as the door swung shut, he tossed me on to the bed, climbed on top of me, and ripped off my dress, easily pinning me. He was more than a foot taller than me and weighed at least fifty pounds more. I was nineteen years old and became pregnant as a result and had an abortion. I never told the rapist, nor confronted him with the fact that he had raped me.

I just stayed away from him for the rest of the year, at the end of which he returned to the United States.

Then in 1981, two years after my graduation from university, I fell back into a horror story. I met a charismatic older man who persuaded me that we should move to Ireland together. This was to be my first cohabitation experience and I was excited about my new life. Once we arrived in Ireland, he began almost immediately to physically and sexually assault me. This began with intermittent episodes of violence, eventually escalating into almost daily assaults. My friends were hours away across the Irish Sea, and I was trapped with no idea what was happening to me and with no one to turn to for help. For eighteen terrifying months I lived with him in a cottage outside Cork, Ireland—a remote location, without a telephone— where he beat me and sexually assaulted me with increasing ferocity. I tried leaving twice or three times, going to a hotel for the night, but I had no one to tell my story to, and each time I returned, terrified he would track me down and kill me anyway.

I had just been appointed as a junior professor in my first academic appointment and was thrilled by the rush and deep satisfaction of teaching for the first time. I lived a bizarre double-life between this nine-to-five world and the terror that engulfed me at home (all the other hours of the day). There he burned me with cigarettes, choked me unconscious, tied me up and raped me, suffocated me with pillows, and submerged me under water in the bath. He told me the violence was all my fault, and incredible though it sounds, I believed him. For a year and a half, I was alternately terrified for my life and convinced that the violence I was subjected to was the result of my own failures. Eventually my desire for life won out. One night I finally ran in my nightclothes down the country lane we lived on and threw myself on the mercy of a horrified neighbour.

I was twenty-four years old. It was International Women's Day, 1983. I had just snatched back my life.

Today, I don't think about my experiences of sexual violence as especially unusual. Many girls and women have suffered through one or more abusive experiences. With the wisdom of hindsight, I can now see that each experience set me up for the next by further diminishing my self-esteem and my confidence in my ability to take care of myself. This is a common pattern. Research suggests that the chances of being sexually assaulted rise exponentially after the first incident,[1] especially if it took place during childhood and the victim learned to keep silent.[2]

Also, in common with other women, I experienced many other commonplace sexual violations, often in workplaces and sometimes in social settings. Compared with being raped or forcibly sexually assaulted, being kissed against my wishes or even having parts of my body touched without giving permission seemed relatively minor, trivial even. I do remember feeling like I must be some sort of catnip for the older men who hired me into part-time jobs—retail, grounds maintenance—as a high school student. They didn't seem to be able to keep their hands off me, but perhaps that was my fault, I thought. I lived by my wits (don't go alone back into the storeroom when the manager is around, don't go into the boss's office to return the complex keys, just open the door and drop them on the floor) and tried to both keep my job and keep the predator at bay. No big deal. In hindsight I can also see that I carried my relative privilege as a white middle-class girl with me into all these situations. This probably protected me from the most extreme behaviours I might have faced if I had been further marginalized and vulnerable.

Despite my privilege, I knew I had no route to complain or fight back. That was unimaginable. As I now look back at these years of violations, I recognize that my peers and I did not talk about these everyday experiences. We did not share them even with our best friends, fearing the shame of being "the only one" who experienced such behaviours. We certainly did not share them with our families; I knew with certainty that if I described to my mother having been grabbed and groped at work that this would lead rapidly to her telling me I was a slut who must have been "leading him on." Our mothers carried the rape myth too. Even today, many of the deepest and most useful conversations I have about sexual violence are ones I have with much younger women, for whom the topic is at least less taboo than it was for myself and my peers.

I have a strong memory of an attempt at a sharing conversation with my then-best girlfriend after our first sex education lesson (I went to an all-girls high school). I was about twelve or thirteen. We had been shown anatomical diagrams of human reproduction on the overhead projector in the chemistry lab. It had just hit me like a thunderbolt that what the boy in the woods had been trying to do to me was to have sexual intercourse with me, to rape me.

I remember standing outside the classroom after the class trying to tell my friend, "that happened to me." She either did not understand or was just freaked out, both understandable reactions. The conversation petered out and we went on to our next class. I remember feeling terribly lonely and terrified that I had done something disgraceful, irredeemable. And perhaps something that I could talk to no one about?

It was at least ten years after I left my home town of Chichester before I told anyone about what the minister had done to me there from 1975 to 1976. I revealed only fragments to a couple of my closest girlfriends. I told just one person, my friend John, about my rape by the university athlete. I didn't tell anyone else about that rape—or name it as such—for many, many more years. Only my two closest girlfriends (the same ones I told about the minister) knew that I had lived in an abusive domestic relationship in Ireland; everyone else thought that it just didn't work out with the guy.

I didn't come anywhere close to telling anyone the whole story in those days. I never really allowed myself to think about this explicitly, but I was terrified that if anyone actually knew and connected all the parts of this odyssey, this crazy nightmarish litany of abuse, they would conclude that I was one messed-up, disgusting person. As well, these stories would reveal how close I had come to being lost, to them, to me. I could not imagine telling people who loved me this.

While the silence and secrecy in which I wrapped my experiences was not unusual then, the hard truth is that it is still not unusual now. Certainly the advances of the #MeToo movement have begun to lift the suffocating shame that surrounds personal experiences of sexual violence, finally making it possible for women and men to speak up about assaults and violations. But outside privileged places like Hollywood, many still will not do so for the same reasons that I stayed silent for so long. It's still a lot easier to hold on to our secrets. Because we cannot talk about this, we remain isolated in our shame and fear, and do not reap the benefits of collective support and solidarity.

As continuing revelations about sexual violence by well-known and powerful men unfold in the media, the same questions are being asked either implicitly or explicitly in each story that is told.

Did the victim understand that what was being done was sexual assault? Why didn't the victim report immediately? What are the narratives that survivors of sexual violence tell themselves as they are coming to terms, often over decades, with what has happened to them and who is to blame?

To try to understand better why so many of us struggle with personal disclosure, such as reporting and seeking redress, regarding sexual violence, the rest of this chapter will take a deep dive into how I understood and processed my experiences at the time they happened, and over the ensuing years. Because I was not talking about it, it was a conversation with myself. I asked myself louder and more insistently over time, what did these experiences tell me about myself? Had this happened to anyone else? What was holding me back from talking about it? I didn't know the answers to these questions because I did not share my experiences with others. What eventually made it possible for me to speak up? And what has that journey been like?

Throughout the years I shall describe, I enjoyed a great education with many friends and a growing ability to make a living. My race and class gave me plenty of advantages. Yet I struggled.

I hope that my account helps to illuminate both the pressures to stay silent that are still faced by many survivors and the impact of unresolved—undisclosed, unacknowledged, unprocessed—abuse.

UNIVERSITY

England is a small country, but Durham was about as far away as I could get from my home base in Chichester. This is where I went, in October 1976, when I left my hometown to begin university on the other side of the country. I was relieved beyond expression to escape from the minister, giddy even. Like many other young women living away from home for the first time, I began to have sexual relationships with men. These early experiences were not positive ones. Perhaps I was vaguely aware that some of these problems stemmed from my earlier abuse, but I did not consider this at a conscious level. I think my major feeling was that sex—promoted to us by my high school gym teacher as the eighth wonder of the world—"come on in girls, the water is lovely!"—was not what it was cracked up to be. In fact, it was unpleasant and brutish and unsatisfying.

This changed when I fell in love and had my first committed

relationship. My boyfriend was a wonderful young man, kind and loving to a fault. I never told him anything about my history before coming to university, but I credit him with my ability to find my way through those first eighteen months. But I was a fickle nineteen-year-old, and ended my relationship with John after second year, and for a few months dated other men casually. Then came the date rape. It was John to whom I ran for help that night, still in my ripped formal dress. My debt to him is immense.

In my final year at university I dated a very good man whom I remain close friends with today. I did not tell Peter what had happened to me either before or since I had arrived at university. To my shame, he learned only in early 2016 about my abuse by the minister from one of the papers he reads over breakfast, when my now-public story was picked up by the media.[3] Since then we have talked extensively about my history and both he and Alison, his wife, have been extremely supportive.

In the final year of my undergraduate program, I was also becoming increasingly aware of my anxieties around intimacy. Peter and I had massive, one-sided "arguments," during which I would cry hysterically, assailed by imagined threats and convinced of his impending betrayal, and storm off feeling completely wretched, confused, and alone. Not the confrontational type, I remember his puzzled expression when I launched these tirades, which only made me cry harder and storm louder. It would be much later in my life that I began to understand my flight or fight impulse and its connection to the emergence of my PTSD (post-traumatic stress disorder). At the time, I strenuously resisted any introspection and moved on.

The rest of my life was going well, and I seemed able to easily weather other types of challenges. I successfully completed my undergraduate work in law, despite spending a great deal more time at the athletics centre than in the law library (it was not even close); I rejected the idea of a legal career and made a ceremonial bonfire of my law notes and books; and I spent my first two years post-graduation alternately working as a residential social worker and travelling. Hopelessly unqualified as a social worker, I lucked out with some excellent mentors and tried my best to at least give my clients love and support. I also spent five amazing months backpacking across Africa with ex-boyfriend John, including journeying by truck across South Sudan as it lurched in and out of civil war in 1979 to 1980. It was an incredible experience. And without the pressure and expectations of being anyone's girlfriend I had an easy, contented, conflict-free relationship with my travelling companion.

On my return from Africa in 1980, enchanted by what I had seen and learned on that continent, but sick with malaria and a parasite, I briefly reunited with Peter. A few months later I met the man with whom I moved to Ireland the following year. I had no sense when we left England with our belongings packed into my car—a bright yellow classic 1980s Citroen Dyane—that I was about to enter a nightmare of violence and abuse. For the first six months I worked minimum wage jobs, including one in a grocery store where I tried to organize the non-union labour to protest working conditions and found myself expelled to a tent ("Santa's Grotto") in the parking lot with Santa. This provoked some reflection on what I was doing with my life and, amazingly, with the support of a former professor now teaching there, I found a position teaching law at University College Cork. First as a part-time adjunct and then as an assistant professor with a full-time contract, I managed to begin my career as a law professor. I carefully wore long sleeved shirts and jackets to hide bruises and burns on my arms from constant physical assaults by my domestic partner, and he in turn was careful not to mark my face. Each evening I drove home from the university, through the beautiful Irish countryside to our remote cottage, feeling like I was going crazy, to be terrorized and assaulted, but with no other plan.

I resurfaced in the summer of 1983.

COPING

Back in London, surrounded by friends, I was determined to get my life back on track. Superficially, this was easy—from the outside I looked like a confident young woman who, unlike the generation of women before me, saw no barriers to what I wanted to do or could become. I kept my secrets close. To most of my friends I just said that it didn't work out with the guy in Ireland (I guess that was true). No one asked any more questions.

Something kept me constantly moving forward, looking for the future I so desperately wanted to feel optimistic about. I had many friends. This was the time in my life when I began to understand how much I cherished my friendships with other women, but even with my two closest girlfriends I confided only snippets of the stories and vague references to my experiences of abuse. Both were kind and loving, but we never took the conversation very far because none of us knew how to have it, and to me it felt way too scary.

I was on the cusp of a career as an academic, loving the work I was doing in the classroom and as a researcher (the beginning of my lifelong love affair with interviewing people), and as an activist for children's rights and reproductive rights. There was often uncertainty about where next month's rent would come from or even where in the world I might be next month—my jobs in those days were short-term contracts. I had a constant nagging anxiety about money and brief panic attacks when utility bills arrived in the mail, but I shared this in common with most of my peers. I was a naturally optimistic person and my privilege enabled me to imagine that the time would come when I would have a more stable income, instead of living from pay cheque to pay cheque. And I was living in London, the greatest city in the world! I worked assiduously on nurturing my confidently independent self so that I could live alone, vacation alone, and avoid any decisions about intimacy. In these ways it was easy, it seemed, to push my past under my consciousness and pretend that I was unaffected, my passion for life undimmed.

I was extremely careful now about whom I dated, making a promise to myself that I would never, ever again spend even a minute in the company of a man who scared me or made me fearful or anxious. I resolved that even if that seemed to be *just my* reaction, I would listen to my abuse radar. Instead of doubting my instincts, I realized that I had to listen much more carefully to them. It was not my instincts that had let me down—I had bad feelings about the church minister, the athlete, and my domestic partner early on. Rather I had not had the self-confidence to act on them and insist on a safe, loving relationship.

At the same time, I could never quite connect the four men who had assaulted me with the men I was now meeting and spending time with as friends, colleagues, and lovers. I recognized that if my history of abuse soured me forever on men, then the men who had already abused me would have somehow won. While my expectations for a happy and rewarding romantic life were not high, this didn't make me all that different from many of my equally discouraged single women friends.

Another important coping strategy, a constant throughout my life, was to immerse myself in work. One of the jobs I did in the 1980s, to supplement my meagre stipend as a doctoral student, was for an advocacy group campaigning for the abolition of corporal punishment in schools. STOPP (Society of Teachers Opposed to Physical Punishment)[4] was established to challenge the then-widespread assumption that teachers should be able to physically discipline children, "for their own good." The campaign was well underway by the time I joined as a researcher, and I was fortunate to walk on the path carved by early activists Tom Scott and Martin Rosenbaum. STOPP was in many ways a blueprint for how to run a successful operation to change minds and then the law on a tiny budget. I learned an enormous amount from my time at STOPP and still use those lessons in my work today. By 1986, we had succeeded in amending the Education Act to remove the legal defence of "reasonable chastisement" from school teachers in state schools.[5] By 1998,[6] following an earlier European Court of Human Rights ruling,[7] we would succeed in forcing the government to change the law in relation to private, fee-paying schools.

I loved my work at STOPP and remain eternally grateful to my boss—the redoubtable Martin Rosenbaum, later the director of the homeless charity Shelter and now a producer with the BBC—for teaching me everything he knew about how to mount a low-budget, high-profile, media-savvy, effective campaign out of a tiny office in Bethnal Green. We worked on the issue from a variety of angles: writing innumerable "letters to the editor" at local newspapers (pre-Internet, news print was our primary platform), doing media interviews, and responding to calls from parents whose children had come home with welts on their bottoms after a caning at school. It was obvious—both from the stories themselves and from the research literature that Martin and I stayed current on—that some of these physical beatings had a sexual dimension. This seemed to be especially often the case where the school was a residential boarding school, access to children unhindered, and the physical abuse repetitive. But in those days, no one was talking about child sexual abuse and we had no direct evidence. STOPP's work and the complaints being brought forward all focused on physical abuse.

One of the ways in which it was manifest that there was a connection between corporal punishment and sexual gratification were the letters and occasional telephone messages that mostly seemed to target me and not Martin. Not infrequently, writers and callers described in detail how they would like to beat my bottom. One morning Martin came to the office to find me sobbing at my desk after listening to a very upsetting and abusive message on the answering machine. When he discovered the source of my upset, Martin started to replay and listen to the message. He was a little taken aback when I got up from my desk, grabbed the answering machine and threw it across the room. The machine didn't work very well after that.

Looking back now, I marvel that I never consciously made the connection between this work and my own experiences of sexual abuse. It seems so obvious now, but evidently not one I was ready to make at that time. It is a striking example of how we often cope by compartmentalizing. Nonetheless, working at STOPP introduced me to advocating for the vulnerable against injustice, which was to become a driving passion of my life. What I still did not realize during those years in London was how indelible a mark sexual violence had left on my personal identity.

FLASHBACKS

Despite all this looking away, a couple of important internal conversations were happening for me. I did not share them with anyone, even though I was in and out of therapy at this time.

I spent a lot of time thinking about whether the man who abused me so vilely in Ireland was innately evil and whether there was such a thing as a "bad person." Was he a victim of his own life circumstances, some type of family or personal or socialized dysfunctionality that caused him to behave in such a monstrous way? Or was he an innately evil person whom I had had the misfortune to run into and then found it so hard to extricate myself? Were there other "bad people" out there whom I must be vigilant about protecting myself from?

I went back and forth on this. I think a lot of people who have been raped and assaulted have this debate with themselves.[8] What was my answer then, and now? I could not then and do not now accept that some people are innately evil. There are always reasons. But—and this is very important—that does not mean that they should be excused responsibility for their actions. We all have choices, however hard to make.

During this same time period I was becoming increasingly aware of my fears and anxieties about intimacy. I dated, but felt much more comfortable being single, and especially if any kind of decision-making (for example vacations, or just social decisions) was involved. I had a number of "on and off" relationships, neither monogamous nor intended to be, with a tacit understanding that there was no commitment. Although this was what I wanted at that time, it was totally dissatisfying, and I found myself less and less interested in dating. I had a pin at that time which I wore on my coat with pride: "The more I see men, the more I love my dog." My springer spaniel Thomas went everywhere with me, including the STOPP office, where he sometimes barked in the background during media interviews.

As I lived my otherwise carefree and contented life in 1980s London, I began to experience with some regularity the crowding in on my consciousness of unwelcome but vivid memories. There were some that played over and over in both my dreams and my awake mind. One of these was the three or four minutes during which I finally escaped from my violent domestic partner in Ireland. Because it was International Women's Day, I had been planning to go back into Cork City (about a forty-five-minute drive away) and attend a movie that evening with my girlfriend Mary. In fact, I don't remember ever being allowed to go to any social event without my boyfriend, and I wonder now if I really imagined that he would let me drive back to meet Mary that evening. Perhaps I was looking for a way out by provoking a confrontation.

I told him of my plans, and of course he did not allow me to leave to meet Mary. Instead for several hours he yelled at me, telling me what a terrible person I was and describing a litany of my crimes; he punched and struck me, burned me with his cigarettes, and pulled out clumps of my hair. This was a fairly routine occurrence; often these episodes would erupt out of nowhere and would last anything from two to five hours. The barrage of physical and emotional abuse would be over only when he got tired, and sometimes I was kept in a chair subjected to this abuse late into the night.

Each episode was punctuated by short periods of respite, when he would sit glowering at me but not speaking or throwing punches, just smoking and fuming. That fateful evening, when one of these "breaks" happened, I suggested I take out the vegetable compost that we collected in the tiny kitchen and empty it into the outside composter. I have thought a lot over the years about where I got the courage even to ask this, since it could easily have provoked a violent outburst. I think I must have reached the point that I knew that if I stayed with this man in this relationship, one of these nights he was going to kill me.

To my amazement, without looking up, he just shrugged and nodded. I can still see him sitting there, looking down at the ashtray and smoking his roll-up cigarette.

I knew exactly what I was going to do now. I picked up the pot we used to collect kitchen compost. My hand was shaking on the door knob as I pulled open the front door of the cottage. I tossed the compost and its pot into the darkness and I ran. Ran up the tiny, unlit country *boreen* (lane) that we lived in to my nearest neighbour, about two hundred yards away, and banged on the door. I shall never forget my neighbour's horrified expression when she opened her door to me. I was dressed in my nightclothes, clumps of hair from the assaults on my shoulders. She let me in and my nightmare was over.

Other memories that sometimes rose up in my mind threatening to overwhelm me, often at night if I was unable to sleep, were of the months of trying desperately to get away from the minister who assaulted and stalked me in my hometown of Chichester. One scene in particular appeared frequently in both my dreams and my waking consciousness—as I walked home from my job as a dishwasher at a local restaurant, taking a short cut down a back alley with my heart in my mouth, he would appear out of the darkness and grab me (this happened on a number of occasions). Like many survivors of assault, I had already developed an extreme physical reaction to any unexpected appearance or intrusion. Someone simply walking up behind me as I was preoccupied with whatever I was working on meant I would jump out of my skin. At the time I thought this was just a regular reaction that lots of people had. It would be years later that I recognized the sudden racing of my heart and profuse sweating when someone simply walked up behind me as PTSD.

There were other memories of the months I spent trying to escape from the minister that intruded on me regularly. At my parents' insistence, it was arranged that I stay overnight with him and his family at a house they rented briefly in the summer of 1976 in France, I think probably to pull off this very plan. The house was conveniently located directly on the train route he knew I would be taking back to the UK across Europe after a visit with family friends in Zurich, Switzerland. "How kind of the minister," I heard again from my mother, when I protested that I could easily travel from Zurich to home in a single shot without needing to stop overnight. I was trapped again.

I arrived at the local train station in the late afternoon where the minister collected me and drove me back to the house. After dinner, I made excuses about being tired and retired to bed as early as possible. Once in my assigned room, I moved every piece of furniture other than the bed in front of the door. Which was just as well. After everyone else had gone to bed, the minister spent a long time trying to persuade me to open the door, then trying un-successfully to push his way in. The furniture barrier held and he eventually gave up.

I had a sickeningly clear memory that began to return to me regularly of the weight on top of me of the college athlete as he raped me after our "date." We were friends because we played on the men's and women's university basketball teams. He needed a girl on his arm for his college ball. I ended up being the girl under his crushing weight on his tiny college bed. I remember leaving his room—where he had passed out immediately after ejaculating inside me, and I had to push his unconscious body off me—and going directly to wake up my friend John, banging on his door in the early morning hours. I told John that I thought I was pregnant because the athlete had not used protection, and I was at the point in my monthly cycle when I was most fertile. I was correct; I was pregnant.

Perhaps the most haunting and painful memory of all that replayed over and over in my head during those years, and still sometimes today, was of sitting on my mother's knee and telling her about what had happened to me in the woods. The sensation of twigs and leaves pressing into my bare back as the boy who as-saulted me pulled down my underwear and got on top of this small child. His penis pressing into me between my legs—I can feel that still. As I tried to tell my mother what had happened later that same day, I had no idea what it was that I was struggling to describe, but I was aware that it was a *bad* thing because the older boy had told me to "tell no one." I was a child unsure of whether to tell, but feeling somehow that I should, and wondering, would I be in trouble?

I remember my mother's visceral, physical shock. I was still sitting on her knee, and she flinched as my words came tumbling out. I still cannot imagine how terrible it was for her to hear this story. But she quickly pulled herself together. She told me that the boy who had done this, who in a very small community was easily identified, was "very naughty." I still didn't know if it was my fault, although my parents did seem angrier with the boy than with me.

I never talked to my parents about this again and, except for a vague memory of a mention of consequences for the boy, they also never spoke of it to me again. It was as if it had never happened. I don't recall any new restrictions on my movements. As a young child I roamed freely through the woods behind our house and I am sure would have chafed at any limits. I think my parents assumed— wishfully—that I had forgotten the whole incident. But of course, I had not.

TRIGGERS

It was during these years in London that I first came to realize that graphic and disturbing scenes from my earlier experiences that I had otherwise completely switched off, were seared into my memory and could overwhelm me at unexpected moments. As I browsed in Liberty's department store in Regent Street London one day in about 1986—I think I was sheltering from the rain, I certainly had no budget for shopping at Liberty's—I saw a spool of the same patterned fabric that my domestic partner in Ireland had regularly used, in the form of a scarf, to tie me up before raping me in our bed. Feeling nauseous and with my hand over my mouth, I ran from the store. This was my first experience of a trigger reaction, and I felt humiliated and ashamed. I had no idea what was happening to me. I could not make sense of this with my rational brain (the one I preferred). Why would this obscure detail return to me? And what other details lay as yet unawake inside my head, which might leap out at me without notice and cause me further embarrassment? Was there something actually *wrong with me?*

I had a fair share of unexplained rages and emotional melt-downs during these years with whomever I was dating. Since I was not committed to any of these men I dealt with my embarrassment in the aftermath of such a scene by moving on. I also experienced a number of brief but gut-churning panic attacks when I thought I saw my Irish domestic partner as I travelled in London by bus or tube.

It would be another decade before I recognized that sometimes my emotional and physical reaction to an apparently trivial event or interaction was very inappropriate and made the connection to PTSD. The first time this realization dawned on me was in the mid 1990s, and I had just moved to a new home in Kingsville, Ontario. It was springtime, and everyone was out doing yard work after the winter. A man was working on trimming my next-door neighbour's trees, one of which was growing over the fence between the two properties. Naturally and reasonably, he hopped over the fence between the two properties, tree clippers in hand, to trim the branches hanging down over our side of the fence. I was also out working on the garden. When I saw him on our side of the fence, I became hysterical, completely losing control. I still remember vividly how this felt. I felt threatened, violated even by this man who had come into my yard without my permission. I have no idea how long I screamed at the poor man, but at some point my then-husband came and escorted me away. I spent the next few hours curled in a fetal position inside the house, unable to explain to him why this had happened and feeling completely alone.

This was the first time I can remember being completely traumatized by an innocent and mundane event that, in hindsight, must have been a PTSD trigger for me. My reaction was outside my control and an irrational, out of all proportion response to an equally out of proportion feeling of intense fear and threat. It was an awful feeling and still is. What helps me now is my capacity to understand and anticipate many of the triggers and my response to them. In those early days I just felt like I was going crazy.

WHY I DIDN'T REPORT

There is an abiding assumption, often repeated in public discourse, that if a sexual attack has occurred then the victim or her parents would *obviously* report this to authorities. This is a misplaced and erroneous belief which is painful for survivors to hear.

My parents never, to my knowledge, reported the attempt to rape me to local police. Such a thing would have been very unlikely in the 1960s, based solely on the word of a very young child. Truthfully, I am not even sure we had any local police; this was a very small and isolated island community with few services. I have a memory of my mother telling me that my father angrily confronted the boy's father and told him that "he would go to prison if he did it again." I had no idea what that meant but knew it must have meant that what happened was really bad. Did that mean that I would go to prison too?

For decades, I didn't even consider reporting the abuse by the Anglican minister after he abused me, despite the fact that the abuse took place on dozens of occasions, and I had detailed memories of when, where, and how. It's hard to separate out all the reasons why. I think that the most important were a combination of shame, confusion, and a fear that I would not be believed. At the time of the abuse, I believed the minister to be a man of God. When he first told me that I should kneel in front of him and put his penis in my mouth, I had never seen a man's penis before. An authority figure to me, he told me that God wanted me to do this and that this action would somehow help me to resolve my doubts. Was it true that God wanted me to do this? He seemed so certain, so confident.

The disconnect between what he made me do with him in private and his public role left me confused, terrified, and ashamed. As far as I knew, in the years after I left home, he was a minister still, holding a position of authority and power. Who was I to challenge this? He seemed so unafraid of detection in his overt behaviours and in some of what now seem preposterous public acts—stalking me around Chichester, lying in wait for me in the dark, showing up regularly at my home to take me for "driving lessons," and "losing" his swimming trunks in the water while swimming with me at an empty beach. Did that mean that he was really doing nothing wrong? Or just that he was supremely confident that I would never tell anyone?

It was many years later that I realized that the sexual act he repeatedly forced on me had a name, fellatio. Yet the more sexual experience I had, the more disgusted I felt about what he had done to me, and the more terrified of disclosure. I'm not sure which felt worse—the idea that I would not be believed if I were to tell anyone this story about a man of God, or if I were believed, what would that person think of *me*?

When I was date-raped in 1977, I don't think the word "rape" even entered my mind as a description of what had happened to me. This wasn't my boyfriend; the college tradition was that a guy without a girlfriend would prevail upon a friend to be "arm-candy" for his college ball, as it was apparently unacceptable to go alone. Sex was not part of the deal; arm-candy duty did not even class as a date. At the end of the evening, he was so drunk that I was afraid he might not make it back to his room without help, so I escorted him back there. The instant we stood inside the room, he pinned me to his bed, raped me, and then passed out. But the word "rape" did not occur to me, not for years. Why not?

In the 1970s and 1980s we did not attach the word "rape" to sexual attacks by people who knew one another. It would be 1991 before the law in England recognized that a man could rape his wife.[9] My peers and I had zero consciousness about sexual consent. Girls of my generation who went, as I and many others did, directly from an all-girls high school to a co-ed residential college had no preparation for the morass of sexual consent issues we were about to face. No one talked to us about sexual relationships, consent, boundaries, or how to ensure our personal safety. I cannot imagine how much devastation and distress was the result, with my own date rape just one example.

Researchers describe a pattern of normalization of abusive sexual behaviour in groups such as university dorms or fraternities, or among a peer group. Victims may trivialize their experiences of sexual violence as minor, unimportant, or in some way "normal."[10] Not reporting is a conflict avoidance response. It is also consistent with the prison of self-doubt that many of us feel trapped in after experiencing sexual harassment or assault.

As a university student in my second year, I was just beginning to have consensual sexual experiences. I had as yet no understanding of the dynamics of power and domination in sex. My analysis was simpler: I thought that you took your lumps when it came to encounters in dorm rooms with boys. As I told myself over and over, I should never have gone to his room in the first place. I had felt some responsibility to get him back to his college room without passing out, he was so hopelessly intoxicated. Bad idea. Stupid me. So I didn't for a moment consider reporting to college authorities or the police what he had done. I knew he had done a bad thing, but I believed that the consequences, both morally and practically, were all mine to deal with. I ran into him again a number of times after this evening at the university athletics centre, but we never spoke about the night he raped me.

I also did not even consider telling him that he had made me pregnant, or about my subsequent abortion. This was 1977, and abortion had become legal in the UK just a year earlier. Access to abortion services was far from established or straightforward. Plus, I needed to have the termination during the university holidays (I could not risk going into hospital during term-time, as someone would be bound to find out). I needed to find a doctor who would help me without too many questions asked and without my parents finding out. The solution I hit upon was practical but ironic, under the circumstances.

In high school, I had often slept over at my best friend's home. Her father, a well-known and highly sought-after local gynecologist, beat his wife, my friend's mother, regularly. She would often take refuge in our bedroom when he was drunk and violent. I had no doubt that the gynecologist would remember that I was well aware of his abusive out-of-office behaviour. I believed that he would facilitate a termination procedure for me at my preferred date because of the secret I knew about him.

I cold-called him at his office. I gave the receptionist my name and persuaded her to tell him that I wanted to speak to him. Less than a minute later, I was put through to the big man directly. I explained that I was pregnant and wanted a termination—I never even considered explaining how I came to be pregnant, and unsurprisingly he did not ask. I asked him to arrange for a termination for me in my hometown over the Easter holidays. He asked no questions and agreed. He told me his assistant would follow-up with the details, which she did a few days later when I called again from the pay phone in the stairwell at my dorm.

Having this plan in place saved me an enormous amount of anxiety and heartache. But the loneliness and trauma of both the decision and the procedure were devastating. I knew I couldn't have a baby and stay in school, and I certainly did not want this guy's baby. But as I watched my body start to change in those first three months of pregnancy, I wept for the child I could not have and longed for the one I would have at some future time in my life. And in 1977 abortion was still so taboo that I could talk to no one. This experience gave me a lifelong commitment to fighting for reproductive rights for women and girls.

I went home to Chichester from college for the Easter holiday as planned. I intended to keep my pregnancy secret and succeeded until just a few hours before leaving my parents' home. I was prepared to take myself to the hospital, where I was to stay overnight—in those days termination was an in-patient procedure. I had already given my parents a cover story about going away to London for a few days. But in those final hours, I broke, sobbing with fear and guilt, and I told my mother that I was pregnant and going for an abortion. I did not explain to her how I had got pregnant, and she never asked me. She told me she was too ashamed to come and visit me in the hospital, although she did in fact come to visit me that evening, glancing around furtively. When she drove me home from the hospital the following day, she told me that I was a slut. I didn't even consider telling her that I had been raped. She would not have believed me. I was not sure I believed me.

My biggest shame, and perhaps the most difficult to explain, is why I did not report to police the violence I suffered at the hands of my boyfriend in Ireland. I knew that this was a very dangerous man and have no doubt that he went on to violently assault other women. But I simply could not bring myself to describe his extraordinary violence to a third person. I had tried once before, about six months before I finally escaped from him. I spoke to an American woman who was visiting at the law school, imagining she might be more worldly-wise and open to hearing about domestic violence than my other, all-male, colleagues. To my horror, she responded by telling me that if I was "done" with him, she would be interested in dating him. My world collapsed in that moment. I went back to the cottage I shared with my abuser.

The night I escaped from him, I went to friends in Cork City who sheltered me in their home for a week until I could return to London for a short break. I began to make plans to find an apartment with my friend Mary, who had recently arrived from Harvard to spend a year at the law school. My Cork City friends knew of the violence and how dangerous this man was, but none suggested I go to the police. Why not? This seemed too obvious to even merit a discussion at the time. It was 1983, this was rural Ireland, and I was living with a man out of wedlock, so therefore morally culpable. I was also a manifest outsider, as a British woman living in southern Ireland in the 1980s. These friends are still close friends, more than thirty years later. They have recently pointed out to me that Irish police would probably have taken little or no interest in a call about domestic violence from me. I'm sure that is right, but my failure to even consider reporting him still fills me with shame.

I didn't report for the very same reasons I have described for not reporting in the earlier instances. Confusion, shame, and anxiety that I would not be believed or, worse, understood. I was terrified of being asked: why did I live for eighteen months with a man who regularly beat me?

But there was an important additional reason that I did not report in this case, one that is not unusual for survivors considering coming forward. I was scared to death of him. I was certain that if I reported him, he would come after me. He had often told me when we lived together that if I left him, he would find me and kill me. I believed him.

The week in Cork—the last week of the teaching term—before leaving to go to friends in London for the Easter holiday, I was in a state of constant terror. I had left our shared home with nothing other than the nightclothes I was wearing, so my friends negotiated to transfer some of my belongings back to me. In the meantime I borrowed clothes and bought some underwear. When I returned from London after the holiday, my Cork friends had arranged for him to leave my car in a street beside the law school which I could see from my office window. Inside the car were some of my belongings—clothes and books—and, by far the most important, my dog Thomas, whom I had left behind when I had fled. Walking to the car that day my brain was racing, and I was filled with dread. I could see my dog's face at the window watching me approach. I got into the car and drove away to safety.

For years after, when I returned to live in London to attend graduate school, I regularly imagined that I saw him and would break into a sweaty panic. I would see his face in the face of strangers on the tube, sitting on the bus, in the pub. It didn't seem to matter where I was—I still returned to Ireland to visit friends—but my feeling that he was around every corner was just as bad in London as it was in Dublin. To report him to authorities felt like putting myself right back in his crosshairs. I was not brave enough to do it.

MOTHERHOOD

No reporting also allowed me to pretend all these experiences were firmly behind me. Then in 1986, I found myself accidentally pregnant. I knew that the father was a colleague with whom I had been having an on-again off-again relationship. At first I was scared at the prospect of what I knew would be raising a child alone, but that passed quickly and was replaced by an unexpected euphoria. I wanted this baby. I was ready to be a parent, I thought (despite having no idea what that really meant, and knowing that).

My daughter was born in July 1987 and, from the very first moment, I was in love. It was a turning point for me. I was stretched to my limit emotionally, financially, and physically—I was always exhausted—but I was experiencing real happiness for what felt like the first time. Life was developing some clarity. I had a kid now and needed to take care of both of us (and our dog). But my optimism and belief in being able to do this kept me going, and I was doing okay.

It was a little more than four years since I had run out of the cottage in Ireland and up the lane. I knew I was doing better in a way that would help me to face the past that I had been avoiding thinking about for so long. By the time Sibyl was six months old, I began to see a psychotherapist, feeling better able now to begin to face some of what had happened in the past. Maybe.

I was coming to understand the impact of the assaults on me and how to manage some of my memories and worst triggers. My daughter was my focus, and relationships with men were pretty unimportant to me in those years. As the years had built up since my escape from my abuser in Ireland, I had slowly started to feel safer. One of the consequences was a gradually enlarging reflection about my responsibility for preventing the men who had abused me from doing the same to others.

I was particularly haunted by the thought that the Anglican minister who had abused me would continue to have access to young girls from a position of power and authority. In relation to my other assailants, there seemed less I could do. I had no idea how to find the boy who had tried to rape me in the woods. I had managed to convince myself that my former domestic partner, given his extremely violent disposition, was either in prison or dead (in truth, I was still too frightened to go looking for him). My college rapist, an American athlete, was presumably a continent away, probably married with a family by now, and I saw little purpose in going after him. But the idea that a church minister might still be forcing fellatio onto young girls and abusing his position of trust? I knew I had an undeniable moral responsibility to do something about, like it or not.

CHAPTER 2

PUBLIC DENIAL

The #MeToo movement is beginning to make a difference to our timidity and fears about stepping forward, but generations of gender-based violence require a wholescale cultural re-evaluation. Myths remain pervasive, about malicious false reporting, women as temptresses, accusers seeking fame and fortune and—the most dangerous of all—the consent myth. They play out in how victims are treated, how allegations of sexual misconduct are responded to by legal authorities and by institutions (who prefer to keep complaints away from police and courts), and in the multiple deficiencies of the systems used to process complaints and punish offenders. This means that most women are still not talking about sexual violence, even though one in three of us will experience sexual assault, abuse, or rape in our lifetime.[1]

I did not report to church authorities any of my personal experience of sexual abuse by the minister for almost twenty years, and I never reported the three other incidents described here. Why not? This is the first of a series of poorly understood realities for survivors that I shall try to explain in this book.

Historically, we have minimized and distorted the scope and impact of acts of sexual violence by men against women and girls. This has been possible because of a deeply gendered and distorted narrative about the roots of this behaviour. Challenging sexual violence requires a rejection of the underlying misogyny that permeates cultural understandings of "why" men sexually assault and rape women and girls. Many if not all of the pervasive myths surrounding the dynamics of sexual violence are based on gender fictions and stereotypes. Women are sluts who are "asking for it"; we seduce men and lead them astray (this often associated with young women or girls); we are unreliable storytellers, deceitful, even liars; we are "regretful sluts" who complain about sex with men because we did not enjoy it and now feel guilty about it. Each of these prejudices is heightened against women who already experience other oppressions and biases including women of colour, Indigenous women, gay, bi, or trans women, and working-class women.

These distortions result in a huge underestimation of both the scope and the impact of sexual violence against women and girls. They affect how we evaluate the importance of preventing violence against girls and women and how we understand the pain experienced by "women in a society that puts less value on their safety and well-being than that of men."[2] For what other crime do we accept an underreporting rate of 90 per cent?[3] Or the fact that of the less than half of the incidents of sexual assault that do get reported to police result in a charge, less than half proceed to court, and that this number is halved again for convictions?[4] These are choices we have let our law enforcement systems make.

Sexual violence is not about sex but about the use of power and domination. I don't think all men are sexual predators, or capable of sexual misconduct, but I am pretty sure that if women (rather than men) were 90 per cent of sex offenders[5] we would have a different system, and a lot more offenders would be in jail. Understanding sexual violence through the lens of power, built and sustained by misogyny, casts our understanding of sexual "consent" in a whole new light. As we see repeatedly—in my story and in the stories of others told in this book—there can be no consent where there is a relationship of power, in assaults involving men with power over their victims, whether they are professors, teachers, clerics, sports coaches, or managers.

The stories we tell reflect depressing similarities. The first is the multiple disincentives to report, including the risks we take in reporting acts of sexual violence to authorities and the high likelihood of those reports falling on deaf ears. Sexual violence is our dirty secret—we know about it, but we don't like to talk about it. So let's begin by talking about why.

WHY WE DON'T REPORT

Our stories about experiencing sexual violence are painful, ugly, and upsetting, and they are very difficult to tell out loud. Patricia

Weaver Francisco describes holding on to the story of her rape like carrying around a bomb—every time she told someone about what had happened to her, she caused a small explosion.[6] Similarly, in *The Red Word*, the narrator describes her reaction to being asked if she had been raped like this: "'Rape' (is) a sharp word, a greedy word. It (is) a double-sided axe brandished in a circle above the head. It (draws) all kinds of attention to itself."[7]

Whether a rape, a sexual assault, abusive sexual behaviour, or harassment, every narrative of sexual violence told out loud describes power being used by one person over another. It describes one person as hurt, often grievously, by the other who is the perpetrator. This framing of blame is also part of the "explosion" set off in the recounting.

For years before I made my decision to "go public" about my personal experiences of sexual assault and abuse, I had tried to pluck up the courage to speak about this to friends. I would make a plan to do so. For example, when a story about rape or sexual assault was in the news that I anticipated might open up a conversation on this topic, I would choose to meet in safe spots like our homes or private booths in a restaurant or a bar. I would even rehearse what I was going to say. But over and over again, I felt like the words were literally stuck in my throat. I could not force them out. I often felt like a giant rock was pressing on my chest, constricting my breathing. I just couldn't do it.

I am accustomed to speaking up about difficult issues, and in my professional life I frequently address audiences who are not supportive of my arguments or positions. I have for decades worked as a mediator on high-stakes conflicts that are often volatile and emotional. I do not feel anxious or intimidated by these situations; I just want to do the best job I can. Yet I could not talk to *my friends* about my personal experiences of sexual violence. Why not?

If I could compellingly challenge just one narrative about sexual violence with this book, it would be the pervasive and misguided belief that if someone experiences rape or sexual assault or harassment, "all" they need do is "just" report it to authorities. And that if they do not, or delay, then nothing really happened. The persistence of this myth means that we do so much less than we need to encourage survivors to report and to understand the many barriers and disincentives they face. I want you to understand that *no one in their right mind* would make up a story about sexual violence and report it to authorities. There are about a million better ways to get rich and famous.[8]

Let's look at the recurring themes in the experience of reporting sexual violence. When survivors are asked about the hardest part of telling our story—and perhaps, why did we wait until now to tell it?—we talk about the same barriers, over and over again.

Shame and self-blame

If disclosure to friends is an emotional minefield, reporting to a stranger or a person in authority who may show little or no empathy is even harder.

We are scared of being disbelieved or dismissed. We wonder how we will feel when we see this disbelief on the face of the person we are telling, or hear it in their clipped responses and follow-up questions. Speaking to a figure in authority about a private traumatic event is almost always painful and intimidating. So much rides on it: a sense of self, a reaching for justice, and a determination to stay silent no longer. The shame we feel about having been the object of someone's gross and invasive behaviour floods back as we try to describe what happened. At some level we have each internalized the domination—and the deep sense of personal shame—inherent in all acts of sexual harassment and assault. As well, telling our story challenges social taboos about talking openly about sexual violence. Complainants reporting their own experiences place themselves in a very vulnerable position. And once the words are out, there is no taking them back, no matter how undesirable the reaction is. The bomb just went off, and there are no re-takes.

Multiple studies attest to the barriers to reporting sexual violence. The first and most obvious is the deep personal shame and embarrassment of the victim.[9] This sense of personal shame reflects entrenched societal norms about "bad girls" who are sexually assaulted or harassed. I know from personal experience that telling a survivor of child sexual abuse "it was not your fault" does not dispel the feeling that surely we must have done something wrong or bad to now be in this situation? I struggled with this feeling for many years, and it persisted long after my adult brain understood the power dynamics of child sexual abuse.

In a revealing study for the Department of Justice[10] based on interviews with survivors of both child and adult sexual abuse, Melissa Lindsay reports that adult sex abuse survivors are almost twice as likely to feel shame as child survivors.[11] This means that it gets harder to report as we get older, and that shame is a learned, socialized response to being a victim of sexual violence. The older we get, the more we worry about how others will judge us, something I, and I know others, struggled with for many years before "coming out" as a survivor. I can easily relate to the blogger who describes how for years she was held back by a fear of "not wanting people to judge me or look at me differently."[12]

Karen Weiss[13] writes about how the shame experienced by survivors of sexual violence is often exacerbated—intentionally or unintentionally—by questions from a person to whom they report that imply that they were responsible in some way for the attack:

"Were you flattered that he was showing you so much attention?"

This reinforces the tendency to assume some blame:

"I was stupid to go into his room"

"Could he have interpreted my listening politely to his stories in the break room as my being interested in him sexually?"

"Should I have said something earlier, like that day he said he liked my dress? I just thought it was creepy and did not want to confront him, but maybe he thinks I led him on?"

To minimize what happened:

"He is harassing me, but should I just ignore it? Is it really that bad?"

And even to take personal responsibility:

"We had sex when I was drunk—I didn't want it, but isn't that partly my fault? I am sure I said no, but just how loudly and how many times? Did I fight back hard enough?"

These and similar self-blaming statements stem from the cultural expectation weighing heavily on women and girls that they need to "take care of themselves" and be self-sufficient. As another student blogger poignantly put it: "How many times (do students) think 'I know better' the next morning as they process their feelings of violation?"[14] In these ways, girls and women continue to be imprisoned by a narrative that they are the temptress—the slut—who is the culpable party.

Other research suggests that many women do not understand their experiences as rape and struggle to recognize that an "offence" has taken place,[15] even where the facts are apparently clear. Giving an unwanted sexual experience a label such as "rape" or "abuse" often provokes feelings of embarrassment and confusion.[16] In *The Mockingbirds*, Daisy Whitney's book about a campus rape and its consequences, Amy has sex for the first time but can remember nothing about it (she was drunk). Her first instinct is to feel shame, embarrassment, and also regret—this is not what the first time was supposed to feel like. Her older sister, Casey, sees it differently. Amy tells Casey, "I had sex. Twice, evidently. So it was a stupid hookup. So I'm a slut." Casey says: "It sounds as if he had sex with you while you were sleeping. Alex, it sounds like he raped you."[17] Such confusion continues even when the victim is a law student—in a survey of law students, familiar with the legal definition of rape and assault, 13 per cent said that they were "unsure" at the time whether an experience they were now anonymously reporting as non-consensual was sexual assault.[18]

For many years after my date rape at college I had a hard time labelling my experience as rape. He pushed me down, ripped off my dress, and penetrated me, all without saying a word. Yet it took me years to privately and then publicly call this rape. Why?

No one will believe me

Another consistent fear for those of us considering reporting sexual violence is that we simply will not be believed and especially if we are younger female targets of sexual predators. Anyone seen as more powerless—a person of colour, a trans person—will find their credibility challenged even more. There are many reasons for a listener to resist an account that describes someone with institutional status and power as a rapist, harasser, or abuser. They may be afraid of personal consequences and of damaging the institution's reputation. Accepting the narrative of abuse and domination requires the listener to accept that the perpetrator has done something very bad indeed. It's easy to see why not believing a complainant is a far easier course.

This anxiety resonated through the experiences of the high school students who tried for years to convince their school principal and superintendent that their wildly popular dramatic arts teacher was abusive toward them. They felt powerless, and they were. For many years, rumours had swirled around the charismatic teacher of dramatic arts at a Windsor high school. This teacher was seen as a local "superstar" by the school board and many in the local theatre community and credited with making or breaking the careers of the young aspiring actors attending his program.

But talk of a darker, abusive side to the teacher's "techniques" was widespread. Few students were brave enough to speak out, other than anonymously. Even where parents heard tales that made them uncomfortable—rehearsals going late into the night, foul language directed at students, sudden angry outbursts and bizarre punishments, and inappropriate physical contact with students sometimes captured on social media—they for the most part ignored these and remained fans of the teacher they hoped would make their child famous.

The controlling abuse that students in the program later detailed in writing was verbal, such as "you are a piece of shit," "bitch," "retarded." It was emotional, such as degrading and ridiculing students in front of others, frequently reducing them to tears; telling students they were "not allowed" to date other drama students; telling young women what they should wear to look "sexy"; keeping students until midnight at weekday rehearsals and insisting they not leave to get food or to go home. Occasionally it was physical, including not only inappropriate physical contact with female students but also throwing chairs and pulling students' hair. There were also signs of sexual relationships with student "favourites" who were sent personal text messages, sometimes in the middle of the night. At the same time, the drama teacher constantly threatened to quit the program if students did not tell him that they loved him.

When I reported these allegations to the school board superintendent, he told me that he would not take any further steps until he heard directly from a student complainant who would attest to a sexual relationship. The barriers to a high school student, flattered and enamoured by the attention of her charismatic teacher, acknowledging a sexual relationship with him (now her parents would know) set the bar impossibly high. Students reporting on a "popular" teacher also faced hostility and backlash from those students who idolized him and gave him the adulation he demanded in order to be one of his "chosen ones." At this time I reached out to several young women whom I knew and asked if they would talk to me confidentially about the drama teacher—they all said no. They were all afraid. Students who made complaints were shunned by other students.

In the Lindsay study,[19] one in five survivors said they did not report because they felt they would not be believed. This was my assumption at sixteen years old when my Anglican church minister began to sexually assault and stalk me in my hometown. Why would anyone believe such an extraordinary story about the reverend? Compounded with my personal shame at what it was he was doing to me, this conviction kept me silent for many, many years. My experience is echoed by many other survivors of clerical abuse who have come forward more recently,[20] the girl gymnasts who trained with famous sports doctor Larry Nassar at Michigan State University,[21] and the women who for years experienced but did not report the sexual aggressions of media darling Jian Ghomeshi to the Canadian Broadcasting Corporation or their university internship programs.[22]

The false reporting myth

Beyond not being believed and being dismissed, some women find themselves publicly accused of lying, and especially when reporting to police authorities.[23] There is a growing trend of sexual predators suing for defamation those speaking out personally and on behalf of others, claiming that they are lying. This a power play to face down and silence both whistleblowers and survivors who want to report.[24]

There is an extraordinarily pervasive and stubborn myth—reinforced by both classic and contemporary stories[25]—that women lie and make false allegations about sexual assault and rape. This myth is further reinforced by the stereotype of women looking to "destroy" the life of the person whom they falsely accuse. A closely related myth assumes that any delay in making a formal complaint multiplies the likelihood that the report is false. These fly in the face of our growing understanding of the dynamics of sexual violence. Like myself, many survivors need years, if not decades, to come to terms with their own experiences and begin to even consider taking the risk of disclosure and reporting.

The stereotype of women as malicious liars has a long history. Misogyny is acted out both in literature, as illustrated in this thirteenth century quote, "What she cannot get, she seeks to obtain through lying and diabolical deceptions"[26]—and in art.[27] By the fifteenth century, the idea of women as innately untrustworthy and meddling in "evil arts"—resulting in women being murdered as "witches"—was well established.[28] Women lie about sexual violence, the stereotype tells us, because they are "regretful sluts,"[29] whose subsequent complaints are acting out their regret at having had sex and their abdication of personal moral responsibility. Even if this historical context did not already exist, the treatment meted out to women who stepped forward to describe assaults by (for example) Donald Trump, Bill Clinton, Roger Ailes, Bill O'Reilly, Clarence Thomas, Jian Ghomeshi, and other public figures makes fear of being represented as a liar well-founded. A Google search of "Christine Blasey Ford," who testified that a nominee for the United States Supreme Court, Brett Kavanagh, participated in an attempt to rape her at a high school party, shows up her repeated online moniker: "rape liar Christine."[30] The women who came forward to accuse Bill Cosby, many of whom alleged assaults from years and even decades earlier, also faced down many public attacks on their credibility and integrity,[31] as did those coming forward to complain about sexual misconduct by US Senate candidate Roy Moore.[32]

The belief in widespread false reporting in cases of sexual assault and rape is completely contradicted by a large and consistent body of empirical data. In fact, false reports of rape and sexual assault are extremely rare, demonstrated by official statistics kept by law enforcement agencies in many countries. Consistent estimates are that only 5 to 8 per cent of reports are categorized as "false," but numbers drop further again when cases not pursued—but in which it is assumed an assault did take place—are separated from those believed to be false. A meta-analysis of US studies shows that where complaints judged as "baseless" (meaning the reported incident does not meet the legal criteria for a crime, but is presumed to be truthful) are separated from those judged "false" (the reported incident never happened), so-called "false" reporting falls below 5 per cent.[33] And of course the "never happened" cases are still the result of a subjective judgment on the part of a police officer who may be holding on to his or her own "rape myths."

Police charging practices in sexual assault cases are a startling reflection of the pervasive nature of rape myth. A 2016 *Globe and Mail* study[34] into police handling of sex assault claims by 840 Canadian police forces found that there is a national "unfounded" rate—cases considered to have insufficient evidence to proceed to charge and prosecution—of almost 20 per cent. Cases are deemed "unfounded" cases—and figures vary widely between regions and forces—by individual police officers, a judgment informed by their personal assumptions and biases. In theory, an "unfounded" classification does not mean the victim is lying or that their rape did not happen, but that the decision-maker believes there to be a poor chance of conviction. Deciding that a case cannot be pursued is not supposed to mean that the complainant is a liar, but the "unfounded" classification plays into the false reporting trope. "What does unfounded mean to you?" asks criminologist Holly Johnson. "What does unfounded mean to anybody? It means 'You're lying.'"[35]

One woman who reported a case to police described to me her reaction on being told—after months of silence—that her complaint was "unfounded."

> It was really hard to hear that . . . as soon as she (the policewoman on the case) told me that they're not even going to lay a charge— that really hit me. I think that has impeded my process of healing and accepting what has happened to me.[36]

The problem is circular; the myth of false reporting is sustained by prejudicial discretionary decision-making that disregards the reality of reporting barriers and disincentives and casts suspicion on all women who report sexual violence.

Consent mythology

Myths about consent play into the idea of women as both liars and regretful sluts, now looking to absolve themselves of responsibility. Understanding that "no means no," and that an absence of yes also means no, is not a complicated idea. Anyone with sexual experience can recognize this. Yet it is over the mechanics of consent that we see the most intense battles being fought in the struggle to bring our thinking into line with the lived experience of sexual abuse and assault.

My favourite metaphor for sexual consent comes from Thames Valley Police in the UK. Here is my summary of their excellent on-line video, which analogizes consent to a cup of tea.[37]

> If you ask someone if they would like a cup of tea and they say yes, then you know they want a cup of tea (unless by the time you have boiled the kettle and steeped the tea they have fallen asleep. That is annoying, but unconscious people don't drink tea). If they say "umm I'm not sure," then you can make them a cup of tea but if they don't drink it, don't make them drink it. And if they say right upfront "no thank you, I don't want tea," don't make them tea and don't make them drink it, and don't get annoyed with them for not wanting tea. Even if they told you last week that they liked tea, that was then and this is now. Finally, if they are already unconscious, don't ask them if they want tea. Unconscious people can't answer a question about whether or not they want tea.

A defence of consent is a standard strategy in sexual assault complaints, widely used to intimidate and humiliate women who report sexual violence. In my own civil case for sex abuse against the Anglican Church, the church claimed that when the minister forced me to give him fellatio at sixteen—my first sight of a man's penis, telling me that "God" wanted me to do this—it was consensual. The actual words used in the church's statement of defence were that this sexual assault on me was "not unwelcome."[38] These words are burned forever into my consciousness. The claim is absurd and repulsive but that does not stop it being humiliating and deeply shaming, playing into all my fears about my own unworthiness as a consequence of these assaults.

Consent is used especially often as a defence where the victim is over the age of consent and the abuse was protracted. In fact such cases lay bare the complex dynamics of power in abusive relationships where consent is impossible.

Dawn and her husband had been active church members for many years in their small town, first in the Baptist church. After Dawn met the local Anglican minister at a funeral, he immediately attached himself to her, calling at her home and telling her she would be welcome at his church. Once Dawn joined the Anglican church, he encouraged her to come to him for spiritual counselling, saying it would help her to get over her "Baptist mentality." They began to have regular weekly sessions. Dawn opened up to him about her history of childhood sexual abuse and challenges in her marriage. Dawn says: "I told him all of this because I believed with my entire being that I was safe with a man of God. I believed that he was the safest for me."

The minister gradually and relentlessly began to press Dawn into a sexual relationship with him. He started to follow her and show up at her workplace. "One day he called to say he had been thinking of me and had something to drop off. Soon after he was standing at my door holding a brown paper lunch bag. He told me to take the bag and open it up in private. I immediately ran to the bathroom, locked the door and opened the bag. Inside was a Gerber baby jar that he had ejaculated in. That's what he meant when he said he had been thinking of me. I flushed it down the toilet. I couldn't believe what I had just seen."

One of the places the minister forced sexual relations on Dawn was the church. Dawn recounts: "I told him . . . this is my safe place, this is where I come to worship. He insisted and got on top of me. I told him no! I said I was scared . . . but he wouldn't stop and I finally gave in."

This exploitative relationship, with Dawn continuously saying no and the minister constantly forcing sex on her, continued for ten years. Then Dawn and her husband moved to a different city, and the minister wanted phone sex. He said she should leave her husband. Finally, Dawn started to see a professional counsellor and told her the story of her relationship with the minister. "She told me that I was being sexually abused by my priest . . . He was breaking his fiduciary duty and that I needed to take this to the police." When the police would not act, Dawn brought a civil suit against the Anglican Church and the minister for sexual assault. Despite this minister's history of such exploitative relationships and harassment, the Anglican Church argued (of course) that there was "consent." Eventually, but only after making Dawn go through years of litigation and complete traumatic discoveries, the church settled with her for an undisclosed amount.

It is difficult to think of any high-profile cases in which the defence does not claim that the women who was assaulted or raped gave their "consent." Just as with the ministers who assaulted both myself and Dawn, claims about consent are a cruel and twisted rationalization of an act of power. In our courts, this fictional world has even included the assertion that it is impossible to force a woman to give a man fellatio, because instead she should bite off his penis.[39]

Seriously?

Reprisals

There is also the real possibility of reprisal against those who raise complaints about sexual misconduct. Some of the first athletes to raise concerns about lack of protocols around sexual abuse at USA Gymnastics have stories of being banned from their training facility and left off the team.[40] Accounts from women about failure to advance in their workplace (or termination) after whistleblowing about sexual harassment are legend.[41] In these and other cases, the significance and impact of reprisal is exaggerated by the self-promoting reputation created by the abuser, for example leading young gymnasts to believe that they might lose their chance to compete at the Olympics, or drama students to believe that their chance at future fame was at stake. Of course, in a competitive environment the stakes for making a complaint are even higher. There have been many sickening and well-documented stories of young actors submitting to sexual advances in order to secure a milestone role.[42]

There is also fear of future reprisals, institutional and personal. In 2013, I became aware that a faculty colleague had established a "cult" of control over many students in our law school via social grooming and threats.[43] Students who resisted his advances or simply stood outside the "cult" talked about their fear, bordering on a conviction, that if they reported the faculty member's abusive and harassing behaviour he would trash their personal reputation and make it impossible for them to get a job in law. The following statement was made by a student whom he harassed when she was considering bringing a complaint forward:

> I worry about any tactics he may employ via Facebook (either himself directly or by his "allies") to try to bully me or denigrate my reputation amongst my peers. I fear for potential harm to my reputation and my future career.

She continued:

> I continue to worry about my personal safety. I think a lot about
> future harms this type of individual may be capable of towards me
> and others close to me.

Typically the risk and significance of possible reprisal is exaggerated by the self-aggrandizing abuser. However, a predatory individual may also spend years seeking revenge on anyone who calls out their behaviours. The numerous stories of the threats and intimidation experienced by women considering calling out Harvey Weinstein, and now documented in Ronan Farrow's book *Catch and Kill*,[44] attest to this.

WOMEN FROM MARGINALIZED GROUPS

In light of these hostile and intimidating conditions, choosing not to report sexual violence is often a rational decision that is in that individual's best interests. On the face of it the possible or even probable consequences—humiliation and embarrassment, personal vulnerability, increased trauma, and damage to one's reputation—greatly outweigh the possible rewards. Especially when it appears that reporting will likely not lead to any meaningful action or follow-up.

Yet consider this—all the disincentives and barriers to reporting sexual violence described here and which are real for a white, middle-class, woman of privilege like myself are far more acute again for women of colour, poor women, Indigenous women, and trans women. Since sexual violence and redress is all about power, the more powerless or marginalized the woman reporting, the more difficult it will be for them to report and the higher the risks. The experiences of women of colour illustrate the impact of intersectionality as their gender and race make them especially vulnerable.[45] Tarana Burke, the black activist who started the #MeToo movement, cuts to the chase when she says that "the stakes are higher" in reporting sexual violence for many women of colour.[46] Simply put, there is (even) more risk of bad outcomes. Black women are seen as sexually promiscuous, an ugly stereotype dating back to slavery where women's bodies belonged to their white masters.[47] Latina women are continually sexualized and eroticized in popular culture, portrayed as the "hot senorita."[48] Indigenous women are assumed to be drunks.[49] If the man whom they are reporting is white, not only is he far more powerful than they but there is an assumption that their efforts to require his accountability are "uppity" and need to be "put in their place."[50]

Women of colour who report—or who even consider reporting—sexual harassment or assault have to anticipate that they will be treated differently to white women, in ways that impact self-worth and psychological safety and add a further burden of stress.[51] "(Y)ou live each day in a constant state of being "on guard."[52] This burden is shared by trans women, who wage a constant struggle to have their identity recognized and accepted by the world. Prejudice against trans women means their credibility may be doubted before they even say a word out loud.

Women who are not white and middle-class face the additional problem of getting public media sources to take their stories seriously. When accounts of decades of allegations about popular black artist R. Kelly began to emerge there seemed to be less interest in this case and his victims—largely black also—than in other cases involving white women.[53] Stories about white girls and women seem to be more likely to produce horrified reactions than stories about black, poor, Indigenous, or trans women being abused. We know that sexual harassment is rife in workplaces where women work for minimum wage,[54] yet mainstream media has paid far more attention to accounts of Hollywood stars who have been sexually assaulted. And of course we know that the economic consequences of reporting are much higher where a woman supports her family on her wage.

INSTITUTIONAL RESPONSES TO REPORTING

Another theme that runs throughout the stories in this book is the culture of denial and protectionism deeply embedded in institutions where sexual abuse and predatory behaviour by powerful men has long flourished with impunity. Some of these institutions are now well recognized—the Catholic Church and, more recently, Hollywood being perhaps the best examples. But there are many others, including sports clubs, residential schools, public schools and universities and, of course, other churches.

By the time the school board took action to investigate the multiple complaints from students and parents it had received and always dismissed against the high school drama teacher, it had been almost six years since I first heard stories about his abuse of students. It is astonishing what it required to eventually produce responsible, responsive action from the school board—the hours spent on phone calls and emails and meetings by parents, students, and a teacher in the same department, who took early retirement, exhausted and in despair that anything would ever be done, as well as my own efforts.[55] This second teacher also made a complaint to the superintendent, but it was never even acknowledged. She told me:

> The phrase heard constantly around the school—among students, teachers and even parents—was "nothing will be done." Eventually the students created a Facebook page, and they called it "Something Must Be Done."[56]

But I was starting to realize this was not unusual. By the time I worked on this case, I had already learned that attempts to get an institution—whether a church, a university, or a school—to provide an effective moral and practical response to complaints of sexual misconduct against a powerful "insider" typically face concerted resistance from internal officers, requiring enormous resources of personal time and energy by both personal complainants and whistleblowers. I learned this during the successful civil lawsuit I brought in 2014 against the Anglican Church, whose minister had sexually abused me as a teenager. I learned it again in 2013 and 2014 when I spent fifteen months pressing my university to act on multiple complaints of harassment and abusive behaviour by a tenured faculty member.[57] I learned it again in 2017 when my university hid behind a non-disclosure agreement and, in a classic case of "passing the trash,"[58] allowed another university to hire this individual. When I informed the new institution of the circumstances under which he left, the University of Windsor refused to tell the truth and stood by when this individual sued me personally for defamation in 2019.

So how does an institution typically respond to a complaint of sexual misconduct by one of its members—either brought forward by the victim or an advocate on their behalf? In my experience in each role, the response usually takes three parts. The first is usually deflection. Typically:

"Really, are you sure?"

There might be questions that seem unrelated and inappropriate, for example:

"How long have you two (or 'they' if I am reporting on behalf of someone else) known each other? Didn't you date at one point?"

"Poor guy, is he in love with you (her)?"

"Had there been drinking?"

This is the beginning of the second stage of the institutional response, what Amber Tamblyn calls the "interrogation."[59] There is an assumption that there must be a back and forth in which the person reporting will be questioned, often quite aggressively, and each claim taken and interrogated. Questions like these often signal that the person to whom we are reporting is unaware of the underlying power dynamics of sexual violence. It also means that if we are going to press forward, it has just become our responsibility to help them to understand these dynamics. The most direct answer to these types of questions is "why are you asking that question?" But it is usually necessary to respond to the deflection and the assumptions being made about sexual misconduct. For example:

"I believe they have worked together for two years. They dated briefly when they were first introduced." Or, "no they have never dated."

"I am not really in a position to evaluate his feelings but I am very concerned about his behaviours."

"I think there was some social drinking that evening, yes." Or, "I can only speak for the complainant and she has told me she did not have any alcohol that evening."

The third prong of the response to a complainant from the institutional actor—who is perhaps a workplace or club manager, someone in the church hierarchy—is typically a series of admonishments or warnings.

"Do you realize that these are very serious allegations?"

"I am not having a conversation about this, we have proper procedures to follow."

These questions must appear reasonable to the person asking them—working on the accepted assumption that "there are two sides to every story"—but for the person reporting they are usually upsetting, especially if they are reporting their own abuse or harassment. No one would argue that a report of sexual violence should be accepted without asking questions, and probably a lot of questions—but it is the type of questions and how they are asked that is so often problematic.

What accompanies the warning stage are usually various "requirements." Examples include:

"Nothing can be done without a corroborating witness statement" (how often does forced sex take place in front of hostile future witnesses?).

"Only a complaint of *actual sexual intercourse by the complainant herself* will be sufficient to trigger an investigation" (as I was told by the school board superintendent).

"Are you prepared to follow our procedures? If so, this discussion should end right now. Or if not, please do not take up any more of my time with these allegations."

This last point is an important and overlooked factor in designing effective institutional complaints systems. Brady Donohue has often pointed out to me that a woman reporting sexual violence will be met with an expectation that she is ready to undertake a "formal" complaint, whatever that might look like (for example, a workplace grievance, co-operate with a police prosecution, or a disciplinary complaint). In reality, most women will need time to reflect and a supportive space before they can make that decision. They probably need to speak confidentially with a counsellor and consider all the implications of bringing a formal complaint, including that her original statement will become the reference for every subsequent enquiry, so, as much as possible, she had better be emotionally prepared to do this. How can a woman know whether she wants a prosecution when she reports a sexual assault to a desk sergeant on the night of her assault? Yet if she is not ready to make a formal complaint, she is commonly immediately pre-judged as lacking in credibility.

The three-part pattern of response by institutional officers described here has been a constant in my experience of reporting allegations of sexual misconduct, assaultive behaviour, or sexual harassment to a person in authority, both my own and on behalf of others. It is interesting to interrogate the two much better experiences I have had, which are separated by fifteen years. In each case, the person to whom I was reporting (one a professional caseworker in a regulatory organization, the other a lay member of a church committee charged with investigating complaints against clergy) immediately made me feel understood, taken seriously, and that my report was important to them. They were open to hearing what I was telling them without judging me or my concerns. No one said "I believe you," but—and this is crucial—I did not need or expect that. Instead, it was sufficient that there was no default to skepticism, dismissal, or disbelief.

Encountering the far more typical and discouraging three-part pattern of response, many women then abandon follow-up or further efforts to report. These dynamics create a culture of silence around reporting or even discussing sexual violence. The difficulty of the reporting experience filters down to others inside the same institution, discouraging them from coming forward and resulting in significant underreporting and "lumping it"[60] for victims.

There is also a remarkable similarity in the ways each of these institutions compound the power of predators and abusers by hiding them "in plain sight" through resisting or throwing obstacles in front of requests for investigation and appropriate action. Sexual abuse and misconduct is itself an act of power and domination, which can only be perpetrated by those with some measure of power, whether physical, psychological, political, or resource-based. Inside an institution, this will be behaviour by insiders with power and status who are further empowered by a culture that insulates them against complaint, because any complaint upheld against them would damage the positive reputation of the institution. This is the reinforcing cycle that leads institutional complainants to often tell me: "It's hopeless. Nothing will ever be done to stop him." It is a hopelessness I have felt myself, many times.

One of the revelations of the #MeToo movement has been just how long complaints have been made against some powerful predators without any meaningful action. In cases such as that of actor Bill Cosby,[61] complaints about the conductor at the Metropolitan Opera James Levine,[62] the actor Kevin Spacey,[63] and the producer Harvey Weinstein,[64] allegations about their sexual misconduct were made for years, sometimes decades, before anyone in authority took them seriously.

PRIVATE GRIEF TO PUBLIC ADVOCACY

Aside from threats to our credibility, sense of self-worth, and personal safety in stepping forward to report, we also confront external cultural myths about women and sexual violence. Stubborn public beliefs about sexual violence surround us—so remote from the reality of the survivor experience that we feel like we are being written about in a different language altogether. These beliefs are evident in news stories to movies to family conversations to casual jokes. Part of the risk that women take when we disclose or report sexual violence lies in this disconnect between public understanding of sexual violence and our own lived experience. Reporting sexual misconduct by powerful members of powerful institutions raises yet more risks and obstacles. Internal trauma, hostile public mythology, and institutional protectionism and denial make a formidable triumvirate.

The net effect is that we treat each incident of rape and sexual assault, inside institutions or in the wider culture, as an isolated incident, as an individual issue rather than a deeply embedded cultural problem. Silence about sexual violence—because of shame, reticence, and fear—means that "the clear evidence of its pervasiveness is obscured from our collective vision."[65] The consequences of not talking are that so many of us hold on to unresolved personal pain, perpetrators escape consequences, and institutions continue to easily protect abusers, even in the era of #MeToo.

If, in contrast, we understood sexual violence as a part of our collective, societal conscience, in the same way that we recognize "the war on cancer" or "the war on poverty" as a group effort, this would change the current norms of reporting and responding to sexual misconduct. This does not require a default to believing but an absence of judging.[66] This includes the recognition that sexual violence is a phenomenon deeply embedded in both our patriarchal culture and the hierarchical structure of institutions, whether in families, churches, schools, and universities, or any other setting in which individuals exercise power. It is neither new, unusual, nor surprising.

This means moving from private grief to public advocacy. Rebecca Solnit vividly describes the 87,000 rapes in the United States as "dots so close that they're melting into a stain, but hardly anyone connects them or names that stain."[67]

Let's name that stain.

CHAPTER 3

FIGHTING BACK

In 1990, when my daughter was two and a half, my life took a new turn. I spent a semester at the University of Windsor, Faculty of Law, as a visiting professor from my UK law school. I enjoyed the students, who were a little older than my students in the UK since this was a second degree for them, and I appreciated the smaller number of teaching hours that allowed me to spend more of my time working on research and writing. I was much less enthusiastic about the weather—I had never seen so much snow before—and I missed my friends back home. But the change was good. It also allowed me to take a break from the increasingly fractious behaviour of my daughter's biological father, who balked at paying child support and had started showing up at our London home at random hours of the day and night.

A TOE IN THE WATER

At the very beginning of our visit, we met a University of Windsor law professor, Richard Moon, who was assigned to show us around. Dick and I began a relationship, and by the spring we had decided to get married. I had received a job offer from the City University of Hong Kong, where I would help design and launch a new lawyer's qualification program. I had taught students from Hong Kong in my UK classrooms and knew that there was a real need for a more accessible and inclusive local route to qualification. Dick was also offered a position at the law school. Dick was becoming a wonderful, loving, and committed father to my daughter. We took the plunge at Hackney Town Hall in August 1990, and a few weeks later, sadly without my dog, who had to stay behind, our now three-person family unit left for two years in Hong Kong.

I told my new husband something of what had happened to me with my past experiences of abuse, and he was very loving, kind, and supportive, but of course also horrified, finding my accounts deeply upsetting. I knew that I was still holding on to many secrets. I began to think more and more about my responsibility to report the minister. But I was not yet ready to act.

I was also becoming dimly aware of some further signs of trauma, although I had no name for them as yet and did not confront them consciously. They included a worsening hair-trigger temper (maybe I was just bad tempered? under stress?) that rendered me incoherent whenever I felt unsafe or believed that someone might be taking advantage of me. There were a growing number of incidents in which I would leave a room, run, or even drive away from a heated argument, impelled by what felt like an uncontrollable flight impulse. Also increasingly noticeable during this time was my need to control my environment. I never sat down in a room without facing the door and having easy access to it. Just small things, but I now realize probably all symptoms of or tendencies exacerbated by emerging PTSD.

As the 1990s turned into the 2000s, talking about sexual violence was slowly becoming more acceptable. A space began to open up for scholarly research to investigate and report on its epidemic proportions. This evidence of the prevalence of sexual violence has been a significant factor in changing our public discourse. Gradually, my sense that it was *just me* and therefore *must be* my fault began to recede, at least in theory. Numerous research studies attested to the reality that many, many women experience sexual and physical violence in some form and some, like me, more than once. In a 2011 national survey in the US, almost one in five (18.3 per cent) women and one in seventy-one men (1.4 per cent) reported experiencing rape at some time in their lives. Approximately one in twenty women and men reported sexual violence other than rape, including sexual coercion or unwanted sexual contact, in the twelve months prior to the survey. We were learning that rape often occurs when the victim is young or very young—for example 12 per cent of women report being raped before they were ten years old (just like me) and another almost 30 per cent before the age of seventeen.[1]

As this research accumulated, I also began to notice the media covering violence against women more explicitly and frequently. But as more stories about the prevalence of sexual harassment, sexual assault, and rape began to appear in the news, I looked away. At this point in my life I actively avoided discussions on this topic, afraid that I would be unable to disguise my level of upset and risk unintentionally betraying my secrets. I wanted to be able to talk about these important developments for women, but I felt very anxious that if someone said something about the dynamics of sexual violence that I knew from my own experience to be misinformed, I would want to contradict them. And this would expose me as a survivor, something I was not yet ready to do.

I was also becoming clearer and more assertive about my feminist values. I began to look for ways that I could become active in discussions about sexual harassment and abuse without anyone assuming that I was "one of them" (the victims). I first put a toe in the water in 1992 in Hong Kong, where I organized a conference on workplace sexual harassment, something that had no legal recognition in Hong Kong at that time.[2] The conference was sparsely attended and the very idea of sexual harassment predictably pilloried in the *South China Morning Post* as a Western notion. But it felt good to stand up and speak publicly on this issue. It was close enough to what I knew about abuse of power while not disclosing any of my own experiences. It felt like a safe place to try out a public persona speaking out on sexual harassment.

Little by little, my professional work was beginning to merge with my personal journey. I was drawn to advocacy on behalf of individuals and causes not well understood by the mainstream culture. Before I left Hong Kong in 1992, I established a Free Legal Advice Clinic for women in a women's centre (part of the Hong Kong Federation of Women's Centres) located in a sprawling public housing project in Kowloon. The local press dubbed me "Divorce Lady," suggesting I was encouraging Hong Kong Chinese women to leave their husbands. The local Bar initially scoffed at the idea of the legal clinic, saying that local women would never talk about their personal family lives with the ex-pat lawyers who to begin with were my sole volunteers (with my law students acting as translators). By the time the clinic was ready to open, I was in my final few months in Hong Kong. I was pregnant with my second daughter and attracting stares whenever I was out in public. I was regularly reminded that Hong Kong Chinese women did not go out in public when they were heavily pregnant. Nonetheless I traipsed my ballooning belly around the housing project pinning up notices in the week before the clinic opening. On an unforgettable night, very shortly before the birth of my second daughter, the clinic opened to a line of would-be clients that snaked around the block. Over twenty-five years later, it is still going strong with volunteer lawyers, now from across the Hong Kong Bar.[3] I had the enormous pleasure of visiting the much-expanded service and its dedicated workers in 2018.

FINDING THE MINISTER

It was during my two years in Hong Kong in the early 1990s, with Dick's encouragement, that I resolved that I needed to try to trace the Anglican minister who had abused me. I wanted to ensure that he was no longer in a position to use his authority to abuse others who placed their trust in him.

I began by looking at the parish in Chichester where I had met him in 1974. He was no longer there. The Internet was only just emerging in the early 1990s and was no help in locating him. One day, I called a central national administrative office of the Anglican Church in the UK and asked how I could trace a particular minister. I was told that the church published a worldwide directory of Anglican ministers each year. I ordered the 1991 edition. A huge tome of a book arrived at my Hong Kong apartment several weeks later. It didn't take me long to find him. Meirion Griffiths, parish priest, Perth, Australia. Bingo. No longer in the UK. Did that mean anything?

I called the diocese office in Perth from my Hong Kong apartment. I heard the tremble in my voice as I said that I wanted to make a complaint against a priest involving sexual misconduct. I was told, kindly and surprisingly undefensively, that I should send in a written statement and was assured that it would be taken very seriously. Fair enough. A good start, I thought. And thank goodness. Just making that phone call left me edgy and drained.

Over the following weeks and months, I started to try to write out my statement. It felt like wading through wet cement. As soon as I started to write, I felt exhausted, like my limbs were made of lead. I wrote little by little. Then the computer I was writing on crashed, and I had no copy. I couldn't face starting again. I tried to tell myself: "Just do it!" It didn't work. I procrastinated endlessly (not my usual style). The birth of my second daughter just before we left Hong Kong to return to Canada in 1992 gave me another excuse. I was moving our family across the world, and I could not find the time and space I needed to do this, I told myself. For now, I gave up trying.

Back in Ontario, my life was consumed with raising two young children and re-establishing my academic career in yet another country (my fourth!). Then in 1995, the news in Canada became dominated by the murder trial of a man named Paul Bernardo.[4] Bernardo was charged and eventually convicted of the rape and the murder of two girls, Leslie Mahaffy and Kristen French, whom he and his wife, Karla Homolka, had snatched off the streets of St Catharines, a sleepy Ontario town. Despite a publication ban, US outlets and the burgeoning Internet ensured that the gory details of the trial testimony describing Bernardo's sadism were shared widely, along with stories about the cooperation of his spouse, Karla. The role played by Karla Homolka in the rapes and murders and the extent of her personal responsibility for Bernardo's actions became a public obsession. Was this woman culpable in these appalling crimes?

When I read about the trial testimony, it seemed obvious to me that Karla Homolka was subject to extraordinary controlling abuse by Paul Bernardo. Some of her described behaviour was eerily familiar to me from the time when I had lived with my violent domestic partner in Ireland. As the trial dragged on and the debate over Karla Homolka's culpability intensified,[5] I became increasingly distressed by my inability to explain to my women friends that I believed Karla Homolka to be a victim of abuse herself. Some women felt that Karla Homolka was falsely claiming victim status to avoid responsibility. But to me, her detailed stories of her efforts to constantly ameliorate the rages and violence of her spouse rang so true.

Despite the fact that feminists and especially women scholars in my academic legal community were analyzing and talking about the Bernardo case, it was very difficult for me to participate. I was shocked at how easily I understood what Homolka was experiencing when I read her testimony in the newspaper, day after day. She even described a specific tactic that I, too, had adopted with my violent domestic partner—keeping a supply of "sorry" cards ready for writing apologies for unknown but apparently enraging transgressions. When I read this particular snippet from Homolka's testimony in the newspaper on the Toronto subway in 1995, the flash of recognition was so traumatic that a panic attack forced me off the train and up to the surface to recover.

I became preoccupied with how to speak more openly about my own experiences, and the perspective they gave me on the ugly Bernardo and Homolka trial. I was also really scared about how this would go. It was an opportunity to say "that happened to me and I understand that." I could try to explain that the dynamics of control that I had personally experienced offered a way of understanding what had happened to Karla Homolka. But feelings ran high about this trial. Homolka was demonised by many, so would speaking up make me the subject of the same anger?

One day, following a long discussion about the case and Homolka's culpability, I shared some of my personal stories of assault and abuse with a small group of women colleagues who were also, by this time, personal friends. Although they listened kindly, they were visibly shocked and seemed to have little idea what to say. The subject was quickly changed.

I had learned the first lesson about public disclosure of abuse. None of my women friends knew how to respond to me. Later that evening, one woman spoke to me privately offering personal support. I really appreciated that, but this first experiment in openness had not gone well. I felt like an aberration, like I had just admitted to having some filthy disease. But it was a first step, and I have learned over the years that survivors need a lot of small first steps.

THE PERTH PROCESS

I had still not written my statement that the Perth diocese needed to begin the process of investigation of Griffiths and his potential prosecution under church or canon law.[6] It was now more than six years since I had first spoken to them from Hong Kong. I kept circling, circling, circling—it weighed heavily on me.

At the end of 1998, I got together a new resolve. I contacted the diocese of Perth again to confirm that Griffiths was still there; he was. As well, the diocese had now established a special Panel of Advice on complaints against clergy and church workers. I was given the name and email of the committee chair, a psychology professor at the University of Western Australia named Christabel

Chamarette.[7] From our very first communication, Professor Chamarette was supportive and affirming of me. She was too professional to say so directly, but I knew she believed me. I mean really—why would a law professor suddenly decide to make up a story about a minister in Perth Australia concerning events more than twenty years earlier?

Finally, one September Sunday in 1999, Dick took our two girls to a baseball game in Detroit, planned as a way to give me the physical and emotional space to finally write out my statement. It came pouring out. I wrote four single-spaced pages of detail about how Meirion Griffiths won my trust as my church minister and then sexually assaulted me and stalked me for almost a year. In the final paragraph of my statement, I wrote about how ashamed I was that it had taken me twenty-five years to speak out. I also wrote about my conviction that I had "a duty to tell this story, on many different levels." I also accepted that "now I have started this ball rolling, I have to see it through."

The response from the committee was swift and efficient. Griffiths was shown my statement, and he responded with his own. This was the first time I had seen a response from a sexual predator to accusations against him. Griffiths's statement exuded what I now recognize as the typically conflicted tone of someone unable to completely face up to what they have done to another person's life. It was at the same time both acknowledging and denying. For example, he acknowledged "I did for some time seek out her company actively as she describes . . . I acknowledge that such behavior was inappropriate." But he continues, "I strongly rebut all allegations of oral sex, forced or otherwise." At one point in his statement he declares "To suggest that I coerced sexual activity on her *first* (his italics) interview is outrageous."

The diocesan committee seemed unimpressed with Griffiths's response. They decided that they would proceed with a formal complaint under canon law. In effect this was a declaration that they were dissatisfied with Griffiths's account. This next step required me to make a statutory declaration affirming my statement and witnessed by a notary, as well as to provide the name of someone in Western Australia who could attest that I was who I said I was. I had a female colleague visiting Australia on sabbatical, and I plucked up the courage to write and tell her why I needed her to confirm my identity to the Perth Panel of Advice on complaints against clergy and church workers. That was a hard email to write and it must have been a surprising one to receive—but she was very kind and, of course, did exactly as I asked.

The following month, November, a long-awaited event was happening in my family. We were going to Hunan Province in southwest China to bring home a 10-month old baby girl we were adopting from an orphanage. I put the Perth process to the back of my mind and joyfully departed with my family to collect the little girl who would become my third daughter, Hopey. I thought little about the minister or Perth in those two weeks, consumed with our new child and watching her bond with her two sisters.

We arrived back in Canada shortly before Christmas. On our first morning at home, I was sitting on the sofa with my baby girl on my lap, feeling dazed in that jet-laggy way, but content. The phone rang on the little table beside the sofa. I picked it up. It was Christabel Chamarette, calling from Perth.

"Julie, I am calling to make sure you got the Archbishop's letter."

"Oh hi . . . um, I'm not sure, what letter is that?"

"Julie, he's resigned. Griffiths has resigned. The diocese does not employ him any longer and will never employ him again. It's over."

I vaguely remember placing Hopey—whose ability to sit without supports were pitifully underdeveloped after spending ten months in a crib in the orphanage—at the other end of the sofa and then coming back to the phone.

"Ummm . . . would you say that again?"

A moment later the sound of my littlest child sliding off the sofa reminded me that I was a new mother again. I put the phone down and picked Hopey up, none the worse for wear. After this, she quickly learned to sit up unaided. And I am forever glad that she was there to share this moment with me.

The archbishop's letter—dated December 9—was in the pile of mail I had not tackled since our return the previous day. It said "I am very grateful to you for being prepared to make your complaint known in the way that you did. I hope now that you will be able to live with some peace of mind." I felt jubilant. He would no longer be able to harm other young people—or so I thought.

Although in 1999 I believed that Griffiths had been removed from a position in which he could continue to abuse girls, I found myself thinking more now about my experiences of abuse than I ever had before. It was as if the Perth process had let the genie out of the bottle for me, and I could not put it back.

A critical part of this journey was growing into my role as the mother of three daughters, whom I am committed to protecting from sexual violence. I realized very early in my life as their mother that that meant each of them knowing they could always bring anxieties and questions to me. No more secrets, as I had held.

First I told the daughters of a close friend, who were older than my own kids, something about my own abuse to open up the possibility they could bring any similar experiences to me or to someone. This step was precipitated by a concern that one of them was in an abusive relationship with another teenager. I wanted her to know she could talk to me. I did not give a lot of detail about my own experience but tried to convey that many, many girls and women were subject to sexual violence, and it was important that they could talk to the adults they trusted about any behaviours that frightened them or were abusive.

I then told each of my own three daughters when they were, in my view, old enough to be able to understand what I described to them about the endemic nature of physical and sexual violence, and that I had experienced this myself when I was younger. My emphasis was not on those details but on keeping them safe and reassuring them that I would always answer their questions. I hoped this would be an ongoing conversation and commitment to openness for all of us as they grew up. I regarded these private conversations as my responsibility as a mother of daughters and as an "auntie" to some special young women I had known their whole lives. These conversations continue to this day with them and an ever enlarging group of young women.

Another milestone was meeting, in 2001, the person who would become my second husband, Bernie Mayer. By then I had told most of my story to just one person, Dick, my first husband, but it was not a topic that we dug into further. Dick was very supportive when I looked for the minister and finally wrote my statement, and he was naturally empathetic. But I knew that further and more detailed discussion would be upsetting for him, and we barely spoke about the impact of the abuse on me. When I met Bernie I felt for the first time that here was someone I could tell the whole miserable saga to, and moreover it felt somehow urgent for me to do so. Over the course of two long nights, the second time we met, at a conference in Washington, D.C., I told Bernie the entire wretched story, in detail. He didn't just listen with empathy and compassion, he asked me many, many questions, which felt affirming and necessary. For the first time ever I felt as if I could talk about this history without constantly worrying about the listener being appalled or distraught. It was incredibly liberating. Suddenly I was taking control of my story, and I wanted to do something with it to empower others.

In 2002, Dick and I separated, and Bernie moved up to Canada from his Colorado home. This brought my stepson Mark, and later his wife Ashley, into my life, which has been an unexpected and joyous gift. When Dick and I formally ended our marriage in 2004, we both remarried; Bernie and I in our backyard on Lake Erie. Inevitably this was a time of great upheaval for my family and my focus was on them. But slowly another important part of my recovery and healing was emerging.

WHAT MR LOUIE TAUGHT ME ABOUT PTSD

I grew up horse-mad, a little girl who drew horses, read stories about horses, saved her pocket-money to buy more books about horses, and looked for friends with horses who might let me ride them. For a few years the only access I had to riding was a donkey that lived in our village. I somehow persuaded the owner to let me ride the poor beast up and down main street. I had a riding lesson once a year, on my birthday (this was a hobby too costly for my parents to support). My father told me that if I could save up twenty-five pounds, he would put up the rest to buy me a pony. I guess he was pretty confident I couldn't do it. He was right—in the late 1960s and early 1970s twenty-five pounds was an unimaginable sum to me.

After university, as I bounced between temporary jobs and travelling, I had a spell as a teacher in a residential school for girls which had a stables in the grounds. In response to my query, I was airily told by the (alcoholic) "headmaster" (I was the only other teacher) that of course I could take the girls riding. Wonderful! There were just two problems: I did not know the first thing about horses or tack or equine care or safety; and the girls, my charges, saw the horses as a means of escape from their lock-down. We had a number of adventures, but somehow everyone survived and no one galloped off over the horizon. When I left the job, I put away my passion for horses again and went back to my life.

My oldest daughter started riding when she was small (my wish fulfillment?) and I began ten years of taking her to the barn in all weathers and watching her turn into a beautiful rider. I petted the horses and graded papers and read while she rode. Then in 2001 we bought her her own horse, Duel, something I had long wanted for her, partly because I could not have it as a child. Six months later, Duel had a freak accident and had to be euthanized. My daughter was devastated, and so was I. I couldn't stop crying. I had expected to be upset of course, but weeks later I was still sobbing about it. That was when it occurred to me: perhaps I needed to finally learn to ride?

That decision turned out to be important in ways I could never have anticipated for my own recovery. Beginning with a school horse, I started taking riding lessons and then graduated to riding alone between lessons, and within a few months I was hooked. I was doing something I had always wanted to do, and now I was learning properly. My daughter was very supportive—I'm sure having your mother decide to start riding at your barn is not straightforward for a teenager—and I had a wonderful first teacher, Julie O'Connell. By the time my daughter left to go to university, I was riding her amazing horse Houdini, who taught me to ride, mostly with patience, and he and I had moved to a barn run by friends that was slightly closer to our home.

I have ridden ever since. In good weather, I ride most days. In bad weather, I ride at least three times a week. So this is a big part of my life. I have had a series of wonderful teachers. The only interruptions have been my treatment for recurring cancer, of which more below. But there has been both a dark and a healing side to this sport for me, which has come to represent another step in my understanding and management of my PTSD. I was determined from the beginning to *do it all;* that is, to learn to ride including jumping and cross-country eventing, which is the most dangerous element of English riding. It would be normal to be a little afraid when you first start jumping a horse over fences, especially if you are starting, as I was, in your forties. It was also normal, given who I am, for me to be competitive and want to do it all.

But I slowly began to realize that this was different. I experienced excruciating self-doubt about my ability to ride. I analyzed and critiqued my riding over and over again, always ending with dissatisfaction. I was scared when I jumped, but made myself do it anyway. I began to experience physical symptoms. As I drove the fifteen minutes to the barn, my stomach would convulse. I would experience nausea (extremely unusual for me). My heart would be racing as I turned into the barn. When I rode, if my horse spooked and did something unexpected my heart would race and my stomach would feel like it was coming out through my mouth. I knew these reactions were completely out of proportion. I wondered what was happening to me. But I persisted.

By 2007, I had been riding for six years and was competing my own horse, Mr Louie. One day I drove to the barn to have a lesson with Jenn Irwin. Jenn was a very successful competitive rider and eventer, and she had worked with me for some years as an outside coach, someone with whom I would take a lesson every few months. Jenn knew me well and I loved riding with her. We began an exercise. I felt that I was not getting it right and said so; Jenn contradicted me and said I was doing well. This back and forth continued and finally she told me to stop. "What is going on here?" she asked me. "I don't know what it is, but you are letting something get in the way of your riding. You need to leave it at the barn door."

This was a moment of acute realization. I was being irrational and reactive. Just as I had been by this time at numerous riding shows, big and small, when I munched on Gravol the whole day to calm my stomach. My disproportionate and extreme reactions to riding fears and lessons were somehow tied in to my PTSD. Something was triggering me, over and over again.

Jenn had seen something that needed to be recognized, and I am grateful to her for her prescience. I began to read a little about sports and PTSD. It did not take long to work out that the rush of fear that should have been simply motivational adrenalin when I faced a jump or another riding challenge had become associated with the fear I had felt for my life before, when I was living with my domestic partner in Ireland. It wasn't motivational—it was crippling.

While studies show the positive effects of participating in sport for people with chronic PTSD, there is also data that demonstrates what I was experiencing. Where a sport involves exposure to negative sensations that trigger traumatic memories (in my case, physical fear for my life) there can be a heightened effect. One study explains this as the result of the attentional focus that comes with sport's participation which can give rise to both positive but also negative feelings of self-esteem, invidious comparison with others, and a re-experiencing of the original trauma.[8] "Participants may be exposed in and through sport and exercise to negative sensations and to triggers of distress, intrusive memories, or even retraumatization." My physical symptoms were typical for a panic attack for someone with chronic PTSD. I also realized that each time I jumped a fence, I said to myself under my breath "That's for you, D. (the name of my violent partner)." I had been doing this for years by this point, but each time I was finished my jumping round I put it out of my head and never thought about it again—until the next time. The traumatized brain is a strange and mysterious thing.[9]

As is common with PTSD triggers, once I could identify what was happening it became much easier to deal with the consequences. As Karyn Freedman puts it in her book about rape and PTSD, this awareness "gave new meaning to my past actions and I began to feel more normal."[10] I am delighted to say that I now drive to the barn with a steady stomach, ready to absorb myself in a sport that has become my go-to for mental relaxation as well as physical exercise. The extreme and persistent physical symptoms of fear have disappeared. I can now relish the adrenalin rush of jumping fences, and my struggle with the irrational and immobilizing demons of riding is over.

In 2010 I faced a new challenge; I was diagnosed with breast cancer and had surgery, followed by chemotherapy and radiation. It was a difficult six months, with my oldest daughter away at school and my middle daughter in her last year of high school. But we came through it together as a family. As we celebrated the end of my treatment at Christmas 2010, little did we know that we had a much longer cancer journey before us. For now, I was healthy again.

With the dawning awareness my earlier experiences of sexual violence had affected me in more ways than I could ever have imagined came another realization—disclosing to my friends that I was a survivor of sexual violence was a key element in my own recovery. I still found this really difficult and had many false starts and aborted attempts to do so.

I became preoccupied with a new question: should I go public about my history of sexual abuse and assault in a way that used my status as a law professor to open and influence a more informed and realistic conversation about sexual violence? I was aware of course that sexual assault and rape were associated with a *certain kind of woman*, and their narratives were often distorted by pejorative ambiguities about their manner, dress, and sexual history. The barriers to speaking up were immense, and these "reinforce the shame that we struggle against and widens the gap between who we are and how others see us."[11] As I pondered this question and what I might do, another shoe dropped.

NOT JUST ME

In July 2013, I spent a week with my mother, who was ill with cancer, at her home in Chichester. This was the same town that I had lived in during my teenage years and where I had been assaulted by the Anglican minister. One evening, I overheard a news story on the local TV news show my mother liked to watch. As I carried my mother's tea tray back and forth between the kitchen and the sitting room where the TV was on, I overheard the news reader making a reference to what seemed to be a well-established story. The story involved multiple allegations of sex abuse by a number of different Anglican clergy, some of whom had by this time been criminally convicted. They had all worked for the diocese of Chichester.

The air stood still in the room. My mother was watching the TV in a sleepy, mesmerised way. I stood above her chair with my heart hammering in my chest, my eyes fixed suddenly on the TV. I learned from the news story that there had been a 2011 inquiry into a network of child sex abuse by clerics in the diocese of Chichester.

This enquiry, conducted by Baroness Butler-Sloss, a respected jurist whose work on child protection I had read as a graduate student, had concluded that the diocese had shown "a lack of understanding of the seriousness of historic child abuse."[12] At this stage, one minister, Colin Pritchard, had been convicted, and a second, Roy Cotton, had died before being charged. Incredibly, Cotton already had a conviction for sexual assault when he was ordained a priest, and both men had previously been investigated following complaints and not charged. The news story I caught by complete chance that evening at my mother's home covered the formal apology offered by the Anglican Church for the Chichester abuse.

It wasn't just me.

The story had so many other people in it. And the story was

much bigger than me, bigger than I could have ever foreseen. I went online and almost immediately found a website, Stop Child Abuse,[13] which David Greenwood and other lawyers and survivors had started to raise awareness of their call for a public enquiry into sex abuse and its cover-up by the Anglican Church in England and Wales (a call which would eventually be successful).[14] I wrote to David that same evening, wondering if I might be able to help by speaking publicly about what had happened to me in Chichester.

> I am writing to you because I am blown away to realize as I read the various news stories today that Chichester was a cauldron of sexual abuse by clergy, and I have never been aware of this before. I am very willing to play whatever part might be helpful in help-ing others to come forward, pressing for an enquiry etc. I have wrestled with my demons over this period of my life for decades and now feel brave enough to be public in whatever way might be useful to others.

David Greenwood replied almost immediately. This was the beginning of an important professional and personal relationship that continues today. In the first few messages, David was encour-aging and supportive but made it clear that his preferred strategy was to bring as many lawsuits as possible against the church. He believed that this was the most practical and effective way to make the church accountable to the victims of clerical sex abuse. He did not believe that the church would "do the right thing" for moral reasons, and instead it would have to be fought through the courts. This hunch turned out to be correct. I would be, David argued, "a dream client"—an apparently highly credible plaintiff.

But when David first raised this, I was completely disinterested in the idea of a lawsuit. In fact, I was strongly opposed. As a law professor and a frequently appointed mediator in civil disputes, I was painfully aware of the risks and potential traumas of litigation and did not intend to go down that route. Besides, I had already tracked down the minister who abused me as a teenager, and he had been removed from the clergy. That part of the story was, I be-lieved then, closed.

How wrong I was.

CHAPTER 4

GOING PUBLIC

In these years I would occasionally find myself alone, without kid or work distractions. Usually this meant driving on highway 401 in my home province of Ontario, along which I sometimes drove to work as a mediator, or taking a flight to another city to deliver a speech or a seminar. For many years, I used this alone time to return over and over again to the question that encapsulated my anxieties and preoccupations about my history of sexual violence: Could I speak up about my experiences in a way that moves the conversation forward and is empowering for others?

I sometimes made elaborate plans on these trips (for an op-ed, a speech, a call to other women survivors to come out together on the streets) but never carried them out. Looking back now, I realize the importance of #MeToo in making this an imaginable thing. Since 2017, the #MeToo movement and disclosures about sexual violence by people with public profile and influence have proven effective in advancing a different kind of debate about women and sexual violence, one informed by real people with real experiences.[1] But I was still in pre-#MeToo days, and *going public* seemed like an outrageous fantasy. A compelling one nonetheless.

Personal *coming out*—the disclosure of something that has historically been seen as shameful—has a long history in activism. The most recognizable example of this phenomenon in the last thirty years has created a seismic shift in public attitudes toward sexuality. In large part this seems to be a response to the personal stories of recognizable public individuals (an athlete, an elected representative, a media personality). Reinforced by this, personal coming out to friends or family became much more common and this has further impacted attitudes. In 1993, Pew Research reported that 61 per cent of US adults said they knew someone who was gay or lesbian—by 2015 that figure was 88 per cent.[2]

This history demonstrates that the more people speak up about something assumed to be shameful—sexual identity, abortion, mental illness, the examples are numerous—the more the dominant culture is forced to re-evaluate the shame historically associated with it. Eventually, putting human faces to formerly taboo topics challenges prejudices and changes attitudes. But not everyone is equal in their ability to speak up. Some have good support, some have none. Some have the privilege of education and class and white skin and the knowledge that they begin with a "believability advantage" over their sisters. Some face consequences inside their families that are more devastating than others. Some have chosen for many private reasons to keep their secrets hidden. In 2013, I had many of these privileges. This meant I could not simply shrug and tell myself not to worry, someone else would do this. As a law professor, I thought my public persona might be useful in normalizing a conversation about sexual violence. I also recognized that, as a tenured professor, I did not have to worry about my job security. I had a ready-to-go platform at my disposal (my classroom and my law school). And I had learned enough from years of activism on different issues to enable me to plan a public coming out for maximum impact.

Speaking up would mean that I could live up to my own strongly held principles about using my privilege for good and challenging social constructs of shame. I was also beginning to realize that speaking up would empower me too. I was by this time working extensively as a third-party mediator in a wide range of conflicts. I often saw firsthand the power of authenticity and open disclosure and the ways in which this had the power to undermine patterns of hatred and presumption.

How might my own family respond to my going public about my history of abuse and violence? How might it affect them? Bernie and my daughters reassured me and generously told me that they would be proud of me. It was no coincidence, I believe, that the timing of my eventual coming out was just after the death of my mother in 2014 (my father was already deceased), and so I did not have to worry about her reaction.

There was just one problem—the idea terrified me.

FACING MY FEARS

As I turned the idea of this coming out project over and over in my mind, I struggled with other, deeper anxieties. A reason I had long given myself for not being open about my experiences of abuse was that those who loved me but still had no knowledge of this would be deeply distressed to learn about what had happened to me. Why would I force this ugly knowledge on them? This had kept me from speaking to even my closest friends for many decades. Most still knew nothing of any of this.

Once I had identified as a survivor of abuse, I could not take it back. It could change how some of my colleagues and students thought about me in ways that I could not control. I did not want my story about sexual violence to become synonymous with my identity, to be known as the *abuse professor*. I worried about how the whispering exchanges might go when I walked into a room. I wondered whether some of my colleagues might be so upset by my disclosures that I would have to manage their pain, as well as my own. I imagined that some of my male (and even female) colleagues might find it hard to make eye contact with me after I blew the lid off law school's traditional ironclad discretion in all matters personal.

As I tried to think all this through, another question that concerned me was whether public disclosures about my sexual history would change my relationships with students. My (then closeted) gay male professor friends had raised the same questions when they first considered coming out in the 1980s and 1990s. How would their students react to this disclosure? My concerns were similar but different. Would there be students who would be triggered by my disclosures and suffer pain as a result? Or would students with their own history of abuse now feel a special connection to me, and would this feel excluding to other students? Would I inevitably be subject to some hurtful comments? And just how uncomfortable would everyone feel as the accepted role boundaries disintegrated in the face of this new information about me? I could not answer these questions.

I had no role models for whether it was appropriate for researchers and scholars to use their personal experiences in this way to open up a public conversation. We value academics for their ability to be dispassionate and objective as they parse data and argument. Would we value their expertise in the same way if their data and argument included their personal—in this case, deeply personal and private—experiences? Was there a risk that I would be seen as using the credibility of my position for personal advantage? Might I be accused of self-promotion or attention-seeking? Was it okay for an academic to base her activism on her personal story? I had a lot of anxiety that I would not be taken seriously because of my personal connection to the issue—a familiar way of denigrating personal experiences as emotional, especially those described by women and people of colour—and that this might damage my larger reputation as a scholar.

Finally, and most frightening of all—how did I know if I would be strong enough to actually stand up and do this? To let off the bomb? To say the sharp word? The red word?[3] *Rape*.

Eventually none of my concerns, either personal or professional, convinced me to back away from coming out, but they allowed me to procrastinate for a long time. In the end my sense of responsibility as an educated, solvent, well-supported person got the better of me. I kept coming back to what I might be able to do by speaking up about my own history of abuse, for example, encourage other survivors to speak up, and disrupt stereotypes about *who* gets abused. Instinctively I believed that identifying myself as a survivor of rape or sexual assault would be empowering for me and that openness was the antidote to the shame and self-doubt I had experienced as a survivor. At minimum, going public, even in a limited way, had the potential to create supportive relationships among myself and other survivors.

I knew how to write a coming out speech, an op-ed for a newspaper, and could do a competent radio interview. My career was, by then, well established and even the worst reactions were unlikely to significantly undermine my credibility as a scholar. If colleagues misinterpreted my motivation as publicity-seeking, then so be it. Among many other myths about sexual violence, the idea that anyone would want to be famous for being a victim of sexual violence was pernicious, and I knew I couldn't be controlled by it. I really did not know how my students might respond to my disclosures, but I assumed that with mutual care and transparency we could together work through the issues that would arise from my disclosures. Increasingly, those seemed to be risks I had to be prepared to take.

I was still scared, but I was ready. Now I just needed to find an opening, and back myself into a commitment I could not break.

SEXUAL ASSAULT AWARENESS DAY

In January 2014, I was supervising three third year Windsor law students who were working on a paper about how law schools dealt with complaints about sexual assault. One of these students, Brady Donohue, was also leading the organization of Windsor Law's Sexual Assault Awareness Day, which first took place in 2013. Brady's brainchild, the idea of Sexual Assault Awareness Day was to raise student awareness of the prevalence of sexual assault and rape, both on campus and in the law school, and the extent to which this problem is suppressed and ignored. In 2013, before the #MeToo movement began to change public consciousness, this was an audacious and brave innovation in a climate that barely acknowledged, let only discussed, sexual violence. Brady had also started a blog, "Pantyhose and the Penal Code,"[4] intended as a forum for frank discussion on the barriers faced by women in the legal profession, including the requirement that they wear pantyhose, but especially sexual assault and sexual harassment.

All three students were in my office one day discussing plans for Sexual Assault Awareness Day in 2014, including whom they might invite to speak and on what topic. The previous year, speakers had focused on legal issues, such as why it was so difficult to secure a sexual assault conviction, how to convince a jury, and so on. I knew that this was not what Brady really wanted this year. She wanted, instead, to encourage a more open and personal conversation that broke the silence about personal experiences of sexual assault.

Just do it, I told myself.

I was sitting at my desk. I moved my chair away from my desk and faced all three students squarely.

"I'm a sexual abuse survivor. I've also been raped—twice actually. If you would like, I would be willing to talk about those experiences on Sexual Assault Awareness Day."

Time stood still. The three students stared at me. They looked stricken. I immediately regretted my choice of words. It sounded like it would be horrible, coming out that way. I babbled on.

"I would be talking about it in an empowering way, of course . . ."

Brady spoke first.

"Seriously? You would do that? Are you sure?"

"Yes. I'm sure."

I had done it. I was committed. Although it all still felt a little surreal and certainly scary, I knew I couldn't back out now, and that actually felt good.

The date for that year's Sexual Assault Awareness Day at Windsor Law was set for March 5, 2014. The students originally designed a poster for the day with the date and time of the session that simply said, "Featuring Professor Macfarlane." When they showed it to me, I said that I thought the poster should be explicit about what I would be talking about. They looked fleetingly anxious, but agreed. We came up with "Professor Macfarlane will break the silence [the event theme] surrounding her personal experiences of sexual violence."

As soon as we had finalized the poster and it began to go up around the law school, I realized that I needed to tell some of my close colleagues personally before they saw them. I didn't want them reading this news off the poster and feeling upset. I made a mental list of everyone I felt I needed to check in with, and I did the rounds. This was hard, but important both for them and me. I forced myself to walk into their offices, a tight smile on my face. Their responses were sometimes awkward and stilted, often a little baffled, but always supportive. One more hurdle crossed. It was real now. I was going to do this.

THE HARDEST SPEECH I EVER GAVE

As the day of my speech crept closer, I could no longer delay writing it. By this time in my career I had delivered literally hundreds of speeches. I thoroughly enjoyed speaking to audiences large and small, engaging them and trying to keep their attention. My long-established approach was to use notes with a list of bullet points or slides with the same shorthand structure. It was natural for me to find the words in the moment, to be relatively spontaneous, and to improvise around my structure. I no longer had any nerves or anxiety about speaking in public, having done it so often.

But this was different. Nerves would hardly describe how I felt when I anticipated looking out over the room where I would tell my personal story. For the first time ever, I felt that I needed to write out what I would say, word-for-word. I was afraid that if I did not, one or both of two things might happen; I would not make sense, and I would not get through the speech. This was an odd realization, to be tackling something so very familiar in an entirely new way. So, I drafted my speech, word-for-word, and then sent it to a few trusted friends as well as my husband and daughters for their input.

Everyone was so supportive and encouraging. I obsessed, of course, about how to frame what I would say in a way that would be most clear, most empowering (emphasizing survival and moving on) and least toxic for others to hear. I was painfully aware that there would be other women in the room listening who were survivors of sexual violence. Just as Karyn Freedman reflected on her first public reading of her story, "How many women in this room . . . are holding their breath right now? How many are feeling unhinged?"[5]

I knew I had to focus on some but not all of my experiences—this was just a thirty- or forty-minute speech—and I thought hard about which of my experiences would be most meaningful and relatable for my audience of students and some faculty. I knew I wouldn't make all the right calls, but thought hard about some details, for example, whether to mention that my university date rape had resulted in a pregnancy and an abortion (I left that out for fear of making it harder for someone opposed to abortion to hear what I was really saying), or how much detail to give about the assaults by the minister.

I refined the speech in a few places with the input I received, but basically it was the way I wanted it right out of the gate. It was like I had been waiting to do this for decades (well, I had). Next, I started to practice delivering it out loud. I wanted to detoxify it, so that I could feel okay about the words as they came out of my mouth. I knew that this would help me not to break down and to be able to get through it. So I practised out loud many times, with the help of my so-patient husband.

I was ready. The hour before the speech, Brady came to check on me in my office, her face clouded with anxiety. "I'm fine, I'm good," I reassured her. I really was. A calm had settled on me. Bernie and my youngest daughter were also there with me and two dear friends, Perry and Gillian, who had driven in from our small town to Windsor to listen and support me.

I delivered my speech on the evening of March 5, 2014, to a packed room of students and faculty in the law school. I felt literally held up by the arms of everyone in that room. Here is how my speech began:

> It's been more than fifteen years since I first started thinking about talking publicly—somewhere, somehow—about my prior history of sexual assault and rape.
>
> I've been too afraid.
>
> The reasons are obvious—it's hard to talk about traumatic experiences. It's embarrassing to talk about sexual assault and rape.
>
> I worry about upsetting people.
>
> I worry about the reaction to me—will people look at me differently? What conclusions and judgments will they draw about me?
>
> Nonetheless, for many, many years I have kept returning to a deep conviction that it was important for me to come out and be public about my experiences.
>
> I believe that it is important for at least some of the survivors of sexual violence to identify themselves.
>
> Part of the reason is to demonstrate that these things happen to many, many people—and not necessarily the people that you expect.
>
> Part of the reason is to shake the stereotype often attached to those we call the "victims" of sexual assault—that perhaps they were just in the wrong place at the wrong time, perhaps they were preyed upon because they were seen as vulnerable, or fragile, or helpless—and present instead a real person, who has a real life: In this case, me.
>
> [And part of the reason is] because there are many, many women like me—we are strong, and we now have successful lives, healthy relationships and we are one hundred per cent credible.
>
> I want you to understand today as I tell you some of my difficult stories that I have really, truly survived.
>
> But I have stayed silent, and afraid, for a long, long time.[6]

Aside from my voice, the room was absolutely silent. No fidgeting. The eyes of everyone in the room were trained on me. I was conscious of my husband and my youngest daughter sitting about halfway back to my left. My long-time colleague Myra Tawfik sat in the front row, right in front of my podium. Myra was so still, she almost seemed not to be breathing.

In the next part of my speech, I tried to explain what I hoped to achieve by coming out.

> I hope to set an example to everyone who is here, as well as beyond this room, of the difference it makes to break our suffocating, paralyzing silence about sexual violence that keeps us as a society, and us as a law school community, stuck in a place of avoidance, minimization, and denial.[7]

I talked about being raped at university, and about being sexually assaulted by the Anglican minister as a teenager. I did provide details—the details I had spent time worrying over in my preparation. Details were important, I concluded, not because I wanted to be graphic or upsetting but because I felt that if we do not talk concretely about what has happened in an assault or a rape, we reinforce our larger difficulty with talking openly about sexual violence.

I tried to honestly and realistically describe my confusion, fear, and isolation when these assaults took place. I reminded my audience that it had taken me decades to reach the point that I could, today, speak up about these experiences. It might take any one of them who has had experiences of abuse a long time too. But I added:

> You do not have to wait as long as I did. There are people who will support and stand up for you, who will believe you, and, most important of all, protect you.[8]

The very last part of my speech was the part that I had had the most trouble getting through when I practised. It always made me cry because it spoke my deepest truth about these experiences and how they had changed me. That night, my eyes were filled with tears but I marched through that final section:

> I have told each of my three daughters when they were, in my view, old enough, something about my experiences in order that they might be able to recognize and name sexual assault, rape, sexual predatory behaviors, and physical and sexual violence. I have done this so that they can always know that they can come to me if anything like this ever happens—or feels like it is about to

happen—to them, or to any of their friends.

Today you are all my daughters—and sons. Whatever your own experiences, what you have heard me talk about today will change you. Women and men, we are all part of breaking the silence and changing the culture.[9]

The room embraced me.

CONSEQUENCES

The stone I cast into the calm of my law school's silence on sexual violence created a lot of ripples.

The speech achieved a lot of what I had hoped. Looking back, I think the most important consequence of what I did that night was that it began to normalize the widespread experience of sexual violence. My speech is now part of our law school story. Students who were not in the law school at the time know about it. They talk to me about it. My disclosures have bonded me to other women with similar experiences, whether or not they choose to be public themselves. Students now often write papers for me about their own experiences of sexual violence, using some of the ideas I talk about in the classroom, including process design, confidentiality, safety, and participation, whether using legal or institutional processes. I am glad that I can offer a safe place for them to describe their experiences and explore how they—and the system they will work in as lawyers—might deal so much better with sexual violence. This has made a different kind of conversation in my classroom imaginable and possible.

Many of my fears about the repercussions of coming out did not materialize. Any sense of personal embarrassment faded away quickly. I just got used to it. I think I resigned myself quickly to the fact that both friends and strangers now knew a lot more about me than I (or they!) had ever expected they would. I was briefly miffed when the *London Times* described me in an article written about my abuse by the minister as "sex claim woman,"[10] but my sense of humour soon took care of that. My greatest fear was that my students and colleagues would never look at me the same way again, but in practice I do not find myself discomfited by it. It would be a little like feeling embarrassed because the existence of my biological daughters makes it obvious I have had sexual intercourse. That would obviously be silly. Now that my story is known, the secret part of me is now also the public part of me, and that feels right.

Making the speech brought me a deep and lasting feeling of affirmation and relief. I was no longer hiding an essential part of myself. It remains astonishing to me how long it took to take this step, which was so positive and important for me. It had been more than thirty years since I stepped back into the light in 1983 and left my violent domestic partner, ending my chronicle of sexual abuse. Many women attest to the same feelings of personal affirmation and emotional relief when they speak publicly and to family and friends about the abuse they have experienced.[11] Public speaking is not for everyone, of course, but survivors consistently describe a feeling of catharsis from speaking up, even if to just a small, close circle.

The speech prompted a number of female law students to come forward and disclose that they had been assaulted or harassed by other students. For a few weeks, the law school roiled in the turbulence of these disclosures. The students who had organized Sexual Assault Awareness Day and to whom many of these disclosures were being made began to feel overwhelmed. For a few weeks, we turned the giant whiteboard in my office into a map of all the complaints that had been brought forward and the interconnections (for example, one law student, named by several different women, appeared to be a serial rapist).

Unfortunately, as is often the case with a new activist strategy, we did not have a clear idea about our next steps. We had not thought enough in advance about the limits of what we could offer those who came forward with disclosures of assault. In 2014, my law school had no internal processes for dealing with allegations of sexual assault and harassment, and the central university processes were unwelcoming, bureaucratic, and inadequate. The students and I asked the law school administration to speak with the women who had come forward and that they message the student body at large about the availability of counselling and support services. "This is out of control," I was told angrily by one senior administrator, as the consequences settled in. My speech had broken the silence— but silence was the status quo, and changing the status quo throws everything off balance. After some tense discussions, a supportive and acknowledging message was sent to students by the dean. My

2014 speech and its aftermath serves as an example of how it is relatively easy to embrace a single event or individual coming forward and far more difficult to recognize and respond to the endemic and systemic nature of the problem.

I was now ready to become an activist on other cases. I was beginning to hear from other women, some high school students and some university students. I had not anticipated that this would happen; in 2014, before #MeToo, stories of personal disclosure were still uncommon. In this way my coming out speech not only brought me personal relief and affirmation, it also marked the beginning of my public activism on sexual violence.

CHAPTER 5

FROM LAW PROFESSOR
TO LITIGANT

W hen David Greenwood first suggested to me, in July 2013, that I bring a lawsuit against the Anglican Church for historic sex abuse, I dismissed the idea. From my professional work over the previous twenty years, I understood only too well the pitfalls of litigation, its capacity to distort feelings, recollections, and justice and to keep people in trauma long after a more healing and healthy process could have enabled them to move on with their lives.[1] I had long advocated for humane, equitable, meaningful alternatives to litigation, as a researcher, educator, and mediator. I studied litigation and those caught up in it as lawyers or as parties. Why would I want to be a litigant myself?

Over the following months, my discussions with David, as well as with my oldest daughter and Bernie, persuaded me that the most effective way for me to do something was to add to the pressure of mounting numbers of lawsuits against the church. David's strategy in bringing these lawsuits—to draw attention to the church's responsibility for sex crimes committed by clerics—was one I recognized from my earlier work as an advocate on children's rights issues. Having spent a lot of time in those years looking for the "right" plaintiff for test cases, I could see that I brought some important credibility as a litigant. As well, what I now knew about the systemic nature of child sex abuse and cover-up in my hometown of Chichester changed the equation for me. I realized that my story needed a different, more robust, and more public ending. It was not simply about stopping one particular minister from committing abuses. The scale of both the abuse and the long-term cover-up by church was mindboggling.

Early in January 2014, I told David that I was ready to go ahead and commence proceedings against the church:

Dear David,

The first of my New Year resolutions is to ask you to take this case forward for me against Rev Meirion Griffiths and the Anglican church.

David replied in under an hour.

Dear Julie,

I will be in touch shortly with the plan.

Happy New Year.

Within two weeks, I had completed the paperwork to engage David on a conditional fee agreement, meaning, I would not pay for his work unless and until I won the case.

It was a surreal experience for me to find myself a litigant in a lawsuit. What I did not realize at the outset was that no matter how familiar I was with the bizarre and ferocious positionality of lawsuits, the experience I was about to begin would exceed my worst expectations.

From the outset, I instructed David to explore settlement with the church, knowing that my financial goals were modest—I just needed to pay him for his work. Once we had successfully settled my case, I could move on to my real purpose, which was talking about the case publicly and trying to motivate and encourage other survivors.

David offered the Anglican Church an opportunity to settle with me before issuing proceedings, that is, before beginning a lawsuit against the diocese of Chichester for my repeated sexual assault by the minister (their employee) from 1975 to 1976. Given that my case had already been considered by an Anglican diocesan committee in Perth, resulting in the minister's resignation, I naïvely believed that the church would probably settle before action—that is, accept some responsibility and via their insurer (which the Anglican Church, in the form of All Churches Trust, owns) offer a settlement to avoid having to defend the case in court. This belief was bolstered by a possibly even more naïve assumption that they might look up the plaintiff (me) on Google and realize that given my particular professional specialism (research on the aggressive use of litigation tactics by the legal profession)[2] I would be an unwise plaintiff to dick around.

I was one hundred per cent wrong. My first inkling that this might not play out quite as I had expected came when the church showed no interest at all in talking to David and me. My second clue was that while I was shocked by this David was not. Slowly, it began to dawn on me that my confidence that the other side would not play chicken with me was misplaced.

This was the beginning of learning that the Anglican Church will go to the wall with an aggressively adversarial and highly legalistic strategy even where they are fully aware that the abuse complained of took place. The only explanation I can offer for my offended sense of shock is my boundless and often ungrounded optimism that people will *do the right thing*. I was about to enter the bizarre world of an ancient religious organization that has long tolerated abuse by its priests and now sees nothing wrong in utilizing arcane legal arguments to defeat claims that they know to be valid. Of course, the church was going to play hardball with me, because they always did—because our legal argument had some obvious weaknesses.

THE LIMITATIONS DEFENCE

In response to our letter-before-action, the diocesan lawyers informed David that they would plead the statute of limitations to defeat any legal claim I brought forward. I was suing the church for historic sex abuse in a jurisdiction (England and Wales) that maintained a statute of limitations restricting the length of time after an assault that a civil claim may be brought—and I was well out of time. It had been forty years since I had been assaulted by the minister, well outside the three year period prescribed by the English Limitation Act of 1980.[3] This required my claim to be brought either within three years of the day I turned eighteen years old (1980), or within three years of the time that I had "knowledge" that I had an actionable injury.

Most countries have had (and some still do) a statute of limitations for bringing a civil suit or criminal prosecution for sexual assault and rape, setting a limit on the time that can elapse after an attack and before a claim is brought. Time periods vary between jurisdictions, as well as between criminal cases and civil claims. The premise of limitation periods in these cases is that knowledge of the theoretical possibility of legal action and a personal resolve to step forward and begin a claim are indistinguishable. Once the victim realizes they have a legal case—for sexual abuse, assault, rape, or harassment—they will contemporaneously step forward to report. Justification for a limitation on legal actions reflects the entrenched myth that victims are only credible if they come forward to report immediately after the assault. A fainter but present rationale is that if too long a period of time passes following the alleged assault, it may become difficult to reliably and accurately reconstruct events so long after they occurred. Perhaps, yes. Unless trauma burns those memories into your brain.

England and Wales, where my claim was filed, still had (and has) a limitation period for civil lawsuits like mine, where a "plaintiff" wants to sue an alleged perpetrator. David (who had fought many such cases) and I were ready to make arguments against the limitations defence, aware that a court could make exceptions and that there was case law to this effect.[4] A growing number of jurisdictions—including California and more than a dozen other US states,[5] Canada, and South Africa—have now removed all such restrictions for civil cases. Many more are following suit.

Still more countries, including England and Wales, Canada, and some US states,[6] no longer have a statute of limitations in *criminal* cases where the state prosecutes the accused (a fact that will later become relevant to my case). Where limitations do continue to exist in criminal cases, they typically range from two to seven years, with longer periods for more violent crimes such as rape. There has been widespread public attention to this issue since the dozens of allegations of rape and assault brought forward by women against legendary entertainer Bill Cosby. At that time in California, felony sex offences had to be brought within ten years and most of Cosby's accusers were out of time. The successful prosecution against Cosby was based on the one case that was still within the time period: Cosby's assaults on Andrea Constand.[7] The Cosby case has created further pressure for reform, and in 2016 California passed a law eliminating limitation periods for prosecuting sexual crimes.[8]

However, many US states continue to have an expiry date on sexual crimes.[9] In another high-profile case, police in Sweden faced a time expiry on allegations of rape against Julian Assange, the founder of WikiLeaks, who lived in the Ecuadorean Embassy in London from 2012 to 2019.[10]

Statutes of limitations work to the advantage of perpetrators and the institutions that protect them. There is chilling evidence of the lobbying efforts of the Catholic Church to oppose repeal of the statute of limitations for sex crimes in a number of US states.[11] Despite these efforts, the tide is turning. The gathering pace of changes in the law regarding time limitations in both criminal and civil sexual assault cases reflects a more complex understanding of the reasons why survivors typically do not report an assault and will only do so when they have begun to recover and take stock. The disclosures by Wade Robson and James Safechuck of their prolonged sexual abuse by Michael Jackson as children is a high-profile example of the same phenomenon.[12] Evidence submitted by police to the Victoria, Australia, Parliamentary Commission on the Handling of Child Abuse by Religious and Other Organizations demonstrated that the average length of time that elapsed before a child experiencing sexual abuse reported to police was twenty-four years.[13] They were intimidated by the way rape victims are treated in the criminal and civil justice system, where they are subject to hostile treatment and intrusive and insensitive cross-examination.[14]

My civil case against the church was filed in March 2015. In August 2015, the church raised the limitations argument in their defence to our claim. Just as we expected, the church, now represented by their insurer, Ecclesiastical Insurance Group (EIG), argued that as a law professor and even as a law student, surely I must have known that I had a legal case? From the defence:

> The Defendant will contend that she [*this is a reference to me*] has or ought to have been aware, from an early stage, of her entitlement to pursue a claim in respect of the alleged abuse by MG and has not provided any proper explanation for her failure to do so at an earlier stage.[15]

To address the limitations argument, I wrote a memo for David titled "Reasons Why I Didn't File a Lawsuit against the Anglican Church Until Now: a 10-step Chronology."[16] It set out the sequence of events that finally brought me to a decision to begin a lawsuit. As I explained:

> [A]ll these steps towards my eventual decision to bring a lawsuit against the church, this decision-making process had nothing to do with my own legal knowledge. In making each decision and taking each step I am a *survivor of abuse,* trying to work out how to keep myself safe and gradually taking responsibility for speaking up to protect others—and *not a law professor.*[17]

The memo ended:

> It has taken me a very, very long time to reach a point of emotional readiness for this final step. I still experience a great deal of emotional turbulence and distress each time there are further developments in the case or I am required to do something additional (such as writing this statement). But I am ready now.[18]

THE CONSENT DEFENCE

The second major defence to our claim was also, in hindsight, sadly predictable. The Anglican Church, represented by Ecclesiastical Insurance Group, argued that I had consented to the sexual advances of the minister. The statement of defence stated that while the minister's "touching" (as they called it) might have been "inappropriate," it was "not unwelcome."[19]

I read that line over and over again. For a few minutes, I was just stunned. And then I was furious with myself. I had been sixteen and seventeen at the time of the assaults, so legally I could consent to sexual activity. I should have anticipated that the church would argue consent. But for some naïve reason I had not, and I was blindsided.

The week after I first read that phrase about my abuse being "not unwelcome" was very difficult. Like any other survivor bringing a claim forward, I expected to be frequently and intensely triggered while I spent so much time reading and thinking about the abuse. It was a traumatic time for me.

I came up with a metaphor to help my family understand what this experience was like for me, and why I had days during the litigation when I was extremely edgy and emotional. "PTSD," I explained, "is a bit like a jolt of electricity. When it happens, it shakes up your world both cognitively and emotionally—everything feels impossible. Being in this law suit now and reading all these horrible putdowns and dismissals of my experience feels like my fingers are stuck in the electricity socket, sort of buzzing away." This metaphor helped both them and me to accept and even somewhat normalize what was happening.

Consent. So blatantly absurd in my situation and so many others. The contention that a victim of assault actually consents to her own sexual violation is often described as "rape myth." The core of this idea is that a woman fantasizes about being sexually violated and is now denying her enjoyment of the act. Rape myth extends to many other false beliefs and misinformed stereotypes about "believable" victim behaviour, including running away and reporting immediately. Judith Lewis Herman has pointed out that rape myth serves as yet another (extremely effective) means of silencing of victims: "If secrecy fails, the perpetrator attacks the credibility of his victim. If he cannot silence her absolutely, he tries to make sure no one listens."[20] Even where there is no suggestion of consent, women who are sexually assaulted are often blamed for wearing inappropriate clothing, not taking proper caution, or simply spinning lies. Rape myth sustains the long-held assumption, conclusively disproved by numerous research reports emanating from law enforcement agencies,[21] that women routinely lie about rape and sexual assault and present false claims.

Rape myth is commonplace in defending both civil claims of sexual assaults and prosecutions for sex crimes.[22] Bullying complainants about whether they in fact "consented"—and suggesting that this is evidenced by, for example, not running away from their attacker, accepting a ride home with him that night, or texting him the next day—is commonplace. This primitive idea of "consent" harkens back to an era when women were widely mocked for talking about the importance of consent to sexual activity. As recently as 1993, *Saturday Night Live* ran a sketch about a game show called "Is it Date Rape?" which peddled familiar myths about the impossibility of requiring consent and how this would take "all the fun" out of sexual relations.[23]

The disconnect between the lived reality of victims and the legal system is most noticeable in the context of sexual abuse that is abetted by the power embedded in a professional or institutional relationship such as student/teacher, athlete/coach, or congregant/minister. Consent claims where there is a clear imbalance of power—between adults or between adults and children—have no credibility. In such cases, the dominant power of the perpetrator over the victim changes the nature of what it means to "consent" and indeed the whole definition of "rape." "[R]ather than defining rape as engaging in non-consensual sex, it would be defined as engaging in an act of sexual abuse of power, dominance, and control."[24]

MY TIPPING POINT

While the church's use of a limitations argument and the "consent" defence were their major legal arguments, their statement of defence contained further offensive material. The church argued that it would be impossible to know if the minister's abuse had actually had an impact on me given the other difficult experiences of my life, and referenced my other experiences of sexual violence and that I had recently been diagnosed with breast cancer. All this was upsetting, but a uniquely galvanizing moment arrived in the form of a letter from the Office of the Archbishop of Canterbury, Justin Welby, in November 2015.

David had written to Welby after raising my case with him personally when he met him at the General Synod. The written response to David included this line:

> I should be grateful if you would convey to your client the Archbishop's concern and apology on behalf of the whole Anglican Church for the shameful and distressing events mentioned in your earlier letter.

And then the sentence that tipped me over the edge:

> As a lawyer, you will be very aware of the constraints under which we in the profession have to work in dealing with these miserable matters. The scope for personal and sensitive engagement is very limited.

It may seem peculiar that amid the many intrusive, dishonest, and hurtful statements made by the church, this would be the final straw for me. But this assertion perfectly crystallized for me the church's wilful hypocrisy and the insincerity of their so-called apology.

It was unwise, to say the least, to try to persuade me that the church had no control over its lawyers and simply had to do what they told them to do. In some ways, it was almost funny. I had written a well-known book about lawyer/client relationships in 2008, based on years of empirical research.[25] It was a useful cover for the Anglican Church to pretend that they had no choice about their adversarial strategy, and perhaps another person without my background might have swallowed this. But given my background, I was not a good person to use this bogus argument on.

As any first-year law student will tell you, lawyers take instructions from their clients, not the other way around. Legal services are a simple transaction exchange—clients pay lawyers for their services and seek out their advice. Some lawyers press their advice, but the final decision-maker must be the paying client. He who pays the piper calls the tune.

When an insurer *subrogates* (takes over) the legal interests of a client, there are conventions regarding the management of litigation strategy by the insurance representatives. Insurance companies would not turn a profit if they paid out every claim, and their clients are expected to accept this. But it is obfuscation to claim that a large institutional repeat-client like the Anglican Church does not have the power to set standards and instruct their insurance representatives. If the Anglican Church wants its insurers' lawyers to behave in a highly adversarial and aggressive manner on its behalf, they can so command. If they wish them to pursue settlement in meritorious cases, avoid offensive and spurious defences, and respond to a lawsuit with empathy and a desire to see justice—they can do that too. Moreover, as I was going to learn over the next few months, the relationship between the Anglican Church and Ecclesiastical Insurance Group is a corporate one. The Anglican Church owns a majority share in EIG, its representatives sit on the EIG board making policy, and the church directly benefits from EIG's profits.[26]

The letter from the archbishop's office was a blatant attempt to offer David the traditional lawyer's "handshake" and make him complicit in the claim that there was nothing that could be done to rein in the insurer. I knew David would not be sucked in, but the tone and the dishonesty of this assertion infuriated me.

I went upstairs to my bedroom and crawled into bed, drawing the covers over my head. I could not believe what was happening. My world was upside down. What I knew to be true—not just personally, but as a matter of my professional work—was being denied. I felt shattered, drained. This was my lowest moment since we had started the lawsuit.

But after wallowing in bed for an hour, I suddenly sat up. Now I was enraged. I was going to call them out. I was going to show that the church was being, at best, disingenuous and, at worst, deliberately obfuscating their relationship with the lawyers and insurers and claiming to be powerless. I was going to reveal that their protestations of remorse, as they continued to aggressively defend sexual abuse claims because the lawyers "made them," were no more than crocodile tears.

I had a plan. I googled the *Church Times*, which I knew to be the world newspaper of the Anglican Church, and found the email of a submissions editor named Rachel Boulding. In the course of the next two hours, I wrote about two thousand words about the hypocrisy of the church's claim that they had no choice but to do what their lawyers told them and fight survivors tooth and nail. I emailed it to Rachel. I called it "Not for the Fainthearted," a reference to the consequences of taking on the church in litigation for historic sexual abuse. I heard back from Rachel first thing the next morning.[27] The *Church Times* wanted to publish my article.

Two extraordinary journalists, Rachel and *Church Times* editor, Paul Handley, worked with me over the next four weeks and navigated many obstacles to publication. Following good journalistic practice, Paul and Rachel showed my article to the diocese of Chichester, who threatened an injunction unless we removed the name of the diocese from my article. By now there was a concurrent police investigation of the minister by the Chichester police and the Crown Prosecution Service,[28] and they too required changes before lifting a threat of injunction. We went through dozens of drafts. There was also an effort to pressure me personally to withdraw the article, with the police scolding me that there was another "fragile" complainant who had come forward who would withdraw if I published the article (this complainant had told police the same story as mine about the same minister a few months earlier, prompting a police investigation).[29] As David and I suspected at the time, this claim turned out to be speculation by the police designed to put emotional pressure on me ("the other lady is so distressed and fragile"). This was confirmed when the other lady wrote to David and thanked me after my article was published.

I was in London for a week at the same time as Paul, Rachel, and I continued to negotiate the content of the *Church Times* piece with the various objectors. I also spent one afternoon being examined by the psychiatric "expert" appointed by the Anglican Church. Dr Anthony Maden was in fact no expert in childhood sexual abuse, known mostly for his work on female homicides. The use of partisan, regularly retained experts is a notorious feature of civil litigation[30] and evidently one that the church also stoops to. My examination was a brutal experience, despite being ready for him: I introduced myself as "Dr Macfarlane" when he first addressed me as "Julie," asked him questions about his qualifications and role, and openly set my phone down on his desk to record the conversation as we began. It was very clear that Dr Maden was fishing in my personal history for other explanations for the impact of the sexual abuse on me to minimize the damages the church would be asked to pay. This experience solidified even further my determination to do something to change the process systemically.

Paul and Rachel continued to painstakingly negotiate an acceptable version of the article that no one could stop them from publishing. During that time, the *Church Times* had a barrister on call, ready to defend against an injunction. Paul acknowledged, "we don't usually do this sort of thing and we don't have a legal budget: contesting the injunction would be £15,000 which is a little out of our ordinary costs, to say the least." They never once backed away from publishing the piece.

"Not for the Fainthearted" (the article finally came out under the title, "An Abuse Survivor's Tale") was published on December 11, 2015.[31] While we had been forced to make some amendments, the article did not pull its punches on the critical issues that had motivated me to write it.

As an academic, I have researched, written, and spoken about adversarial litigation tactics and strategies for many years. I am writing now to describe the litigation games that are being played in the name of the Church, which further traumatise survivors like me—even as the Church claims publicly to be sorry for these crimes. This is a breathtaking hypocrisy.[32]

I wrote about the church using a consent defence—"(T)he Church and its insurer's representatives perpetuate discredited and offensive myths about sexual assault"—and a limitations argument ("they hide behind archaic legal defences") to try to knock out my claim. I also wrote about the church's claim that they were remorseful, but had to do what their lawyers told them and fight each claim.

> The Church claims that it cannot control how legal claims brought against them are handled . . . In reality, an institutional client like the Church negotiates a policy and claims protocol with its insurer, and can ultimately control the management of claims and disputes . . . By permitting the lawyers, instructed by their insurers, to play games on their behalf, the Church is complicit in both their behaviour and its impact.[33]

Earlier versions of the article had called out the corporate relationship between the Anglican Church and EIG. At this time, little attention had yet been paid to this issue which was brought to public prominence by the research of another survivor, known as Gilo.[34] I was forced to remove this section to get the article published, but this symbiotic relationship was later covered and confirmed by BBC reporter Martin Bashir.[35]

I ended with this statement:

> Finally, I have been strongly discouraged—to put it mildly—from publishing this article. It has been difficult to sustain my commitment to speak openly about these issues in the face of pressure from many quarters to say nothing, and just focus on my own case.
>
> I recognise that this publication may make settlement of my own matter even more difficult. But my higher goal here is to expose the chasm between the public statements of the Church and their complicity in this immoral approach to sex-abuse litigation. If this article achieves that goal, it will have been well worth it.[36]

There was a huge response to the article. For weeks, my inbox was full of messages from both survivors and church members thanking me for what I had written. A flavour of the reaction, here is a typical response from a *Church Times* reader and a priest in the Anglican Church:

> I was involved in a case recently where again the Church behaved in exactly the two-faced and hypocritical way you described so powerfully. It was clear that their (the lawyers') attitude to my friend was "He can't afford to sue us, so ignore him" but that if he'd suddenly found someone willing to fund his case, they would have attempted to settle immediately!
>
> I thought this was outrageous, especially in light of the pious statements being made by our Archbishops and others. So I wrote to Justin Welby and told him so! And to his credit (and against the advice of the lawyers presumably) he then met with my friend which I thought was brilliant. And the church did subsequently make a settlement which my friend was happy with. But clearly this is always going to happen until the church, as a matter of course, instructs its lawyers to subjugate legal/financial concerns to the principles we're supposed to live by and die for as Christians.[37]

The *Church Times* article was picked up by other media, and I talked about the case on British national radio.

And all of a sudden, the church wanted to talk to us about settling my case.

YOU'RE THE PLAINTIFF?

Immediately following the publication of the *Church Times* article, EIG contacted David to ask for a settlement meeting. We agreed, of course, and I began to make arrangements to fly to the UK (EIG eventually agreed to pay my costs to travel).

It was winter 2016, and I was teaching my regular law school class on Dispute Resolution. Both as a matter of courtesy and for logistical reasons, I decided that I needed to give my students a heads-up that I might need to travel to the UK that term if a settlement meeting took place, and I would perhaps need to reschedule a few classes. I had to decide what to tell them.

My instinct was that I should be completely open about what

I was going through in the lawsuit. It would be interesting both for them and for me. I could not ignore that the course I was teaching this semester—Dispute Resolution—was about the process of negotiating a settlement in a lawsuit. Here was the perfect case study—my own. How could I not tell the students what was happening and, perhaps, get them involved in planning, anticipating, and strategizing with me?

But should I? Some of these students might have been aware of the speech I gave two years earlier, before the lawsuit began, for Sexual Assault Awareness Day. Other than this, unless they subscribed to the *Church Times* or followed UK news, this would be the first time they would be hearing that their professor was a plaintiff in a lawsuit against the church for sexual abuse.

One day in class I took the plunge: "I need to give you guys a heads-up that I might need to be away one or two classes this term—and we shall of course try to reschedule those so we don't miss any time together. The reason is that I am—I am, umm—I am the plaintiff in—umm—a sexual abuse case in the UK. And I may need to be available for settlement discussions. I am also hoping that we can use this case, my case, as a class case study for considering settlement strategies and possible outcomes—"

In an instant, all two dozen students in my seminar class looked up from their laptops. They looked puzzled, unsure if they had really heard what they thought they had just heard their professor say. There were several beats of silence. Then, a hand shot up.

"Professor Macfarlane?" A young man nervously cleared his throat.

"Can I ask, um, as the mediator in this case, who are your clients?"

"Actually, I'm the plaintiff."

He struggled on. "I mean, as the mediator, how did you get brought into this case?" (The students were accustomed to me referring to my experience as a third-party mediator in this class.)

I responded, "I'm the plaintiff. I am bringing a sexual abuse claim against the Anglican Church, who is the defendant. This happened when I was a teenager and still living in the UK."

A feeling of shock descended on the room. Now instead of silence there was a lot of fidgeting and anxious smiles and exchanged glances (which I interpreted as "maybe now she has *really* gone off the deep end—?").

Instinctively, I tried for reassurance: "It's alright guys, really I am fine with talking about this. And if anyone doesn't want to participate in this discussion, I am fine with that too."

They looked both dubious and shell shocked, but I could tell that a lot of intense googling was going on.

My first task as a teacher seemed to be to try to help them adjust to the idea that their law school prof had just disclosed to them that she had been sexually abused by a church minister as a child. I laboured on:

"This is a great opportunity for you to work with me on a real live case! As the plaintiff, I am completely committed to talking with you about the case, and I shall answer any questions you have, okay? And if you would prefer not to engage with this as a case study, you can certainly opt out." I was clumsily and inadequately trying to signal that I did not want to trigger anyone. In hindsight, I regret that I had the intention but no good plan on how to facilitate that, other than "talk to me."

"But if you are able I think you can help me to plan my strategy. I think you could help me think this through and that in the process it will be a learning opportunity for you too. Let me tell you some more . . ."

It was an awkward start, but this was to become one of the most rewarding and inspiring experiences of my thirty-five years of teaching. CBC, the Canadian national media outlet, shot some footage of my class a few weeks later when the students were discussing strategy for settlement, and the atmosphere was electric. Once they had got used to the idea (and no one spoke to me about opting out, although I reiterated this a few times) everyone seemed to be engaged in the task. These students worked with me on preparing for the first settlement meeting which was now set for February 2016, later that term, and subsequently on the proposal that formed stage two of those negotiations. I will be forever grateful to them for accepting what I told them and helping me to be the best negotiator I could be. I hope it really was a good learning experience for them.

THE FIRST SETTLEMENT MEETING

Before the first meeting, I began to develop an idea which centred on the overhaul of the existing claims process which I had found so upsetting and would, I reasoned, be even worse for anyone unfamiliar with litigation culture. In short, I wanted a new claims protocol for handling sexual abuse cases against the Anglican Church.

I was less concerned about my own financial settlement, which I believed (correctly) could be resolved quickly and easily. Much more difficult was trying to explain to the litigators handling the case at EIG my realization that what I wanted was a new claims protocol as a settlement. Their initial reaction was to say, "Oh sure, we can talk about that if you like"—I think they expected a five minute chat at the end of the settlement meeting when we would all speculate politely and vaguely about how the process could be improved. It was clear that they did not really understand what I was asking for—which was that I wanted to be directly involved in negotiating a new claims protocol which would limit or, better, eschew some of the defences and tactics used against me and would offer a genuinely supportive environment for claimants. I wanted these to include, for example, immediate payment for therapy and guarantees that victims coming forward would not be thrown out of their church communities (something I had learned about in the avalanche of mail I received from church members after the *Church Times* article was published).

"Look," I explained over and over, "I am a dispute resolution specialist and I have designed many claims processes over the years. I want to work with you on a new claims process, and have the people who need to sign off on it sign off, and then I want this new process published on the EIG website so your commitments to a better process are public and transparent."

"Really?" said David—at first.

Me: "Yes, really."

But first, we had to sit down with the church and its various representatives and put this idea into a formal written undertaking.

In preparation for the settlement discussions, I wrote an "opening statement" that I would insist on delivering at the start of the meeting. As a long-time mediator, I was accustomed to encouraging parties to create such a statement, which would set out their goals and motivations and hopes for the mediation. Why wouldn't I take my own advice—I needed the same approach here.

My goals were to first present myself as a real person and strip away the passive anonymity that surrounds and obscures so much discussion of sexual abuse. I wanted the church officials and lawyers in the room to see me both as a survivor and as a professional person who understood the iniquities of the claims process and its damage to victims (and the church's reputation). I worked on my opening statement—what I should say and how—with my Dispute Resolution class, as we covered this as a course topic.[38] I felt ready, or as ready as I could be.

I flew to the UK with Bernie, and we arranged for Sibyl, my eldest daughter, to come with us to the settlement meeting, which was held in central London.[39] We rented an apartment in my familiar East London neighbourhood. The morning of the meeting, Bernie took some video which provides some interesting insights into my state of mind. When I watch it now, I am struck by how clear I am about my goals for the day and by my apparent calm and focus. I remember feeling like a bit of a basket case, but my resolve is clear.

"What do you want to achieve today?" asked my husband.

> I want to explain to them why I am motivated not just to resolve my own case, but to change the way claimants are treated when they come forward . . . They still don't really understand that I am not going to settle the quantum[40] until we have a commitment to the systemic changes.
>
> I think one of the things we are going to have to work through today is convincing them that it's not enough to say "yes, yes, good points." I want this to actually get fixed in a way that I am quite certain it can be with enough work and thinking. I think we can make a significant difference if we change the institutional processes.[41]

We assembled in a conference room at the law firm of the litigator retained by EIG and the church to represent them, Paula Jefferson. The first thing we discovered was that she would not be at the meeting. Her husband was sick and she was with him in Spain. Paula participated by phone, which was the most she could do, but it lent a slightly surreal feeling to the whole affair. She was after all the most important player on the church side when it came to making decisions, and I was sorry that she would only be able to listen and not to watch me give my opening statement. The others in the room were a deaconess, who was there on behalf of the church to say "they were very sorry"; a junior lawyer working with Paula; a representative from EIG; and David, Bernie, Sibyl, and I.

We began as I had requested with my opening statement, which I read (the participants had been provided with a summary in advance, so they knew what was coming). I began by introducing myself and my background and acknowledging that I understood a settlement meeting was an opportunity to size up a plaintiff if the matter were to go to trial. I said that I thought I would be credible and effective if I had to testify and was committed to doing so if necessary. I think they got that message.

Next, I reassured the people in the room that settling on an amount of damages with me would not be difficult. It was not my priority. I also reminded them that David and I had already given notice that we would not engage in a discussion of the so-called expert report by Dr Maden, which we saw as partisan and biased. Moreover it was not the work of an expert. No one raised it.

I then turned to what was important to me.

My highest interest here is in changing the way that survivors are treated when they step forward with a claim against the church.

My goal—to which I am 100% committed—is stopping what has happened to me happening to those that come after me; and thereby enabling and encouraging other survivors to come forward. This is consistent with what the church publicly states, over and over, that it wants. It is time to make that assertion by the church the reality of the actual practice of legitimate claim reviews, because it is painfully obvious that few people would or could put themselves through what is required to bring a claim forward—what I am living, in other words. I am sure that you are aware that survivors are regularly and constantly re-traumatized by the process they must endure.

It may well be—and I suspect that this is the case, in fact—that many of the process issues I shall be raising with you today arise from convention, and that your protocols in responding to claims are unintentional, reflecting normative behavior by lawyers rather than conscious choices.

But the restoration of relationships—and that is what the church says is its goal here, and not the intimidation and deterrence of survivors from coming forward—requires intentionality. I am going to try to persuade you to place a new intentionality—one that is characterized by good faith, not by adversarial and hostile tactics—at the centre of what we try to achieve as a result of my case, with today as a first step.

I then spoke about three central issues for me; the church's use of a consent defence; their recourse to arguing that actions against them for clerical sexual abuse were time-limited; and the clear strategy of minimizing the harms done to victims of clerical abuse. The part I enjoyed delivering the most was when I talked about their disgusting consent argument. I saw responsibility for this as shared by the church's lawyers, insurance representatives, and church representatives; in short, everyone in the room.

> We all understand that this (consent arguments) is a standard strategy by the defence in a sex assault case. For example, in your statement of defence it was claimed that the forced fellatio I was subjected to as a 16 and 17-year old over a period of almost a year was "not unwelcome." The psychiatric report is filled with innuendo about my "consent." So was my psychiatric examination.
>
> Let's roleplay this. I am on my knees before the minister, to whom I have gone for spiritual counseling. He unzips his pants and tells me that God wants me to suck his penis (I have never seen a penis before). I am told that this is how I will resolve my spiritual crisis—this is a "test" of my faith that I must pass. So let's script this—how exactly do we think that the "consent" conversation would have played out here? Between the person I regarded as my spiritual mentor and myself at 16, with zero sexual experience and a strong commitment to my faith? Or on the multiple other occasions when this or a similar assault took place?
>
> We are all, I hope, far too sophisticated and sensible here to even entertain such a ludicrous notion.[42]

I paused at this point and allowed myself a glance at the people wearing business suits sitting around the settlement table. With the exception of David, my husband Bernie, and my daughter Sibyl, each of whom was looking directly at me, everyone was looking intently at the yellow legal pads in front of them, their eyes downcast. No one ever raised the issue of consent with me again. My sense was that they were ashamed. As they should have been.

The second issue I raised was the use of limitations defence to knock out historic claims, which I believe everyone in the room recognized was a technical loophole that the church was exploiting.

Finally, I turned to the minimization of impact.

> Third and finally, I want to talk about the default to arguing no or
> extremely limited impact for acts of abuse.
>
> Again, as legally trained people we all understand that quantum
> is always contentious and will always be argued over.
>
> But this does not mean that it is necessary and certainly not
> appropriate to pick as a starting point outright denial or offensive
> minimization of impact. For example, I don't think anyone here
> would seriously suggest that having a minister's penis forced into
> your mouth as a 16 and 17 year old, regularly, over a period of
> around a year, is going to have "no impact"—surely?
>
> In considering the impact, there are of course in any person's
> life—especially someone of my age!—multiple possible causes of
> PTSD. Undeniably. The science tells us that PTSD typically re-
> flects multiple causes. That does not mean—as the psychiatric re-
> port here bizarrely proposes—that if there is no conclusive proof
> of one single event causality, there is no PTSD. This is completely
> at odds with the accepted science.
>
> The report also contends that if I suffered from PTSD, I would
> have been unable to speak out publicly about my abuse, almost 40
> years after it happened, after preparing myself emotionally for this
> for years and rehearsing my text for weeks and weeks in advance.
> Again, the assumption is to minimize the impact on me, in order
> presumably to reduce the church's costs.
>
> Apparently if I am a functional and resilient person, I cannot
> have PTSD and I cannot have suffered. This risible claim would
> be shredded at trial by a genuine expert.

I concluded with the point that got me out of bed that awful
evening and galvanized me to write the *Church Times* article.

> So—let's give you the benefit of the doubt and say that recourse
> to the miserable tactics I have just described is unintentional.
> Because it is certainly not what your client says publicly that they
> want—and of course, your job as their instructed professionals is
> to advance your clients goals—not independent normative behav-
> iors of your own.
>
> In summary—in order to settle this case I want to talk con-
> cretely, practically and realistically about changes in your process

protocols and defaults when defending sex abuse claims against the church.

I have some concrete proposals for what and how.

Paula excused herself shortly after my opening statement, having had a private discussion with her junior. My sense was that her appraisal was "Game over." Before she signed off, she asked if I would send her a copy of the text of my opening statement so she could read it again and refer to it in future. I was happy to oblige.

After that we moved rapidly forward. Video footage shows David and me during a break looking relaxed but still focused on nailing some of our final stipulations for a timetable for designing a new claims process as well as my direct involvement. Another video shows David and me working on the memorandum of settlement that would be signed the following day.

By the end of the meeting, we had agreed on a financial settlement (as I had predicted, that took just twenty minutes of bargaining) and a plan to put together a new Claims Protocol for future claimants against the Anglican church, all of whom must go through EIG. Coming up with a formal and important-sounding name for something that has not been tried before (and capitalizing it!) is an old trick I have learned from years of activism. This involved an agreement to hold a Protocol Review Meeting with appropriate decision-makers present and including David and myself; a plan for developing an agenda for the Protocol Review Meeting; and a final date by which a new Protocol would be completed.

The agreement made it clear that if I was dissatisfied with the new Protocol, I would return to court with my claim. In other words, walking away with the damages we had agreed in principle that afternoon was contingent on my satisfaction with the new Claims Protocol. This agreement did not specify the issues on which I wanted change, but after the opening statement everyone at that meeting knew what I was coming for.

THE SECOND SETTLEMENT MEETING

The lawyers for the church were still having a hard time getting their heads around this settlement focus, but at least now they saw that I was serious.

I had not begun my lawsuit with this idea. I really did not expect to experience the claims process as so completely demoralizing and dehumanizing. I figured if it was this bad for me—someone with a legal background, a good understanding of what is going on, great support—how much harder or even impossible must this be for others without these advantages?

Using an individual case to develop a systemic outcome is a familiar strategy for test case advocates. Test case strategy relies on getting a precedent in an individual case that will change the law for others coming behind—just as the famous case of *Brown v Board of Education*[43] threw out legalized racial segregation in American schools and, in Canada, *Egan v Canada*[44] held that denying spousal benefits to a same-sex couple would be contrary to the Charter of Rights and Freedoms. Private settlement agreements are not bound to follow public case precedents, but they do have the advantage of being able to include more wide-ranging changes and secure a commitment to them. As a mediator I have sometimes encouraged parties making a settlement to think about systemic changes that are important to them—for example, changing the format of an internal workplace promotion process following an individual claim of unfair treatment, or requiring a hospital to review its patient complaints procedure following a malpractice lawsuit. I have always included discussion of this possibility when teaching Dispute Resolution, and the week after my written agreement with the church, my Dispute Resolution class and I were hard at work on a draft proposal for the Protocol Review Meeting.

It was easy to list the topics I wanted to address in the agenda, which David and I had agreed to circulate in advance. In addition to limiting the future use of consent and limitations defences, without-prejudice interim agreements to pay for therapy, continuing pastoral care, limited and appropriate use of experts, the list included procedure on receipt of a claim and efforts to find early settlement; the use of confidentiality clauses or non-disclosure agreements or NDAs; and data collection and monitoring of the new Protocol, once in effect. I talked with my class about the order in which I should raise these issues, whether any of them were non-negotiable, their level of priority, how the buy-in of the church could be maximized, and how to make the most convincing case for the changes I wanted to see. I hired an excellent law student to conduct detailed research on some of the ideas that were being tried in other jurisdictions. David and I went back and forth with first an agenda and then a detailed proposal for each agenda item, which would be circulated before the meeting, and any helpful additional context, including models elsewhere, for each idea.

I returned to London in April and, along with David, met with Paula Jefferson, the EIG lawyer from the first settlement meeting; a public inquiry specialist from another law firm retained by EIG to represent their interests at the upcoming Independent Child Sexual Abuse Inquiry or IICSA (where a segment would be devoted to the failures of the Anglican Church);[45] and the deputy official solicitor for the Church of England. I brought my cousin Elizabeth Macfarlane with me to the meeting. This was less about having Liz there for support—although she was terrific in that role—and more about the joy of revealing to the Anglican Church that I was first cousins with one of the most well-known advocates for the ordination of women and same-sex marriage.[46] I would have loved to have been a fly on the wall when I first informed the church that I would be bringing Liz, the Chaplain of St Johns College Oxford, with me as my support person. She even wore her clerical collar (not her preferred dress mode) to the meeting that day as a special favour.

THE NEW GUIDING PRINCIPLES

The process of negotiating a new claims Protocol—what I described in a subsequent article in the *Church Times* as a claimants' "Bill of Rights"[47]—was remarkably smooth. David and I were extremely well-prepared for the meeting, and it was quickly clear that, although we would not get everything we wanted, most of our "asks" turned out to be hard for EIG to refuse.

The meeting got off to a slightly bumpy start, with the chair (Peter Jones, the lawyer representing EIG at the upcoming Independent Child Sexual Abuse Inquiry) behaving as if I had flown 6,500 kilometres for the excitement of the event and to hear him talk. Once I had clarified my motivations to him, we made good progress, with growing engagement on all sides of the table. At a break, Paula Jefferson and I talked for a while in the ladies bathroom. Paula was still expressing her surprise that the new Protocol was the focus of my settlement, but she was curious now and wanted to know more about why. We continued to correspond about this after the meeting.

What EIG were to call their new "Guiding Principles"[48] would incorporate new process commitments and the principles that underpinned these. Our proposals on immediate therapy for survivors, paid for by the church, and continuing pastoral care were easy to negotiate, as was an undertaking to treat complainants with empathy and respect. We were not able to extract an undertaking to never again use limitations defences, but negotiated strong language and a new procedure to ensure that this would be exceptional,[49] rather than a default position. Some of the language was weaker than I might have hoped for, for example an "in-principle" commitment to the use of joint experts.[50] Some of what was agreed to went beyond our expectations; for example, the adoption of language about "power imbalance" that we proposed be used as critical context in understanding the fallacy of "consent" in this context,[51] and a ready acceptance that there would be no non-disclosure agreements to protect the church, and instead only if the claimant asked for one.[52] I did not know at the time that this single issue—often abbreviated to "NDA"—would return when I reached the final stages of my experience with the University of Windsor over their protection of an abusive professor a few years later.[53]

As we debriefed afterwards, David and I agreed that we had achieved approximately 80 per cent of what we wanted at the Protocol Review Meeting, in other words, significantly more than we had first imagined was possible. The looming of the Independent Child Sexual Abuse Inquiry[54] certainly helped to focus the parties around the table that day, and we made much of the assertion that it would look a lot better if the church were to agree to new and better procedures for victims bringing forward claims of sexual abuse against clerics, rather than being forced to accept change by the inquiry's recommendations. But we also found the insurance representatives ready, relieved almost, to accept these constraints on the unbridled use of adversarial tactics. It was a learning experience for all of us.

EIG has since made much of the fact that they are "first in the industry" to develop such principles for claims handling for physical and sexual abuse matters and an "industry leader." The Guiding Principles went up on the EIG website in May 2016, and I wrote a plain language factsheet version for MACSAS (Ministers and Clerics Sexual Abuse Survivors).[55] Of course, the real impact of the new claims process is unclear without proper monitoring and evaluation. This was a strike for change, but I am well aware that it is possible to render even the most apparently fair process a charade without the will to make the principles stick. I have heard from a number of survivors that they have been able to access therapy and were able to remain in their church congregations. I have also heard from others who report continued bullying by the insurer in settlement processes and efforts to insinuate consent defences. I have attempted, unsuccessfully, to gather some evaluation data via plaintiff's lawyers, but a credible independent review is needed to continue to hold EIG accountable to the agreements made here. Otherwise sexual assault litigation seems doomed to repeat the same injustices over and over.

Ecclesiastical is an international company that also insures the Anglican Church in Canada. During a Canadian case involving the decades-long sexual and emotional abuse of a female congregant—an adult—by a minister with a history of predation, the insurer and the church used consent and rape myth to distort and minimize her evident exploitation (Dawn's case, described in chapter 2). This case was settled in 2019. Despite my repeated reference to the Guiding Principles, I was unable to insert them into the process of negotiations with the insurer and the church. However, Ecclesiastical Canada has since adopted an abbreviated version of the UK parent company's Guiding Principles.[56]

NEGOTIATING WITH THE CHURCH

Negotiating with the Anglican Church[57] is definitely not for the fainthearted, but it is possible.

Many of the issues that we debated in my settlement process are likely to be regulated and legislated as the voices of survivors and their advocates become more powerful. Many hopes rest on the outcomes of the Independent Child Sexual Abuse Inquiry, which is still ongoing. My own view and that of many others is the church cannot be trusted to do its own safeguarding, and the process and redress for sexual abuse must be taken away from them and given to a credible, accountable, independent body with survivor representation.

It was a fascinating experience for me to be the disputant in such a protracted and complex negotiation after twenty years of facilitating settlement discussions as a neutral third party. In some ways it was humbling as I more deeply understood the stress that such processes place on disputants who are obviously emotionally invested in the outcome. I also learned many new things about effective negotiation strategies that I had for many years coached others to adopt. I hope it has made me a better teacher.

I sent my students in Dispute Resolution 2016 the final Claims Protocol with a note of thanks to them for all their assistance. When I read now about EIG bragging about its sex-abuse claims policy "setting the industry standard" I always smile and think "My class and I wrote that."

THE POLICE GET INVOLVED

But after all this work and some success, I was still not done with the minister.

In August 2014, as my civil suit first got moving, and long before the settlement meetings described above, I went to the UK for a much-anticipated family vacation. We found an Airbnb in my old East London neighbourhood, close to where Sibyl and I had lived when she was a baby and just a few miles from where she now lived as an adult. We travelled to London with our youngest daughter Hopey and her friend Skye, and my stepson Mark was joining us there. A few weeks later, we would go to France where we would meet up with Sibyl for a canal holiday, then back to London and up to Scotland with Mark and Hopey. It was going to be a wonderful time.

The night we arrived in London Fields was a delightfully chaotic family reunion. We crammed into the tiny flat we had rented, suitcases and backpacks everywhere. Jet-lagged but up for a celebration, we discussed where we would go for dinner that evening. Then my phone rang.

It was David Greenwood, who had just started representing me in the civil suit. He had just been informed by Sussex police that a few days earlier, a woman had walked into the Chichester police station and told the same story as I had about being assaulted by Meirion Griffiths almost forty years earlier. I was stunned. With some difficulty, I cleared a space of suitcases and bags and sat down, heavily.

"What? Are you sure? She's talking about Griffiths?" Absolutely, David assured me. Apparently there was an uncanny level of similarity regarding details, although ever the professional, David was careful not to tell me what these were. "But why now? This just happened?" "I don't know, and yes" David replied.

What, I wondered, had prompted this woman to come forward now? At this stage, I had not yet gone public in the UK with my story, so she knew nothing about me. But there had been a rash of disclosures of sexual abuse by prominent individuals that summer in the UK, including a notorious predator whom we had all watched regularly on TV for six decades, an entertainer named Jimmy Savile. In the summer of 2012, a year after his death, a police investigation (Operation Yewtree) into more than four hundred abuse complaints against Savile described him as a "predatory sex offender." Perhaps the climate of disclosures about abuse had given this woman the push she needed to make a formal complaint against Griffiths, all these years later.[58]

I didn't know what to feel. I had never imagined a criminal prosecution. I didn't feel that I needed Griffiths to be punished in that way, just removed from access to young people to prey on (it did not occur to me until much later that a successful criminal prosecution and jail was in fact the only way to guarantee this). As I struggled with this, standing in the middle of a tiny sitting room full of people, bags, chaos, and laughter, David put the pertinent question: if there is now a second complainant, would you be willing to work with police to prosecute Griffiths? Well, yes. I knew immediately that having two complainants would present an opportunity for a successful criminal case. I felt I had a responsibility to do this, to take this opportunity for another level of justice, and support the other complainant by agreeing to participate and go forward. So, yes.

David gave me the name and phone number of the officer dealing with the file, along with this message: "It is important that we speak to you as soon as possible." Over the next four or five days, I called the number I had been given by David at least once and sometimes twice a day. Each time I called, I was told—often brusquely and what felt like dismissively—that the officer I was asking for was not available. Each time I left my number and asked for the officer to call me back (this never happened). Each time I called I tried to explain that this was a historical sex-abuse allegation, and that I had been asked by this officer to call and discuss this. Taken aback at the lack of sensitivity in how I was spoken to, I tried to explain that it was upsetting for a sex-abuse victim to be talked to as if they were a nuisance, that I had been asked to call and consider helping police, and that the circumstances were quite emotionally difficult. I know that the way I was spoken to in those calls would have deterred many people from continuing. Trying to follow police instructions and step forward as I had been asked to do was turning into yet another upsetting, retraumatizing experience.

I decided with Bernie that I needed to stop calling over and over, at least for now, and try to enjoy our family holiday. I let David know and went back to my vacation. No one from Chichester police ever returned my calls and messages. Eventually on my return to Canada in September, I asked David to follow-up for me. I also made it clear that if I was going to agree to do a police interview, it had to be with officers trained and experienced in talking to sex-abuse victims. Eventually I heard from the Major Crime Branch of the Windsor police. My interview—conducted and videotaped by two Ontario Provincial Police (OPP) officers, one male and one female, with kindness, tact, and professionalism—finally took place in the summer of 2015, a full year after I had first been contacted by Chichester police. The wheels of criminal justice turn slowly, it seems, in relation to historic sexual abuse. I could not help wondering whether if Griffiths was accused of murder, or even another type of violence like arson or theft, the pace might pick up a little.

After my video interview, I set a calendar reminder to email the officer handling the investigation in Chichester every four weeks. Each month I received a one-line reply: there is no news to report. The first time I received any unprompted communication was in April 2016—almost two years after that first phone call from David—when I was informed that Griffiths was being charged with six counts of indecent assault. Progress at last!

Since Griffiths was still living in Perth, Australia, where I had located him in the early 1990s, the welcome news that a decision had been made to charge him turned out to be just the beginning of what lay ahead. Fortunately I now had a police officer with whom I corresponded regularly at Chichester police who was much more conscientious—and kind—about keeping me informed than his predecessor.[59] Next, the UK authorities had to work through the paperwork with their Australian counterparts to apply for extradition to the UK where Griffiths would stand trial for indecent assault. This took another eighteen months. All necessary formalities for extradition were completed at Westminster Magistrates Court in December 2016, the same month that Bernie and I went to see *Spotlight*,[60] a newly released movie about cover-ups of sexual abuse in the Catholic Church.

On my way home, discussing with Bernie how the film showed priests showing up in different churches after being identified as abusers, I did something I had not allowed myself to do before. I googled Meirion Griffiths. As I stared at my phone, I saw that Griffiths was listed as a minister—with his sermons available on YouTube—at a church called the Uniting Church in Billabong, Perth. Just up the road from the Anglican church that threw him out in 1999. So he really wasn't out of circulation, as I had believed back in 1999 when the Anglican Church terminated him. He just took up in another church.

This discovery made waiting for his pending arrest in Australia and his arrival in the UK even harder. This part of the criminal law process, and the story of the eventual trial of the minister, is told in chapter 7.

CHAPTER 6

HOLDING MY INSTITUTION TO ACCOUNT

(T)he way abuse is handled from the top down, that's the single greatest factor of whether or not a predator is going to be safe, and whether anyone who receives a report of abuse is going to be motivated to handle it properly.

—Rachael Denhollander
"Predators Know Where They're Going to be Safe"

One of the most disturbing questions raised by the sexual abuse scandals that are being uncovered in institutions ranging from churches[1] to sports clubs[2] to the entertainment industry[3] to children's hospitals[4] is this: *How much did anyone know?*

The final unmasking of a person who has abused their power and authority inside an institution to harass, manipulate, and exploit more vulnerable individuals is sometimes described as a shock by other members of the same institution or community. This expression of surprise, sometimes after years of unheeded complaints, often amounts to little more than self-preservation and wilful blindness[5] (for example, "I had heard rumours but . . ."). Among women, knowledge of predatory and abusive men inside an institution is often an open secret. In many cases, it is impossible to avoid the conclusion that people who could have done something to stop a long-term pattern of abuse were aware of what was happening, yet did nothing.

This sense of shock may be genuine for some, when a "successful" (undetected) predator is able to hide among colleagues, parents, or other members who regard them as "a good person" or

102

"a nice guy." Writing about campus sexual violence in Missoula, Missouri, Jon Krakauer shares the story of "Frank":

> Predators like Frank get away with it over and over . . . because most of us are in denial. We're disinclined to believe that someone who's an attentive student or a congenial athlete could also be a serial rapist.[6]

Predatory behaviour includes, but is not limited to, sexual assaults of the type that Frank was accused of. "Predatory" is commonly defined as behaviour intended to exploit, injure, or oppress. At the core of predatory behaviour inside institutions is the exploitation of power bestowed by the institution, either formally—for example a teacher, professor, coach, or cleric—or informally—for example a student athlete or "popular" guy. This power is used to intimidate and silence those who would complain, and to manipulate and take advantage of those who feel they have no choice but to comply. This pattern allows many predators to continue their behaviours over many years, often in the face of credible complaints.

Why are so many complainants disbelieved, dismissed—or both—until there is a deluge, such as the one that finally brought down the high school drama teacher (described in chapter 2)? Is it because the institution is confident that they can just ignore the problem? Is it because of genuine commitment to the institution and an overriding commitment to prevent it being undermined by a scandal, or even destroyed? Is it because the exploitation and harassment of vulnerable people is not understood as a systemic issue inside hierarchical institutions? Whatever the answer, these emerging scandals demonstrate over and over that the needs of the institution trump the needs of victims. Worse still, the structure and culture of many institutions—frequently self-reinforcing, prideful, and hierarchal, along with a general unwillingness to question past practice or tradition—often provide and sustain the conditions that protect predatory behaviours.

As we are shocked by sordid tales of abuse, harassment, and violence inside institutions, it is important to learn lessons from these miserable sagas. I have already described my experience of dealing with the Anglican Church[7] and the many hurdles placed in the way of victims like myself achieving accountability and justice. In this chapter, I shall add a second personal story of going up against an institution—in this case my employer, the University of Windsor—that was extremely reluctant to face the consequences of the harassment of students and the failure of their existing systems. This experience has further deepened my awareness of the extent of the protectionism that seems to outweigh concerns for the safety of students and other employees.

INSIDE MY OWN INSTITUTION

In 2013, I became aware that a faculty colleague was spending a great deal of time socializing with students and posting pictures on social media from parties and other social events involving law students. This professor had developed a "following" of students, primarily among young men who regarded him as influential and cool. One (female) student at the time recalls, "on my first day of class [the professor] introduced himself by saying, 'if you haven't done a shot with me yet, I'm [professor's name].'"[8] He used his influence to orchestrate student support to win a series of internal awards—"Professor of the Year"—that helped him to build a reputation as powerful and important. The professor's "cult" created an environment in the law school that felt toxic and hostile toward women students, many of whom described his behaviour to me as inappropriate and "creepy."[9]

Professors, especially those in professional schools such as law, hold a lot of potential personal and professional power over students. This power can be used for good—for example introducing students to future employers, giving them a letter of reference—and it can also be used to manipulate and control. Many examples of inappropriate control were reported to me by students. They told me that he made it clear that students who kept him at a distance could suffer academically and professionally. They described ways in which he retaliated against students who stood up to him, once setting an examination question in his class asking students to discuss how female students could be sued for defamation. He used social media—a relatively new and influential means of control available to professors—extensively to promote himself and his student "followers" and to denigrate and intimidate others. He was the only professor active on the Law Student Society Facebook page, created for each incoming cohort of first-year students before they arrived on campus in September. This meant that he was known to many incoming students especially to those to whom he gave a lot of attention, who were of course flattered by the attention of a professor.

I was told by a number of students that all this and more had been well-known for a considerable time among students and alumni, but apparently not among the professoriate. I had been wondering for some time if there was more to the story of the "party prof" who liked to hang out with students so much. Then in late 2013 I learned from my associate dean that she had received reports of this professor allegedly harassing two of our female students (she did not name them). My own past experiences probably made me hyper-aware of the way this individual was exploiting his institutional power to inflate his power and influence, and creating fear among those who resisted or challenged his abuse of power, convincing them he could damage their future prospects.[10] I disclosed to my own research assistants, two of whom were first-year students whom I saw as especially vulnerable to the "party professor," that I had been the victim of an institutionally protected predator when I was younger. I did this because I thought if any of the students had experienced problems with him, it might enable them to feel comfortable sharing this with me.

One student spoke to me privately. She disclosed that she had been rebuffing the professor's advances for some time, but they were persistent and explicit, and she was stressed and scared. She was frightened of bringing forward a complaint against him, telling me that she was worried about how he might retaliate against her and to those close to her if she did so. Along with four of my colleagues and a core of scared but determined law students, I then began the extraordinarily arduous and time-consuming process of trying to get the university to deal with a tenured faculty member who was the subject of student complaints about abuse of power and harassment. Following a lengthy investigation, he was eventually informed of the university's intention to dismiss him for "cause" under our collective agreement (despite being a complainant, I was never interviewed by the investigator nor did I receive a copy of the investigation report, despite asking for this multiple times). The university and the faculty association settled his subsequent grievance by (among other terms) giving him a non-disclosure agreement and a letter of reference from the provost, who was designated as the only point of contact for future references. The provost's letter made no reference to his proposed termination for harassment, intimidation, and abuse of power and authority. This meant that he could apply for positions in other university law schools without their knowing anything about the circumstances of his departure.[11] This agreement was secret, and was not conveyed to faculty who might be asked, as I later was, for a reference for him.

I only deduced that the university must have given him a non-disclosure agreement when I received a call in the spring of 2016 from a colleague at an out-of-country law school. He was considering an application for a position from my former colleague and wondered why he had left a tenured position at my university. Neither this law school, nor the second school he applied to for a position (and whom I was contacted by almost a year later), were able to get any information from my university about the real circumstances of his departure. In responding to each inquiry, I told the truth—that he was to be terminated for "just cause" following an investigation. I also explained that I knew directly of one student who had told me in detail about his harassment of her and that I believed that there were others too frightened to come forward. My former colleague then sued me for "defamation."

But I'm getting ahead of myself—there are many twists and turns to this story and its aftermath, which I shall discuss in this chapter. The details of this story illustrate pervasive systemic problems in the reporting, investigation, and redress for complaints about abuse of power, harassment, and predatory behaviour in universities. What is revealed is an institutional culture that tolerates abuse and then protects powerful insiders.

WHAT WE KNOW ABOUT INSTITUTIONS

An important starting point in understanding these scandals is the unique character of an institution. Whether large or small, whatever their mission or mandate, institutions share many common attributes that are critical to understanding why so many have protected abusers rather than victims.

Sociologist Anthony Giddens observes, "Institutions by definition are the more enduring features of social life."[12] Whether large public institutions (for example, hospitals, schools, courts, universities) or smaller institutions, like clubs or churches, they often have a history in their communities,[13] and they frequently play a broader social role as community gathering places (for example youth groups, churches, sports clubs).

Institutional norms about membership—who is considered to be a "member" or associated with that institution in some way, as well as what it means to be a "good member"—are critical to their identity. While these norms vary widely, reflecting different types of institutional mandates and culture, they are all characterized by a collective energy and identity or "spirit."[14] Members (for example employees, congregants, team members, alumni) are expected to accept a set of shared symbols, meanings, and rituals, and typically refer to the institution as "we." Institutions exercise control over their members because they can bestow both acceptance—successful passage through an education program for a student, promotion for an employee, or tenure for a professor; first team membership for an athlete; a leading role for an actor—or in the alternative, exclusion and rejection. Conformity to the values of the institution is essential for inclusion. The high school students who stood outside the "cult" of the abusive teacher and raised questions about his behaviour were shunned by their peers as well as for years ignored by the school board.[15] If you are a competitive athlete, you may get left off the team if you report the coach's sexual misconduct.[16]

In many cases, a complainant fearfully anticipates exclusion or punishment by the institution when they bring forward an allegation of sexual abuse and harassment and may choose to keep silent about their grievance. The stronger the institutional identity of the organization, the more the pressure to conform and the greater the backlash against what is regarded as "deviance"—which would include reporting of the sexual misconduct of a leader or powerful member. Members of the Anglican Church have told me that after filing a complaint about clerical sexual abuse, they were told by their local minister that they could no longer attend church services. While some of the victims of church sex-abuse scandals have no interest in remaining part of their church community, this is not the case for everyone. For these individuals, being told they "cannot" attend church because of a pending lawsuit is both isolating and distressing. It is punishment.[17]

Institutions both large and small also have some shared decision-making characteristics. Institutional leaders—church leaders, the president of a justice system or a university—are typically invested with broad personal power and discretion to make decisions and to act in what they deem to be the best interests of the institution. I have learned that "best interests" are almost always understood as placing the status quo and short-term reputation of the institution above risk of disruption from change. This is sometimes justified as putting the reputation of the institution ahead of the "interests" of a single individual, and above a thorough investigation of a potentially ugly secret. Many institutions are dominated by white male leadership and either minimize or disbelieve women's reports of sexual violence. The churches are an obvious example of an institution that has historically excluded women (as well as members of the LGBTQ community) from significant roles and have sought to exercise control over women's bodies and reproductive decisions. Many institutions are founded on colonialist values that seek to control Indigenous Peoples. The residential schools system in Canada, where multiple sexual abuses have been uncovered, is an obvious example.[18] All this plays into the culture of denial and protectionism and the neglect of victims.

However flawed, institutions are important to their members. They are an important source of our sense of who we are and the community to which we belong. Therein lies much of their power. The emotional impact of being denied justice by a trusted institution to which we have turned for help is described by Jennifer Freyd as "institutional betrayal."[19] Institutional betrayal is part of the experience for many of those speaking out about sexual violence.[20] When a complainant reports sexual assault or harassment to police, their church, sports club, university or school, or to workplace managers, they do so with trepidation because of the explosive nature of the story they tell. But they also carry a valid expectation that they will be treated empathetically, listened to, and that their complaint will be treated as a serious matter and properly investigated. In so many cases (and especially for women who are already marginalized and subject to prejudice), this is not what happens. Instead survivors are frequently retraumatized with harsh and disrespectful treatment and their complaint dismissed or buried. It feels like "a second assault."[21] Stories of multiple women reporting about a single predator—twenty years ago, ten years ago, last week—with no response from the institution are legion. These stories (and others untold) represent thousands of women bringing forward complaints to trusted places who are turned away.

Betrayal trauma theory (BTT) describes how survivors who knew their abusers generally suffer higher levels of trauma than those attacked by a stranger, leading to higher levels of dissociation. Where the institution is important to them, victims are more likely to make excuses for the behaviour of the perpetrator and to minimize their own trauma—sometimes described as "betrayal blindness."[22] A would-be complainant is usually acutely conscious of the damage their claims may inflict on an institution to which they feel personal loyalty, and they may have held off complaining for a long time. Once the betrayal becomes obvious—in the institution's refusal to help the victim or, worse, by the protection of the predator—the emotional and psychological costs are very high. Some survivors describe this as the worst part of their entire experience. Their faith in an institution with which they closely identify is shattered. Unsurprisingly, high betrayal trauma theory is strongly associated with complex PTSD.[23]

Ultimately, we have to understand the institutional instinct to deny and rebuff allegations of sexual assault and abuse through the lens of power. The public image or reputation of an institution is critical to its continuing power and influence over its members, persuading them to continue to buy into the mission of the institution. Institutional reputation effectively determines the institution's success and longevity. Many institutions can only continue to hold power over members (employees, congregants, alumni) and external supporters by maintaining their positive reputation.

Reputations can be made and destroyed rapidly, and they may be volatile. An institution's reputation is built around the reputation of its most important members. This means that protecting the institution is inextricably entangled with shielding such members from accusations of wrongdoing. All of this is threatened by a scandal and perhaps especially by a sexual scandal. With the advent of the #MeToo movement, suppressing complaints is becoming a calculated risk. Aspersions cast on an institutional culture that tolerates sexual violence and the effectiveness of its response to wrongdoing also threaten the reputation of the institution.

Where the institution is a venerable and well-established one, a positive reputation must be protected at all costs; even, it appears, at the cost of taking moral responsibility. David Greenwood, my lawyer in the civil case against the Anglican Church and a veteran of sex-abuse litigation against multiple institutional defendants, argues that many institutions have for decades pursued an intentional strategy to discourage survivors from coming forward, rather than adopt a morally responsible approach. Despite or perhaps because of the number of whistleblowers starting to come forward, their claims are still typically faced down and fought against by institutions. Claimants are forced through distressing investigative and legal processes and then coerced into signing non-disclosure agreements by institutions that are unwilling to take responsibility for the wider impact of a known predator. This is, of course, counter-productive to the health of victims. In David's words,

> If we want a society that promotes wellbeing and helps vulnerable individuals who have been subjected to abuse to heal and get the most out of life, that is exactly what organizations should be doing. They should be going back through their records, checking who had contact with this person. Not distancing themselves from the problem and hoping that no one comes forward.[24]

THE PROBLEM FOR UNIVERSITIES

Universities are a particular institutional creature. The centuries-old history of universities claims a mission that unites its members in a sense of shared purpose.[25] At its heart is a commitment to enhancing knowledge and the freedom to explore ideas that may be neither popular nor profitable ("academic freedom"). Universities must be seen as credible, critical sites of learning and, to thrive, must continue to draw members—both faculty and students—to this mission. There is a clear relationship between the status of a university and the reputation of its degrees and faculty, and the value it offers to students (and alumni, who are encouraged to continue as "members" by contributing to the university). So how do universities square the circle and manage the tension between protecting their positive reputation and protecting students?

Questions about the safety of students on campus, the effectiveness of the response to wrongdoing by members, and a culture that tolerates sexual violence, all threaten the reputation of a university. It is now well established that as many as one in three female students[26] (and an even higher number of female students of colour, Indigenous students, and trans students)[27] will experience sexual harassment, sexual assault, or rape while they are members of a university community. Campus sexual violence has been described as "epidemic."[28] The first problem that underlies the failure of so many established institutions, including universities, to address sexual violence is denial of the extent of the problem. Jennifer Freyd makes the critical point that low reported numbers of sexual assaults on campus are a reflection of a generalized institutional discouragement of reporting coupled with inappropriate and unwelcoming reporting processes.[29] Instead, low numbers of reported assaults are sometimes assumed to indicate a safe campus, rather than the contrary. In 2014, I attended the first meeting of a "working group" established by my university in light of new media attention to the inadequacy of campus sexual violence policies. On my insistence, I came with a student representative (Brady). The chief of campus police was present, and he was asked how many reports of sexual harassment or assault had police received in the previous year? His answer was "three." The participants at the meeting shifted uncomfortably in their seats. Brady and I looked at him incredulously and began to laugh.

CHANGING INSTITUTIONAL STRUCTURES

How my own university handled the case I describe here,[30] illustrates what I believe are five systemic problems for universities and many other institutions. Each reflects particular institutional characteristics as well as obstacles that are part of the broader social culture faced by those who report harassment or sexual violence. At the heart of these systemic problems lies the unequal power of those involved. Those who are victimized are typically low-power, often (although by no means always, of course) female members of a male-dominated and even misogynistic institution. At the same time, perpetrators typically wield significant institutional power that they use to hide their activities and silence potential complainants. Other problems include a real ignorance of the power dynamics of harassment and abuse and a lack of experience of dealing with such issues; a desire to protect the institution's reputation and from imagined (often inaccurately) legal consequences while ignoring others of real substance[31]; and a general feeling of anxiety over taking decisive action.

In telling this story, it is not my intention to "out" or blame particular individuals. I have, though, used titles, because they reveal the high level at which these mistakes and misjudgments are routinely made. I have tried to extract what we can learn about how institutions act to protect themselves, and how those inside the institutions often get dragged along in that slipstream. Because I have seen these same problems play out in churches and in schools, I shall also draw on those examples.

Power and cover for abusers

The first problem illustrated by the story of the professor is that institutions bestow tremendous power on some individuals, who then become difficult or even impossible to challenge. The relationship between hierarchical institutions and those who abuse their power in a predatory manner is mutually reinforcing.

Typically, such individuals cultivate a high-profile and positive reputation created and reinforced by the institutional culture. It is not uncommon for this to take on a cult-like aura, sustained by inflation of their personal importance, power, and even qualifications; for example, the high school drama teacher who convinced students he was their gateway to fame and fortune.[32] A predator will demand complete loyalty and obedience from "followers" who will protect him at all costs. He will also use intimidation and sometimes threats to silence those who question or challenge his authority and charisma. Another common strategy is "grooming" those targeted for harassment, extending to family members and immediate peers, employing various self-promotion techniques.[33]

The institutional power of the perpetrator gives them a unique protection from disclosure by victims. At my law school, it felt impossible for students to challenge a tenured professor, especially one who so explicitly and successfully leveraged that power to suppress their natural reactions to his inappropriate behaviour—in the classroom, in social settings, and on social media. Abusers can easily hide inside institutions in which they hold status and power; for example as a teacher or a professor, a religious leader, or a coach. Their institutional status allows easy access to large numbers of subordinates, enabling them to identify potential victims, groom them by flattering them with "special" attention," and then abuse and harass them.

Because these institutional "stars" are critical to maintaining the image and reputation of the institution, the institution that first invests them with power subsequently provides them with "cover." They appear almost untouchable.

One of the most shocking disclosures of recent years has been the serial predatory sexual behaviour by British radio and TV personality Jimmy Savile.[34] Not only is there evidence that numerous colleagues at the BBC were aware for many years of Savile's predatory sexual behaviour with the girls he invited onto his shows, but Savile himself talked openly about his behaviour, including in his 1976 autobiography, *Love is an Uphill Thing*,[35] which openly describes his acrimonious relationships with the parents of young girls with whom he has sexual relationships. Other high-profile examples include Penn State University football coach Jerry Sandusky;[36] sports doctor Larry Nassar, who worked for both USA Gymnastics and Michigan State University;[37] Jian Ghomeshi at the Canadian Broadcasting Corporation;[38] and George Pell, a cardinal of the Catholic Church.[39] In all these cases, stories of sexual misconduct had circulated for years before the responsible institution properly probed the allegations and confronted the problem. In the case of former Anglican Church Bishop Peter Ball of Lewes, Prince Charles continued to be counted among his friends and supporters even after he had been formally cautioned by police in the 1990s following numerous complaints.[40] Peter Ball was finally brought to trial in 2015.[41]

Top-down resistance to change

Individuals who have harnessed the power of the institution to protect them and conceal their abuse are extremely difficult to dislodge without engaging the concerted will of the institution. Because we have historically failed to recognize the extent of misconduct inside institutions, no amount of advocacy will make any difference until there is recognition at the highest levels of decision-making that the entrenched norms at the top of the institutional pyramid (and the practices that flow from them) must change. Only then will there be the necessary engagement of will to make hard decisions and take decisive action.

I was about to discover that I was starting at ground zero with my own university.

However in the first few weeks after the harassment allegations against the professor became known to the faculty from complaints (along with many other concerning stories of his behaviour around students), there was a buzz of shared energy and indignation that made it feel possible to confront these revelations and compel the university to act. A law school deputation, comprising myself and four faculty colleagues and a small, brave group of law students,

met with university administration including the president and
the director of human resources as well as the university's outside
counsel. Our law school dean fully supported our efforts. The same
group of five faculty signed and submitted a formal complaint
against our colleague on December 18, 2013. The letter asked the
university to "investigate our concerns," which were described as
follows:

> Professor X has created and sustains a climate of intimidation and
> fear among our students . . . among other things, students have
> described their perception that Professor X is cultivating "friend-
> ships" (which are highly inappropriate in nature) with some, while
> expressing extreme hostility towards others . . . (W)e are con-
> cerned that Professor X may be sustaining this climate of intim-
> idation by explicitly targeting, criticizing and shaming particular
> students and faculty who have displeased him . . ., in public for
> example, including on social media. This makes students under-
> standably reluctant to translate their grievances about Professor
> X's treatment of them into a formal complaint.[42]

After the holidays, in early 2014, the faculty complainants were
informed that the professor had been suspended pending an investigation. At the same time, we were instructed not to talk about either
the suspension or the upcoming investigation to anyone. We were
now face-to-face with the first institutional norm that would undermine the entire process—secrecy and lack of transparency.

As the winter semester of 2014 got underway, there was still no
public statement by either the university or the law school about
the disappearance of our colleague from the law school. As a professor with a larger-than-life image and social media presence, his
absence would be noticed by every student. In the absence of any
information, rumours were naturally roiling the law school. For
weeks, I urged that a message be sent to the law school community
informing them of what was happening without any pre-judgment
of outcomes, even drafting some possible messages that I sent to the
administration. But no message was ever sent, and neither the other
members of the law school faculty nor the student body were ever
informed of the existence of the investigation. Homemade posters
about the investigation (authorship unknown) were posted in the
women's bathrooms in the law school alerting students to the in-

vestigation and asking them to come forward. These were quickly removed by the administration. In every one of my numerous communications with senior members of the university, pressing them on the issue of transparency and providing adequate support for students coming forward to report, I was admonished over and over again—*do not talk about this.*

Lack of transparency underscored the fundamental problem: how would any law student step forward to be part of the investigation if they did not know it existed? How would they decide whether they should participate when they knew nothing of the investigation's terms of reference (which the faculty complainants requested, but were refused)? And perhaps most important of all—how would those who wished to participate be protected? Would they be guaranteed anonymity? Confidentiality? Would they have support? Access to independent legal advice? None of these questions were answered and, instead, were met with either stonewalling or vague and unsubstantiated references to legal risks for the university.[43]

Despite being one of the complainants, I was not at any time contacted by the investigator. Months later, at the end of the investigation, I made repeated requests for a copy of the reported outcome. I was either refused or ignored.

Universities, in common with most institutions, have rigid hierarchies of authority, and their leaders have wide discretion over whether to act and how. This hierarchical structure means that to change institutional norms requires powerful insider allies willing to expend large amounts of time and effort. Among my colleagues there was a widespread reluctance to challenge the university's assumption that it could manage this issue without public knowledge, scrutiny, or accountability. Most of the advocacy for new approaches to responding to sexual violence on campus is coming from students.[44] My major partners in the work we did to press the University of Windsor to investigate the professor were students. This work is critical and is having a real impact, but there is a disappointing absence of faculty voices. There is also a worrying pattern of universities appointing junior staff with minimal power to newly created positions to handle complaints about sexual violence.

I have learned that many of those with power inside the institution are unwilling to challenge established norms. Even those with tenure, who are afforded extraordinary protections, power, and privilege, seem reluctant to take a principled stand regarding institutional responses to sexual violence. Perhaps this is because faculty are afraid to be disruptive inside an institution that typically discourages stepping out of line. Perhaps it is because staying silent about or acquiescent with a flawed response is less personally threatening than the alternative; it is certainly less time-consuming. As I wrote in an email to a colleague at the time, "I accept that we may have shared values about this issue, but we do not have the same ideas about decisive action." To me, it was the difference between saying that you were sorry about something, and doing something effective to change it.

Powerlessness of victims

A student involved in the complaints against the professor commented after:

> We felt that we were in a weak position. We felt that as bourgeoning law students, with no money to our name, and no careers to speak of, we were ending our careers before they started.[45]

Institutional norms that regard sexual and other misconduct as a dirty secret no one should talk about are exacerbated by the reality that individuals who experience assault and harassment are almost always those with little power. Of course, this is precisely why they are targeted for harassment. A telling example: when students at a Quebec university publicly protested the behaviour of a faculty member in an effort to force the administration to investigate his alleged sexual harassment, a nineteen-year-old female student who was just one of many protesters wearing a button was personally sued for defamation by the professor, in an obvious (and successful) effort to intimidate her and to silence the protests.[46]

I once received an anonymous message from a student who was not at my university that poignantly describes this "double whammy": 1) the disempowerment of students who are pressed into sexual relationships to win professorial favour and 2) are then threatened with the consequences of disclosure.

> In the past year I was pushed into a sexual relationship with a professor in my department. Eventually it became clear that my marks in his class and my future career all rested on pleasing him sexually. When I entered the program I was clearly not the top student and so the attention paid to me by this instructor and the

offer to (help) get me into a PhD program was great.

When I talked to the department head, I was told that sex was a small price to pay for a beginning to a career . . . I (was then) warned that I was being a problem, that I was the only person to ever complain about this instructor, that if I continued I would likely find that other schools would hear about me being a problem and that I would probably be failed out (of this) program.

When I continued (to complain), I was . . . reminded . . . of the Academic Confidentiality forms we signed as students when we came to (this university). I was informed that if I talked to anyone the school would have the right to sue me for breach of contract. I was told that (a student) who talked to the media years ago has since had her reputation ruined, is known as a slut everywhere, and is broke because of the lawsuits and problems.

I am still stunned at how quickly I have gone from being a valued student in my program to being an outcast . . . I will be so glad to graduate and escape (this university), but the hurt and stress I have been put through in the last year will stay with me for my lifetime.[47]

The problem of power imbalance, and apparent insensitivity to this, is clear in many of the internal processes used by universities in response to allegations of harassment and abuse. In March 2014, a student who had made allegations against the professor under investigation at my law school told me that she had been contacted by the investigator. She was upset because the investigator told her on the phone that not only must she attend her interview alone, but that she must tell no one that she was participating. Several other students involved in the investigation communicated similar experiences and concerns. Disturbed, I wrote to the provost and the vice-president for student affairs, having first discussed my message with my dean.

> I am writing to express significant concerns about the progress of the workplace investigation into Professor X. There appears to be little or no recognition that the student complainants are vulnerable and scared. They have not been advised of any support that they can have or may bring to the interviews which are about to commence. They have been given no information about what procedure will be followed in the interview, how to prepare for that interview, how long the investigation will take (we are approach-

ing exam time) and what the long term approach to confidentiality will be . . . Without any information, other students—I suspect there could be more since this faculty member has been with us for a number of years—are unlikely to come forward. And without proper procedural protections, I would frankly be concerned about them coming forward.[48]

There was no response from the administration. A week later I wrote again, this time sending a bullet-point list of what the student said that she needed in order to feel comfortable participating in the investigation. This list was written by the student herself, following much anguished discussion with me. It reflected the most basic victim protections and provided the university with important information about how to ensure that students could feel safe participating (if they were aware of the investigation at all).

The list included questions about

- confidentiality and future anonymity ("I worry about rumours circulating about my association with the investigation . . . It would make me feel better if this issue were at least addressed with me")
- safety ("I would appreciate the university telling me what plans they have in place in this regard . . . I think a lot about future harms this type of individual may be capable of toward me")
- the support of the university if the professor were to bring a future legal action against her

The student also describes the impact of the entire process on her law studies ("I am concerned about the impact the investigation and my stress associated with it may have on my studies . . . the timing of all this seems to be around my exam preps or exams again, and I fear that my marks will be impacted again").

This time I received a response from the vice-president for student affairs. He proposed that students who wished to be accompanied to interviews with the investigator should be accompanied by the vice-president for academic affairs (a man, whom none of these students were likely to know). I was once again instructed not to speak to anyone about any aspect of the case or investigation.

Most telling was his assumption that offering basic protections to complainants would involve pre-judging the professor, juxtaposing these as alternatives:

> I appreciate and recognize the anxiety and stress students feel when raising matters such as these against faculty members. However, I also recognize that faculty members have a right to respond to allegations that are raised and have a right to be heard. Until an investigation is concluded and all facts are considered, no conclusions ought to be drawn, and this case is no different. Professor [X] has the right to be presumed "innocent [until] proven guilty" just as any other faculty member.[49]

The assumption that providing basic victim protections and supports implies or prejudges the guilt of the accused is not sustainable. This is not a zero-sum game. Victim protection programs have worked for decades on ensuring that complainants are supported and that this in no way undermines or prejudges the accused.[50] In the context of a secret university investigation, the assumption that protecting victims will inevitably prejudge the accused is an old canard that buys into the widespread myth that those accused of abusive behaviour or harassment are frequently falsely accused.[51] It also assumes, incorrectly, that the standard of proof for a workplace investigation into harassment is the same as a criminal trial ("beyond a reasonable doubt," a much higher standard). This is precisely why basic protections for victims who step forward hesitantly and with little personal power are so necessary.

Legalities trump morality

The story of this professor is a petri dish of the troubled relationship that an institution—particularly one with status, established traditions, vested interests in continuity, powerful hierarchies, and little or no experience of responding to abuse of power and harassment—has with internal abusers and exploiters. Once we have begun on a course of protecting status by suppressing information, it may be difficult to change direction. Our shame drives us to immoral solutions.

By the spring of 2014, two of my co-complainant colleagues were proposing that we promote our colleague to another law school he was interested in working in, in the hopes that they would hire him and relieve us of the problem. In the meantime the secret investigation dragged on. Then in early September, having written a letter of transfer to another law school for a student who had been targeted by the professor, I received a panicked email from her: "He's here!"

Still under investigation, my colleague was formally on sabbatical from July 1. Evidently, he was now teaching as an adjunct at another law school. I immediately contacted my dean and urged notification of our colleagues at this school that this professor was the subject of a continuing investigation into harassment and other misconduct issues. Predictably, the administration told her to say nothing. I wrote directly to the president stressing the urgency and the moral importance of notifying the other university.

> I assume and hope that I do not have to labour the point that to fail to notify the [other] law school administration of the situation would be unconscionable. This is starting to feel chillingly similar to the way that the Catholic Church deals with abusive priests.
>   . . . [I]f for some reason you are unwilling to formally notify [the other school] of the risk that is now posed to their students, I want to make you aware that I shall ensure that professors and administration [at the other school] are made aware of the full situation.[52]

The president wrote back confirming he was aware that the professor was now teaching at another school. He continued:

> the University must act within its legal obligations and constraints, and that is what I am currently doing. I would ask that you not have any communications with [the other school] on this issue, but that you leave this as a matter for the University and our legal counsel to address. Thank you for your anticipated co-operation.[53]

I responded:

> I have acted as I said I would if the university refused to. I have disclosed this information to [the other school] and shall continue to do so in appropriate fora. So I am sorry, but I am no longer co-operating with the requirement of silence as I have for the past 11 months. This is a moral not a legal issue and I have acted as I must.[54]

My colleagues at the other school acted quickly and decisively, without involving the student and further distressing her. In late September, I received confirmation that they had removed the professor as an adjunct. The "legal obligations" the president referred to were never clarified to me, and I assume them to be the inflated fears of a defamation suit if the fact of the investigation were to be revealed. There is an overwrought concern that establishing an investigation into misconduct that does not end up making a positive finding may result in a defamation suit against the employer.[55] This can be used as a rationale for keeping any investigation so far below the radar that it might be described as effectively "secret," as it was in this case. In fact, employers in Canada are legally obliged to investigate allegations of (for example) harassment,[56] and conditional or qualified privilege[57] will generally protect them as long as information is not spread maliciously and the investigation is conducted fairly and thoroughly.[58] Otherwise, the threat of a defamation suit could be used to prevent any workplace investigations taking place.

This reaction to a theoretical possibility (there has been no successful reported defamation suit in Canada against a university or other workplace for simply instituting a misconduct investigation) obscures what is arguably the larger and clearer legal responsibility of the university—the protection of students, staff, and faculty. While "legal obligations" are often used as a catch-all justification for not acting (for example, to inform another school, or to inform the community about the existence of an investigation), the larger motive seems to be the protection of the reputation of the university.

Institutions do not typically understand that responding responsibly and effectively to allegations of harassment and predation is a moral issue. On the contrary, decisions are based not on a moral assessment, but a risk assessment: how much silence and denial is feasible, and how aggressively can a potential lawsuit against a claimant be defended? My solicitor in my lawsuit against the Anglican Church was the first person to make this point to me. In his characteristically plain speaking manner, David Greenwood told me "If I am being really truthful about the situation . . . [the Church's] failure to acknowledge and do the right thing . . . is a strategic plan to prevent people coming forward, and make it a cold atmosphere when people do come forward."[59]

Of course, there is also shame in being revealed as an institution that has permitted an individual they have promoted, even extolled, to abuse their power and go unchallenged, perhaps for many years. In such cases there are frequently long lists of victims who have been harmed during this time and records of earlier complaints that have been ignored or dismissed. David's assertion, which I have seen played out in different institutional contexts, is that a calculation is being made about what is the greater risk to the institution's reputation (and pocketbook)—to take seriously credible allegations of abusive behaviour by, for example, a schoolteacher, a professor, or a priest, and set up a proper investigatory process, or to continue to dismiss warnings and suppress any formal investigation. Which of these two courses is adopted by an institution that has received complaints about abuse and harassment appears to have little to do with the nature of the allegations. Instead it reflects a strategic calculation based on a calculated risk assessment. Such a cynical calculation rules out a genuine acceptance of any moral responsibility, which requires a commitment to protect others in the future.

Instead, fear of legal losses (costs, continuing conflicts perhaps with staff associations and unions) overwhelms morality and common sense. There is a strong tendency to separate the "moral" and the "legal" reaction, as the Anglican and Catholic Churches do when they offer public remorse and apologies but pursue adversarial and aggressive litigation against claimants.[60] The success of this strategy may have led to a sense of impunity among many institutions and abusers. I have observed an aura of self-righteousness and entitlement within the institutional culture as well as the behaviour of the predator—a *how dare you* attitude toward the raising of complaints about abuse, harassment, or sexual violence.

Apparently lacking a moral imperative to act, institutions have historically been extremely successful in suppressing sexual assault and harassment claims. But if something is a moral issue, it cannot be trumped or contradicted by a legal fear. If an institution is to have integrity, and continue to command the respect of its members, its internal morality and its legal strategy must be in-step with each other.

Cover-up and "passing the trash"

The breathtaking scale of the institutional cover-up of clerical sexual predators within the Anglican Church has been revealed as a result of the work of the Independent Inquiry into Child Sexual Abuse. When I testified as a "core participant" in the Chichester case study in March 2018, I learned of numerous examples of complaint letters describing sexual abuse by clergy going "missing" or "misfiled" in the Chichester diocese office, a mysterious bonfire in the courtyard of the Bishop's Palace of a number of personnel files, and the existence of a filing cabinet described in a handwritten note as the "Naughty Boys Cabinet."[61] I was about to learn that my own university would pursue the same goal through its own method—silence.

I have already made many references to the university's repeated demand that I (and other faculty and students) say nothing and speak to no one about the complaint against the professor or the investigation. What I did not realize at the time was that there was to be a further significant and long-lasting component to the cover-up strategy yet to play out which would have significant consequences for me.

But first, the good news.

Despite the obvious deficiencies of the investigation, the president made the decision to inform the professor of his intention to terminate him under the "just cause" provisions of the collective agreement at the end of 2014.[62] The timing coincided with a difficult period in my life. In December 2014, I was diagnosed with ovarian cancer following surgery and, in January 2015, began an intense course of chemotherapy. Unsurprisingly, the professor filed a formal grievance under the collective agreement, and the university began to prepare for an arbitration. Following the end of my chemotherapy, I was headed to the University of New South Wales in Sydney, Australia, as a visiting professor for the month of September. I met with the university's lawyers before I left to discuss strategy for the upcoming arbitration. They were trying to determine whether any of the students directly impacted by the professor would be willing to testify in an arbitration hearing, having already found the investigation process traumatic and still in fear of future consequences.

Two weeks after I arrived in Australia, I was in Adelaide, about to step up on stage to give a speech at a conference. My cell phone rang. On the line was my (newly appointed) dean. His first words were: "It's over." The university had settled with the professor, he was leaving, and there would be no arbitration. A huge rush of relief washed over me, and I walked on stage feeling lighter and joyous. What I did not know at this time is that the university had signed a non-disclosure agreement (NDA) with the professor (also signed by the faculty association representing him), committing itself to reveal nothing of the circumstances of his departure.

Agreements to settle harassment and misconduct cases typically ask claimants (or in this case, the employer) to sign an undertaking of strict non-disclosure. This is often presented as a way to protect the identity of the complainant(s). In reality this can be simply and easily accomplished by a confidentiality clause stipulating that the complainant's identity will not be disclosed, but allowing a complainant to choose to speak out in future if they wish to waive this. Instead, an NDA like the one my university gave the professor commits the signatories—here the University of Windsor, the Windsor University Faculty Association, and the professor—to disclosing nothing about the circumstances of his departure to anyone, now or in the future. It will prevent potential future employers obtaining information from the employer about the circumstances of the employee's departure. Instead, it will direct future inquiries to a particular place in the university; in this case the office of the provost. The NDA my university signed included an agreed letter of reference to be provided by the provost, which said nothing about the circumstances of the professor's departure but praised him for his "extensive publication record" and teaching awards.

Following the typical pattern of NDAs, the faculty and student complainants in the University of Windsor case did not sign (and to my knowledge, were not consulted on) the agreement. It was not to protect them, but the university and the professor. While NDAs are often mischaracterized as protecting the complainant, pressure for a "gag order" (as it is often colloquially known) almost always comes from the perpetrator, who wishes to shield himself from future fall-out regarding his behaviours, for example, bad publicity as a presidential candidate[63] or difficulty obtaining future employment. So common have NDAs become over the past decade that sometimes the acceptance of a gag clause or NDA is set as a precondition (by the terminated employee) to even beginning to negotiate a settlement to release the employer from the threat of protracted and expensive legal action.

The reason that employers agree to NDAs is simple—faster settlement before a hearing will reduce the costs of the lawsuit. What is more, the employer might prefer that no one ever knew that they had once employed a person now known to have abused their power inside the institution. An NDA will often be the price of settlement, and for many years few lawyers have challenged this. This is beginning to change as regulators are starting to look more closely at the moral and legal implications of NDAs.[64]

The use of NDAs first became widespread during the tech boom in the 1980s where they were seen as an effective means of preventing the movement of confidential information between tech companies. Gradually, their use extended into all types of employment termination.[65] As public attention to sexual harassment and assault ramped up with the emergence of the #MeToo movement, an early spotlight fell on the US Congress. Its complaints process (directed by the Office of Compliance) required complainants to sign a non-disclosure agreement and to participate in mandatory counselling and mediation. In addition, final settlements were almost always subject to an NDA. The consequence, of course, was there would be no knowledge (other than by rumour) of sitting members of Congress who had been found to have sexually harassed or assaulted members of their own staff or other Congressional colleagues.

> The identities of lawmakers or their aides who reach misconduct settlements aren't disclosed, effectively meaning there is no warning system for other potential victims.[66]

If a perpetrator leaves the institution, NDAs facilitate "passing the trash"[67] to another organization who might hire that person without being aware of the circumstances of their departure from their last position. A recent report in the UK found that 4,000 settlements (at a cost of £90m) have been made with faculty and staff at universities that include NDAs. Some of these relate to confidential information, but many are NDAs used to cover-up "bullying, discrimination and sexual misconduct."[68]

I discovered that an NDA had been part of the professor's settlement with the university when I was contacted the following spring by another law school which was considering hiring him. They had no knowledge or details about the circumstances of his departure. The member of the appointments committee who contacted me had been suspicious about why a tenured academic would suddenly leave a position voluntarily, and had been tipped off by a third person that there was more to this story. I spoke by phone with the colleague who had reached out to me, and I explained the circumstances under which the professor left.

While this law school did not hire my former colleague, he was subsequently hired by the same university, at a different campus. Evidently there had been no communication between the two campuses over this decision. My original contact was very concerned, and introduced me to the dean at the law school that had hired the professor. When we spoke by phone, the dean told me that he was initially skeptical about the professor's application for the same reason as the first school that considered him. He had reached out to my university to try to get more information but received no response—and so went ahead and hired him as a faculty member. He wept during that first phone call, horrified at the implications for his own reputation. Later after taking legal advice he adopted a strategy of doubling-down on his decision to hire the professor.

As a result of this experience, I committed to persuading my university to eschew the future use of NDAs in cases of harassment and bullying or misconduct including sexual misconduct. I hoped that if one university declared they would no longer give NDAs to employees they intend to terminate for misconduct, others would follow. My own research, ably assisted by then law student Jessica Proskos, uncovered a growing body of American case law indicating that courts will not enforce NDAs where there is an issue of "public safety," which is especially pertinent in the context of educational institutions.[69] Jessica and I worked on a draft policy for the university along with the acting provost.

This progress came to a shuddering halt in December 2018. As I recovered from hip replacement surgery in my "bed office," I received a letter threatening me with a defamation suit from a lawyer who said he represented my former colleague.

The formal action for defamation was commenced against me in February 2019, as I re-entered chemotherapy for a recurrence of ovarian cancer. The claim against me was that I had made "false and injurious statements in the public domain," citing my conversations with the colleagues at other schools who had contacted me for an off-line reference and (covertly recorded by them) a conversation with two partners at a law firm that listed my former colleague as a consultant.

The absolute defence to defamation is truth. As a result of my involvement with the students bringing forward complaints and with the administration in the investigation I knew that in this case "just cause" included a number of forms of misconduct. "Just cause" requires serious misconduct.[70]

The only step necessary to quash the defamation action brought against me was to show that I was speaking the truth, an absolute defence to defamation claims. This would have required the university to release the letter referring to their intention to dismiss him for "just cause," as well as acknowledging that they gave him a non-disclosure agreement. But the university refused to do this (and could not be compelled to release these documents in another jurisdiction), or to assist me in any way, or to offer any collegial support. My pleas for help were ignored or unanswered.

With a couple of honourable exceptions, none of my faculty colleagues (who knew the truth, of course), including my co-complainants, offered me support or commiseration. Presumably they were frightened, and a couple of the original complainants continued to insist that they were proud and pleased that the university had got rid of him, appearing unconcerned for other students elsewhere.

As a result of telling the truth about an abusive professor, I was now personally liable to a monetary default judgment against me in another jurisdiction that if brought to Ontario for enforcement would potentially bankrupt me. In addition, I faced a contempt order (potentially custodial) if I breached the blanket injunction ordered by the court about speaking publicly about the case (aware that the injunction was unenforceable in Ontario, I continued to speak out and, having reached the same conclusion, Canadian news outlets continued to cover the story).[71]

Following my repeated requests, the university agreed to send the statement of claim to their insurer, the Canadian Universities Reciprocal Insurance Exchange (CURIE).[72] CURIE took two months to respond, and eventually declined cover in a one-line email.[73] Their initial explanation was that I was not "acting in the course of employment" as the policy required. This was clearly not true; providing a reference on request was obviously within the terms of my employment (as was honesty). It seemed to me that the insurer was genuinely struggling to find an explanation for declining me and that the underlying reason was the existence of the NDA signed by their policyholder, the University of Windsor.

As these stressful months went by, I received a great deal of support from students (including the remarkable Students for Consent Culture Canada)[74] and from faculty across the country. I created a small group of friends and supporters who were now lawyers, labour arbitrators, and judges to help me figure out a strategy in the face of refusal to help me and stonewalling by CURIE and the University of Windsor. One member of my support group was Natalie MacDonald, whom I had taught more than twenty years earlier and we had stayed in touch.[75] Natalie is a leading employment lawyer and veteran litigator, with many important decisions argued and won.[76] She generously proposed that she act for me pro bono to bring a motion to compel CURIE to defend me in the defamation suit. I gratefully accepted.[77] The date of trial was creeping ever closer, and I was now back in chemotherapy and very ill.

First, we attempted to persuade university counsel to go back to CURIE and make the case for my coverage. We felt hopeful for a few weeks—university counsel, whom I had known for many years and I knew to be uncomfortable with the NDA, seemed to be genuinely regretful that this was happening to me—until we realized that no one would take responsibility for either making the case to CURIE or reviewing the decision to decline within the insurance company. I also began to experience reprisals from the university affecting my position and, in particular, the future time I would be able to give to directing the National Self-Represented Litigants Project, which advocates and creates resources for those unable to afford a lawyer and hence representing themselves.[78]

In the next few weeks, Natalie collected affidavits from three key figures in the drama—a student who was part of the original complaint process against the professor, a professional staff person at the law school who had spoken confidentially with one of the professor's targets, and the overseas faculty member who originally contacted me for a reference when the professor applied to his school for a job. Natalie filed these along with a motion in Ontario Superior Court to compel CURIE to defend me in the defamation lawsuit. On Natalie's first appearance in May, a visibly shocked case management judge gave us an expedited hearing date for our motion: July 10.

At the hearing, CURIE argued that professors can only be indemnified where they are acting "under the instructions of" their university employer and not "taking a position critical" of their employer. We felt that their arguments were thin and suggested a measure of desperation. Natalie was brilliant and passionate—and right in law. She argued that it was entirely appropriate for me to respond to a request for an off-line reference and that it was my obligation as a professor to be honest and protect the safety of students. We left the hearing feeling hopeful and nervously awaiting the decision.

Three weeks later I was in London, England, at my oldest daughter's flat, having just testified in the criminal trial of the minister (see chapter 7). My youngest daughter had arrived earlier that day from Canada and was taking a nap in her sister's bedroom. An email popped up on my screen from Natalie's assistant. It had the decision attached. My shouts and screams as I began to scroll through the judgment—we won!—woke Hopey up immediately, although she was a good sport about it. Within the hour I was talking to Natalie, who was presenting at the Women Economic Forum in Cartagena, Colombia, on the topic of NDAs.

Ruling in our favour, Justice Jessica Kimmel made many important points about the obligation of a university employer to "have the back of" a professor acting in the course of their employment. She ruled that the insurer's argument that I could only be covered if I had acted under the explicit instructions of my employer would exclude many employment activities—including providing a reference—from proper protection from legal liability and damages (known as indemnification). Furthermore, Justice Kimmel shredded CURIE's argument that no action that was critical of or at odds with the university's "policy" (here giving the professor an NDA) was subject to indemnification. From the judgment,

> A university is not an institution with a single voice or a single set of interests—the interests of a university will be broad and diverse and may even be in conflict with one another from time to time.[79]

> While the University of Windsor may have an official position . . . that does not mean that others within the institution no longer speak on its behalf just because they have another view or perspective. "Acting on behalf of" does not mean that the specific act be authorized, instructed, permitted or approved by the University of Windsor.[80]

Justice Kimmel also dismissed CURIE's argument that I should not be indemnified for actions that were motivated by moral principles, as follows:

> Even if Professor Macfarlane was motivated for personal rea-sons to make the impugned statements . . . I must still consider whether the substance of the claims raise even the possibility that she was also acting in her professional capacity as a professor at the University of Windsor, and not acting solely in her personal capacity. These two capacities are not mutually exclusive.[81]

In fact, Justice Kimmel points out, my disclosures to third parties regarding an NDA that I was not party to may in fact rebound to the University of Windsor's benefit.

> (T)he fact that it signed an NDA with Mr X and may have an interest in upholding that agreement does not mean that the University does not also have an interest in protecting itself and its reputation by endorsing the practice of its professors providing *honest and truthful off-list references*. Similarly, signing the NDA with Mr X does not mean that the University does not have an interest in protecting itself against claims by students at other uni-versities to whom it may be found to have owed a *moral and legal duty* . . .[82] (T)here is at least a possibility that Dr MacFarlane (sic) was acting in the interests of the university where the disclosures she made . . . *may protect it from reputational damage or exposure to further third-party tort liability.*[83] (my italics)

This point is important in light of current ongoing litigation by students against universities where there is a claim that they have failed to protect them from known abusers whose activities they were aware of for many years.[84] One of these suits, brought against Dartmouth University by a group of students in respect of three psychology professors who were alleged to have turned the depart-ment into a "21st Century Animal House" of sexual harassment, settled in August 2019 for $14 million.[85] The students argued that the university failed to protect them from sexual harassment despite being aware of the activities of the three professors for sixteen years.

When an institution is focused on minimizing the problem and protecting its reputation an NDA is a tempting proposition. It can speed the end of difficult negotiations, it can be falsely framed as protecting the identity of victims, and, best of all, it appears to protect the institution from any future responsibility of any kind for this individual. That it is an immoral solution that perpetuates the cover-up, likely to have long preceded the unmasking of this person as a predatory threat to others inside the institution, is neither acknowledged nor given any weight. It is also becoming increasingly precarious as a legal strategy. Just like the Dartmouth case, legal liability will fall on the university if any students at the school where Professor X was hired (and has since left under unclear circumstances) were assaulted or harassed by him. The enforceability of such a gag order in the context of public and student safety is also under growing challenge in US case law.[86]

NDAs can also become a bad habit for institutions. After the court decision, we went back to trying to resolve my status with the university following their reprisals against me. When Natalie pointed out that reprisals against a whistleblower raised human rights issues, as did the university's justification of their proposal to cut my position back to half-time because of my health issues,[87] the university responded that they would only consider a proposal to resolve my status if I first signed an NDA. "Seriously? Are you guys paying attention to what is happening here?" asked Natalie upon receiving this phone call from university counsel. We were astonished. And, of course, I said no.

Removing substantive institutional barriers to bringing a complaint, recognizing the relative powerlessness of victims, committing to transparency, setting clear moral standards for the institution that are not driven by fear of legal outcomes, and resisting the cover-up instinct are all critical first steps in institutional accountability. But they are only first steps. We must be clear about the obstacles that remain to changing institutional cultures around responses to sexual violence. The closing episode of the podcast "Believed" about the Larry Nassar case makes this point perfectly.

> It's one thing for people to say "I believe you were sexually assaulted," and another to get accountability—for people to fully comprehend that the Larry Nassar case is not just about one bad dude, that Larry did not operate in a vacuum. They (the survivors) are finding that just because people believe them now, that doesn't mean that institutions will be any more transparent, that attitudes will change.[88]

CHAPTER 7

ON THE STAND

O n January 31, 2019, four and a half years after I received that first phone call from David telling me that the police wanted to investigate two very similar stories about him, the minister who sexually abused me as a teenager finally arrived in the UK to stand trial for indecent assault. At early dawn, he disembarked a plane from Western Australia at Heathrow airport, accompanied by two Sussex police officers.

After the euphoria of receiving news in April 2016 that Meirion Griffiths would be charged with indecent assault, the case had dragged along through the fall of 2017 as extradition proceedings were prepared. I had begun to doubt that Griffiths would ever be apprehended in Perth. Finally, in November 2017, I got this message from David: "He's been arrested. He's in custody overnight and put in front of the Magistrate tomorrow." I got a similar message from DC Alan Fenn at Sussex police, who sounded only slightly less excited than me. Thanks to the excellent public information service at Perth magistrates court, obtaining news about what was happening in the case was about to become a lot easier (in an interesting role reversal I was now passing along this information to Chichester police). Somewhat to our surprise, Griffiths was remanded in custody until the end of January, when he came up for a bail hearing. He was then again remanded in custody and began his defence against extradition, which we understood would focus on his age and claims that he was too ill to travel (ironic since by this time I was again in treatment for cancer). He appeared again on April 13, 2018, when the extradition order was finally granted, nine months after his arrest and detention.

It was now more than forty-two years since I had escaped from the minister's abuse by leaving my hometown to go to university. His detention felt like a recognition of what I had suffered in a way that I had never experienced before, with the full force of law enforcement now involved. The sense of finally glimpsing justice felt both poignant and intense.

The actual extradition from Perth to London took over a year longer. It came after numerous bureaucratic delays of the extradition process and efforts to evade this outcome on the part of Griffiths and his family. These had included formal legal arguments that he was too ill to travel—and pressure from his daughter on Christmas Day 2018 to withdraw the charges via a blizzard of personal messages on Twitter, where she had searched and found me. But finally, he stepped off the plane at Heathrow that January morning. This was the first time that an Anglican minister had been extradited for sex crimes from Australia to the UK.[1]

Emotionally, I was now clear that the minister should be held accountable for what he did to me, to the other complainant (whom of course I could not meet or talk to, and I continued to have no idea of her identity), as well as likely many, many others over the years to whom he had access as a figure of authority in the church. I had not begun this journey looking for criminal justice, but now I was surprised at how determined I was that this was right, even in the face of his daughter's pleas.

REPORTING SEXUAL ASSAULT TO THE POLICE

I had begun the criminal process five years before because there was another complainant, and I had misgivings about working with police officers who are often untrained and insensitive to the impact of sexual violence on victims. Even before the 2015 trial and acquittal of Jian Ghomeshi further chilled the climate for reporting, a survey of assault survivors in three Canadian cities reported that 53 per cent of women did not feel confident reporting an assault to police. They worry that they will not be believed, that they will be questioned with insensitivity by police officers who hold stereotypes about sexual violence, that they will not be taken seriously (especially if they are a woman of colour or transgender woman), and that the police will do nothing to investigate. The large number of so-called "unfounded" claims that Canadian police report reflects their reluctance to prosecute where they do not see a clear route to a conviction.[2] There is also data showing that rape and sexual assault claims are chronically mishandled, misfiled, and swept under the carpet in many police stations.[3] All of this adds up to this horrifying statistic: of the estimated 460,000 sexual assaults that occur each year in Canada, only three will eventually result in criminal convictions.[4] Those convictions are the result of months or even years of effort and continued trauma by the victim (or more likely victims, since police are even more reluctant to charge when there is a sole victim).

I have talked with many women about what they expected and then experienced when bringing a complaint regarding sexual assault or sexual harassment to the police. One clear theme is that their expectations reflect their community's experience with policing, with white women coming with higher hopes that they will be taken seriously and protected than their sisters of colour. One white woman told me that she went to police after a sexual assault that left her fearful for her safety because "I grew up believing that the purpose of the police was to protect the public."[5] However like many others, she did not find that belief panned out. A woman of colour told me that she felt "neglected" throughout a lengthy police investigation that eventually led to a decision not to charge her assailant, and she ended up questioning why she had even bothered, given perceptions of her as a woman of colour:

> For me, I'm not this rich white lady who's coming here to say something about what has happened to me, and the police will automatically take me seriously . . . I'm not the "perfect victim". . . it really shamed me into feeling that I shouldn't have even come forward, knowing that I wasn't that "typical" victim profile.[6]

The same woman told me that she does not encourage other women of colour to report to police.

> It's unfortunate that I have to tell them, I would not report it. It's not worth it. It damaged my process of healing. I felt so much shame around my sexual assault already, and adding (what you call) the second assault—that really broke the camel's back.

Some women even report being threatened with legal action for lying. Brady Donohue was a twenty-something undergraduate residence don when she was assaulted by a university athlete. She went to her university campus police to report the assault, but was not in the best mental or emotional state to deal with police interrogation:

> I went there feeling like I just needed to talk to somebody and I didn't really know what I wanted, and immediately, they [the police] started asking me these really intrusive questions and I thought, you know what . . . I can't do this, and I started to cry. And I left.[7]

The following day, Brady went again to campus police, this time with a young woman who lived in her residence who described being sexually assaulted by a different individual. A few days later, Brady heard from the city police. They told her that they did not believe either of her reports—"we think you have made this up"— and that she was fabricating these stories in order to write an essay about sexual assault. They threatened her with legal action for false reporting. Years later, the devastation she felt in that moment was still vivid to her.

> The institutional response was far more violent to my emotional stability, to how I felt about myself, to how I internalized what happened, than the actual assault. When I think about the pain, I don't think about the assault.[8]

Another theme is that electronic harassment (torrents of harassing and even threatening texts and other messages, usually from an ex, which will not stop) is not taken seriously by police, who do not see it as threatening and intimidating (which it clearly is). One woman told me:

> One day I woke up to 50 messages, and 60 missed calls. It was just constant. Emails, Facebook, text messages, voicemails. Blocking and deleting didn't seem to work. There was also a new phone number, a new account that he was messaging me from.[9]

She was told by police that this was not something they could do anything about.

There is plenty of anecdotal evidence that police simply do not understand the dynamics of violent and controlling relationships and how this plays out in threats and harassment. A woman friend came to my home one day after a series of incidents of physical and online harassment and threats from an ex-boyfriend. This time he had called Karrie on her phone and told her to walk outside her home, situated on the shore of Lake Erie. He then drove past her and off the top of a bluff and into the water. Her daughter actually had to climb down into the water and stayed with him until the police arrived and pulled him out of the car (he was inebriated). This stunt was obviously staged to make her feel sorry for him and take him back, and he planned the call and his drive off the edge to ensure that she and her daughter were outside, watching. They called local police who attended. Karrie told them that her ex-boyfriend had been harassing and stalking her for weeks, and she would like to make a statement to police.

Having heard from no one, Karrie began to call the local police station asking if someone would take a statement from her so they could consider pressing charges against her ex for criminal harassment. The first three times she called the police she was brushed off by whomever was answering the phone in the police station that weekend. "They say I'm a witness, not a victim," she told me. Eventually, I took the phone and spoke to the police myself—of course, it helps to say one is a law professor. Karrie went down to the police station, accompanied, at her request, by my husband Bernie, who remained with her while the police took her statement (during which the police contributed various opinions including: "Well you had a choice here. You could have not dated him in the first place."). Eventually, and after a lot more pushing and prodding from various sources, her ex-boyfriend was charged. In addition to driving under the influence, he was also convicted of criminal harassment, enabling her to obtain an enforceable[10] restraint order. Would this result have happened without the intervention of someone who had connections and familiarity with the legal system? Or would my friend have become another of the women whose reports are dismissed, disbelieved, mishandled, and then closed?

All these stories of the experiences of other women strike a chord for me in my own experience of trying to report to the Sussex police—the dismissiveness, the discomfort, the feeling that the person on the other end of the phone really did not want to be having this conversation and that I was being a nuisance.[11] Women consistently describe the central problem in the same way; that police are often untrained on the dynamics of sexual violence and cannot be trusted to treat women who report with sensitivity. Of course, I was one of those "rich white" women described above who has many structural advantages in this process. It is probably a reflection of our relative power that I did finally get police to charge and then extradite the minister for trial.

His trial was set for July in England, five years after that first phone call from David Greenwood telling me that another woman had come forward to tell the same story about the same minister. I booked my flight to the UK to testify. Eventually reaching this point felt momentous and emotional. Could justice finally be done?[12]

THE TRIAL

The trial was held at Winchester Crown Court. Winchester is a small city quite like Chichester, which is about an hour's drive away. It is historic—Winchester's cathedral dates from 1079, Chichester's is four years older at 1075—and both towns are mostly white and middle-class. As the trial began, I met with my wonderful team of friends and family in the court building. Aside from Bernie and me, my oldest daughter Sibyl came down for the day of my testimony, as did my university boyfriend Peter (see chapter 1). Also there, as a cheerleader, was my civil lawyer David Greenwood, who travelled down from Wakefield for the day. I felt very loved and very well supported.

I had been nervous from the beginning of the criminal process about the fact that in England and Wales, indecent assault is always a trial by jury.[13] There is plenty of research that suggests that juries are often influenced by pervasive societal rape myths when determining guilt or innocence in sex crimes.[14] An early measure was the Rape Myth Acceptance Scale, designed by Martha Burt of the Urban Institute,[15] which contains fourteen false and derogatory statements about women and rape (for example, "Any healthy woman can successfully resist a rapist if she really wants to," "In the majority of rapes, the victim is promiscuous or has a bad reputation").[16] These studies typically present participants with scenarios involving rape and sexual assault (the so-called "vignette methodology") and ask them for their reaction, including their attributions of blame to either the alleged perpetrator or defendant and the complainant.[17] These studies also track experiential, personality, and attitudinal variables among the respondents and variations in victim and perpetrator characteristics via the hypothetical situation presented. They note a number of consistent results.

One result shows that men tend to have more negative views about female victims than women do and manifest a higher level of buy-in to rape myth.[18] As well, among both men and women, less blame is attributed to the defendant where there has been a prior relationship between the parties, whether a sexual or acquaintance relationship,[19] or where the victim was incapacitated (for example by alcohol) and unable to "fight back"[20] (which, of course, also has an effect on victims—see, for example, Amy's self-blaming in *The Mockingbirds*).[21] Similarly, less blame is attributed to the perpetrator where there is so-called "female participation" (allegedly "flirty" behaviour or dress of the victim).[22] These discussions of how societal myths about rape affect attribution and victim-blaming are consistent across a number of different respondent groups including undergraduate and vocational law students[23] and members of the public.[24] They are clearly problematic when it comes to empanelling a jury in a sex assault trial.

There are important differences among jurisdictions over how much questioning potential jurors can be subjected to—in both Canada and the UK[25] this is permitted but generally limited—and when they are told of the nature of the charges.[26] As I watched the empanelment of the jury for the Griffiths trial, the only questions they were asked related to their availability for three weeks (a few demurred and were excused) and whether they had heard the names of any of the witnesses or the defendant. The jury members—four men and eight women, all but one white—were told of the charges ("indecent assault") only after they were selected. There was a collective gulp.

By this time, it was almost 4 pm, and the judge thanked the jury members and dismissed them for the evening. I had been watching from the public gallery, which was high above the main section of this traditionally styled courtroom, like sitting in the top circle of a theatre, what my father used to call the "nose-bleed" seats. As I stood up to leave, the defence counsel turned around to face the gallery from the floor below. She was clearly scanning the seats searching for someone, and I quickly realized that that someone was me. I had had to ask permission from the Crown to watch the juror empanelment, and presumably this had been shared with the defence, so she knew I was up there. When she saw me, her eyes locked into mine. I stood looking back at her, bemused by her stern expression and obvious intent to intimidate me before the trial had even begun. After ten long seconds, I bent down to pick up my purse from my seat. When I straightened up again, she was still there, staring at me. I locked eyes again, nodded briefly, and left.

There was no mistaking her purpose. It was an effort to intimidate. I shared this experience with the Crown, and she was unsurprised. But, like the other defence tactics yet to come, it had not worked.

The other complainant

I had spent a lot of time in the previous five years wondering who the other complainant was and if I knew her. If this was someone who experienced Griffiths's assaults and abuse at around the same time that I did, the chances of our being acquainted seemed high. Perhaps she was a member of my church youth group? I tried to remember all the other girls who were part of that group, none of whom I had maintained any contact with. I knew that I could not know her name or speak with her, because if we were to be effective complainants we would have to show that we did not compare our stories at any point or embellish them with details from one another. But that did not stop me anxiously reflecting on this.

I told the Crown prosecutor, with whom I had my first conversation that day, that I wanted to know the other complainant's name so that I would not be taken by surprise or shocked when I heard it in court. I knew that the following day, when I would give my testimony, would be a hard one and wanted to be as emotionally prepared as possible. If this was someone I had known as a friend in my teenage years, I needed the next twelve hours to get used to the idea.

It turned out I did not know her. Her encounter with Griffiths had actually occurred a couple of years after mine ended—an enormous relief. But that did not in any way mitigate the horror of watching and listening to her 2015 video testimony a few days later (after I had completed mine).

A morning in the life of a sex assault complainant

My first task the following morning when we arrived at the courthouse was to study the current floorplans of the minister's home (the "rectory"). It was in the study of the rectory in 1975 that I was first sexually assaulted by Griffiths. Looking at the floorplans, along with some contemporary photos of the rooms, was upsetting and difficult. It looked different, in some ways, but was also so very familiar. My distress as I reviewed the floor plans—which I kept to myself—was obviously not anticipated by either the kind policewoman who sat with me throughout this process, or the prosecution. This was, sadly, just one of countless examples of an apparent lack of understanding of the characteristics of and triggers for PTSD. I calmed myself down and studied the plans. I correctly identified the room that had been the minister's study in 1975 and signed a statement to this effect. I believed that I was about to go into court to give my testimony, after the jury had heard the video statement that I had recorded two and a half years earlier with the OPP.

But no. The defence had applied the previous evening for a section 41 order, on which the judge had to hear legal arguments before my testimony could begin. A section 41 order[27] is the English equivalent of Canada's rape shield law.[28] It is intended to protect a victim from having irrelevant personal details of their sexual history disclosed in open court. It is sometimes described as an effort to avoid discussion of the "twin myths" before the jury.[29] These myths, that multiple studies demonstrate have widespread public currency, are first, that a sexually active woman is less trustworthy than others when she gives testimony and, second, that she is more likely to have consented to a sexual assault or rape.[30] Instead, under Canada's rape shield law and the section 41 procedure in England, a case must first be made that this is important information that the defence needs to be able to refer to in order to make legitimate arguments.

As we waited—for more than two hours—for legal arguments about section 41 to be concluded and a ruling made, it was impossible not to speculate on what part of my sexual history the defence was arguing was "relevant" to my sexual assault. The short answer of course is "none." My sexual abuse by the minister took place during a distinct period of my life (otherwise chaste and innocent) and the rest of my consensual (and non-consensual) sexual life was irrelevant. However, I am familiar with the tactics of defence counsel in sexual assault trials, and I could imagine the defence lawyer trying to assert, absurdly, that if I went on to university after the attacks and had a sexual relationship with a boyfriend, this suggested that nothing bad had happened with the minister. As chance would have it, my university boyfriend, Peter, had travelled to be at the courthouse that day to support me. When I explained to him that the hold-up with my testimony might involve legal arguments over disclosing our dating relationship at university, Peter went white. In the end, this was not the part of my sexual history that the defence was interested in. It was the attempted rape of me when I was around five years old, which I discuss in chapter 1.

How was this remotely relevant to this trial? For the next two days, defence counsel used her success in obtaining a section 41 order to assail first me and next my "disclosure witnesses" (my two oldest girlfriends, Debbie and Damhnait, to whom I had first disclosed the abuse) with questions such as, might I or they be confusing these two events? Might I be confusing the sexual abuse by the minister with my memory of being forced down in the woods by an older boy who tried to penetrate me at five? "No, no, no, no," I repeated over and over again as defence counsel badgered me. In fact, I had told neither Debbie nor Damhnait about what had happened to me as a child at this time.

"But you said in your video testimony that you had had no sexual experience when you claim the minister assaulted you?" said defence counsel. I could see where this was going. "I do not regard the attempted rape of a five year to be 'sexual experience,'" I responded.

Defence counsel changed tack and tried to use this personal information a different way. "But you told your mother when you were five years old. Why did you not tell her when you were sixteen years old that you were being sexually assaulted?" In the two hours I had spent waiting for the section 41 arguments to be heard, this was one of the questions I had anticipated if in fact it was this incident that they were asking to reveal to the jury. I had already made some notes for myself about how I would address it if asked in court. The following is taken directly from those notes.

Why did I tell my mother when I was five about the boy who tried to rape me?

- It hurt and was scary was all that I knew
- I was told "you mustn't tell, you mustn't tell" which made me feel that I should tell

- I sat on my mother's knee and cried and described what happened as best I could

Why did I not tell my mother when I was sixteen that the minister was sexually assaulting and stalking me?

- My mother was a distant figure in my teenage years
- She was highly critical of me in many ways and very disapproving of my evangelical bent (but not the minister himself, who was an authority figure in the community)
- I was deeply invested in the minister as an authority figure, and could not explain or understand what was going on even to myself, let alone to my (distant and critical) mother
- Although I did not recognize what was happening as forced fellatio, I knew it related to sex and I was confused, embarrassed and ashamed.

I would be questioned over and over on this point. "If you trusted your mother at five, why not at sixteen?" I tried to explain the relationship had changed and the circumstances were entirely different. I started to realize that I was having to explain my relationship with my mother, which was a complex one (as it is for many teenagers). Finally and with some exasperation, I pointed out "I think we should also recognise that five year olds tell their mothers different things than sixteen year olds." This finally ended this line of questioning—but there was much more to come.

My time on the stand

I had agreed (with some reluctance, because it felt that I had no advocate in the courtroom) with the Crown prosecutor's decision not to examine me on the stand, beyond confirming who I was and introducing me to the court. This was her preferred strategy because she said that my video statement was extremely clear, and really she did not need to ask me anything further. What I had not expected, however, was that when I was cross-examined by defence counsel that she would be entirely passive, allowing me to be berated over and over again with the same question.

This tactic, designed to break down and confuse witnesses, was used numerous times by defence counsel as she cross-examined me. Occasionally the judge himself became exasperated and interrupted, telling her to move on. For example, when I was testifying about the floor plans that I had looked at earlier, defence counsel quoted from my statement that I "could hear" the minister's wife on the other side of the wall, in the kitchen while I was being assaulted, which further compounded a feeling of unreality. "But the kitchen was not immediately the other side of the wall to the study," asserted the defence lawyer. "Right, there was a hallway in between," I agreed. "Then why did you say it was the 'other side of the wall?'" she badgered, over and over again. I replied that I had not said "immediately" the other side of the wall, just that I could hear her. Finally the judge intervened. "I think Dr Macfarlane has answered that question clearly counsel. Please move on."

Another question I was asked repeatedly in cross-examination was whether the minister had ejaculated in my mouth when I "gave him oral sex" (defence counsel's words). I corrected the question: "You mean when I was forced to give him fellatio?" I was then asked five or six times whether or not he had ejaculated. Each time I said no, not that I could remember. For myself, I imagine that I could easily have made myself forget such a disgusting detail. At the time, amazing though this is to contemplate in the Internet age, I was not even aware that there was such a thing as ejaculation. Again and again, defence counsel asked me the same question (she was probably trying to make the jury think this was an essential detail that I could not possibly have forgotten). Finally, the judge intervened: "She has answered that question many times now counsel, please move on."

In order to keep myself calm and centred (my friends and family and I knew I had to resist the temptation to respond to defence counsel's more outlandish questions with my customary sarcasm), I had a mantra written on a notepad that I took with me into the witness box. It said: "Let the jury see that she is a bully." Each time I felt my patience beginning to crack and outrage creep up on me at the line and type of questioning, I made myself read my mantra. I read it many times, and it helped to keep me from plunging into hand-to-hand combat with defence counsel, which I was ready to do.

I had a second mantra also on that piece of paper, one that my therapist had given me a few years before. It was core to my objectives in putting myself through this, and it was extremely helpful in those moments when I felt victimized and upset. It said:

"Whenever you feel lonely, remember you are doing this for a whole community."

When I had first taken the stand, I had my first opportunity to look at Meirion Griffiths in more than forty years. He was sitting in the box reserved for the accused, behind a sheet of what looked like plexiglass. As soon as I sat down, I very intentionally looked over at him. I did not need to stare, but I needed him to know I was not afraid to look at him and to begin to de-sensitize myself to sitting in the same room as him. That went fine. On several subsequent occasions later that week, when I was moving from floor to floor or room to room in the courthouse, I would suddenly be stopped by either Jo (the police woman who was responsible for taking care of me) or on one occasion one of Griffiths's counsel. They were trying to avoid me seeing him or walking past him. "It's okay," I said. "I haven't come all this way to hide behind a door now." I walked right past him each time. Eventually they stopped asking.

There were some other lines of questioning, during the almost three hours that I was cross-examined, that illustrate the tendency of criminal defence to focus on a world that is not a reality for sexual assault survivors. When I described him masturbating while he drove me in his car, I was asked "Wasn't that dangerous? [to drive while masturbating] Weren't you afraid?" Well, yes, I was afraid, but being in a road traffic accident was not top of my fear list at that moment. When I described how Griffiths often wanted to go swimming in the sea during our "driving lessons" (mysteriously losing his swimming trunks on each occasion), defence counsel queried "Wasn't it a strange idea to combine swimming with a driving lesson?" A few members of the jury had a smile on their lips at this question. If you grow up on the sea in England, you swim all the time. You combine it with every type of outing. Even driving lessons. Even being sexually assaulted.

Another line of questioning illustrated the remarkably primitive way in which defence counsel frequently present sexual abuse or assault as an intellectual question that the victim can consider and then say "no thank you." Defence counsel built up to this by telling the jury that I was a very academic kid ("yes, 'swotty,'" I added), with high academic marks and a thirst for knowledge. Was it not the case, she asked, that I had self-studied Ancient Greek in order to try to read the New Testament in the original language in which it was written? I agreed that, yes, I had done that. And that I had a deep knowledge of the Bible, especially the New Testament? Yes, I agreed. Then why, she asked, did I not realize that fellatio between a married man and a teenager was wrong?

To answer her, I realized that I had to effectively educate both her and the jury that being sexually abused is not an intellectual experience. It is an emotional and terrifying experience, when nothing you have ever known or know seems anywhere close to explaining what is happening to you. There is no relationship between being "smart" and defending oneself against terrifying and unwanted sexual assault. I had no way of understanding or naming what was happening to me in those assaults that took place in the minister's study but also over and over again in his car, in cornfields, on beaches, and in dark alleyways. Explaining or defending myself against these assaults was completely outside my experience and outside my emotional capacity at sixteen. This had nothing to do with whether or not I could read the New Testament in Greek, or that I was an A student and loved to learn.

I began my cross-examination about thirty minutes before lunch and continued for about two and a half hours after. During the lunch break, I was told I could not speak to or eat with my family and friends. I sat in a witness room where I chewed on a grilled cheese sandwich and talked to Bernie who sneaked down to see me. Then it was back into the courtroom and the badgering started up again. At the end of the day, I was exhausted, but holding it together. Sibyl and David, who had both watched the day of testimony, each had to return to their home base (Sibyl to London, David to Wakefield). We had a quick beer together and then took them to the train station.

It was over, I was done. The Crown prosecutor said she was "very happy" with my testimony. From my point of view, I was allowing myself to feel very little. So far, so good. Bernie and I went for a walk on the beach at Portsmouth.

The other story

The next morning, we returned to the courthouse to watch the playing of the video testimony of the other complainant. I had agreed with the prosecutor that I would not be there for her live testimony the following day, mostly to avoid any objections the defence might raise to this in the event of a mistrial, but also because I had been told that the other victim was very anxious about her testimony, and I could not know if having me in the public gallery would be helpful or another source of stress for her. But I wanted to see the video and went into the public gallery to watch, along with the jury.

I had not fully anticipated the impact that watching another woman talk about Griffiths's appalling manipulation and exploitation of his position would have on me. She was, at the time of her abuse, a trainee teacher, but she later became a priest herself, and her faith was clearly very important to her. Just like with me, Griffiths insinuated himself into her life at a time when she was especially vulnerable (she described herself as suffering from depression). He began to physically press himself on to her, culminating with a horrifying assault in her own sitting room which she described tearfully in graphic detail. The tape was cut and edited numerous times when she began to cry and was unable to continue. Her trauma was clear to see, just as painful and wretched as when the assaults first happened decades earlier.

When the tape was over, I walked out of the public gallery and burst into tears in the hallway. All I could think of was that if I had come forward at the time that I was assaulted, perhaps this would not have happened to her. Maybe I could have saved her from this, the worst experience of her life. I knew that this probably was not the case—who would have listened to me in 1976?—but I keep repeating over and over, "I should have tried." This was a far worse feeling than giving my own testimony. Watching what that man did to someone else was devastating. It was a reminder, of course, of what he did to me. And it was a journey into the misery of another soul.

My friends testify

Next up, my two disclosure witnesses. These were my two oldest girlfriends, Debbie and Damhnait, to whom I had first disclosed just fragments of what had happened with the minister in the decade after. Both were testifying live by video link. Both had previously made written statements about what I had told them, and when. After the Crown did a short examination clarifying the basic details, she handed them over to defence counsel. "Handing over" was what it felt like. Damhnait was up first, and I could see her surprise at the aggressive way in which the defence lawyer began to question her. "Do you think that you might be confusing this story with Julie telling you about her childhood rape?" "No. Of course not," responded Damhnait. "How are you so sure?" "Because I remember the conversation and it began by talking about religious faith; I am a lapsed Catholic." Defence counsel continued to press her but I could see, and I imagine so could she, that Damhnait became more and more confident rebutting her absurd suggestions. After about thirty minutes, she was done. Debbie took her place on the video screen, from a different courthouse. Defence counsel began again with questioning her on "mixing up" the two instances of sexual assault. Debbie is known for her pithy retorts if anyone tries to challenge her. When asked if she might be mixing up the two incidents, she responded bluntly, "Well that would be a quantum leap of fantasy wouldn't it?" I left the courtroom with a profound sense of gratitude and love for my friends.

The following day, having already decided not to be in the gallery for the testimony of the other complainant, I thought about making a "goodbye" trip to Chichester, the town I had lived in as a teenager and where all these events took place. I no longer have family there and have no particular reason to go back, other than to enjoy the beauty of the surrounding South Downs. But that morning I realized I really did not want to go to Chichester. I was ready to let go of any remaining attachment to the town. I didn't need any more triggers this week. Instead, we walked around the lovely centre of Winchester and the grounds of the Winchester Cathedral. Later that day, Bernie and I returned to London, to let the trial conclude and wait for the verdict. I had no interest in watching Griffiths testify. And I was ready to get back to some kind of normal life. That weekend we were travelling up to Leeds to meet Sibyl's new in-laws-to-be for the first time.

The jury comes back

The jury retired to deliberate the following Tuesday in the late afternoon, after seven days of trial. They began their deliberations on Wednesday morning, and I was promised that as soon as there was any news, I would get a phone call from Jo, the policewoman. Of course we felt nervous waiting for the verdict. We imagined we might hear something by Thursday or Friday.

At about 1 pm on Wednesday, as I ate lunch with friends at a Stoke Newington café, my phone buzzed. It was Jo. This was much, much sooner than I had expected to hear from her. My heart in my mouth, I picked up the call and walked out of the café on to the sidewalk: "Hi Jo, what's happened?"

The jury had returned after barely three hours of deliberation and told the judge they were "hopelessly deadlocked." Since an English jury can reach a decision by a ten out of twelve majority verdict, this meant that at least three jury members were at odds with the rest, perhaps more. The judge pressed them on whether they might reach a verdict if they spent more time, saying, this is a "most unsatisfactory outcome." Each jury member, Jo told me on the phone as I listened in a daze, had shaken their head "no" when asked.

This was a very short deliberation period and suggested that something uncomfortable and dysfunctional had taken place in the jury room. For some jurors at least, they needed to be done, right away. So, after five years of police work and seven days of trial testimony and argument, after less than three hours, the result was a hung jury. In other words, no result.

Over the next few weeks, I asked myself over and over again how could a jury have listened to the (extremely similar, clear, detailed, and linear) testimony of two women who had never met about the same man, as well as our disclosure witnesses, and concluded that maybe we had made it all up? It felt surreal. My daughters, my stepson, and my daughter-in-law reacted to the news with fury and tears. Bernie, like me, was in a daze. How could anyone ever be convicted of sexual assault then? If a court could not convict in this case, with these facts, and with these witnesses, when could it ever convict anyone?

Another reaction began to creep up on me after about twelve hours of pure shock. I knew that jury trials were plagued by lack of knowledge about the dynamics of sexual assault and entrenched stereotypes about women who report sexual violence. This jury was no different. On the law of averages, some of them might themselves have been violent toward women, and some of the woman would likely have been sexually assaulted or harassed themselves. Or they might have people close to them who had been. They evidently could not have a meaningful conversation that led to a productive assessment of the evidence (three hours was far too short for that to have happened). This bias against sexual assault complainants was the reason that I was doing this in the first place. I wanted to use my own knowledge and familiarity with the legal system to bring attention to this case and, just as in the civil claim, raise awareness and ensure accountability. I knew why women did not bring their complaints forward. I knew what I was getting into. Why should I be surprised? In an odd way, the hung jury outcome only reinforced for me the importance of doing this.

It was clear almost immediately that the Crown would ask for a retrial, and both they and the police were committed to getting a verdict. I told Jo that, yes, I would do it all again. A week or so after we returned to Canada, I heard from Jo and she was able to confirm that there would be a retrial in January 2020. She also told me that the defence wanted to see my childhood diaries.

During my testimony, I had mentioned something I had noticed just a few months earlier when writing my victim impact statement (which I was yet to give since the trial ended without a verdict). I was an avid journaler as a young person and adult. I filled the pages of many diaries, beginning in my early teens and consistently through my twenties and early thirties. I still write spasmodically—writing has always been a crucial way for me to sort out my thoughts and grapple with dilemmas. What I had noticed was that my page-a-day journal, which in those years I filled on a daily basis, stopped abruptly in the year that the minister's abuse began—actually several months before the first assault, probably at the same time I was experiencing the crisis of faith that I went to the minister to talk about. I did not write again until at least a few years later, when the journals pick up again. I was struck by the fact that I was obviously at a loss to describe what was happening to me, even in my safest place—writing.

I had alluded to this during my testimony. So now the defence wanted my diaries, despite the fact that the whole point of my reference to the journals was that they did not include any description of the abuse. I explained this to Jo. She said that they needed to see the journal for the year that the abuse began, 1975, and the year before, 1974, when Griffiths first came to our parish and I would have met him. But there is nothing there that is relevant, I told Jo, and these diaries are really personal, and have great sentimental value to me. The idea of someone poring over them made me feel slightly sick.

Jo was kind and understanding, but the position did not change. She promised me that only she would read the diaries, and that she would keep them safe. She would note and then give anything that seemed relevant—this did not worry me, I knew there was nothing other than perhaps references to Griffiths leading youth group meetings or Bible studies during 1974—to the Crown, who would then share it with the defence. But these diaries were full of mortifying, cringe-worthy stories of adolescence—crushes, fights with my mother, and worst of all, endless teenage self-doubt and angst. How dare they ask to see these?

I pointed out that this was exactly why victims do not come forward to police, because of the massive intrusion into their personal lives. This is reminiscent of the recent debate over whether police should ask for victim's cell phones, to ensure there are no records that the defence could exploit that the complainant does not disclose (for example, contact with the accused). There are reports that many rape and sexual assault cases are being dropped by police if victims will not hand over their phones,[31] and women are coming forward to say why they refused to do this.[32] This kind of trolling for personal information has a rationale, of course—the Crown does not want to be surprised by any new information that the defence has gleaned from their side of a text or email communication (as happened in the Jian Ghomeshi trial),[33] but the chilling impact on complainants who may see their privacy as too high a price to pay is clear. This just adds to the feeling that we, the complainants, are in fact the ones being investigated.

With great reluctance, I mailed in my diaries to Jo. A retrial date was set for January 2020. We all felt so frustrated. I was going to have to do it all over again. But as I wrote to my daughters,

> This (outcome) underscores how far away our society is from accepting the harm done to people by sexual violence, and the urgent need to change our values that currently give all the power to the perpetrators.
>
> But the biggest challenge I have faced as a result of my own experiences has been not to lose my faith and trust in people. To hang on to my belief that the world could become a better place. I have always felt that if I lost my faith in this, the abusers would have won.

The result of the first trial serves as an important metaphor for the problems and the deficiencies of the criminal justice system in addressing sexual violence.

EPILOGUE

Never, for the sake of peace and quiet, deny your
convictions.

—Dag Hammarskjold

W hen I first sat down to write this book, I wasn't sure if I
could do it.

I was unsure if I could write such a deeply personal account
that would be so different to anything I had ever written before.
I was anxious about putting my own experiences at the centre of
the story; I worried that readers would lose interest, or not relate.
I knew that I wanted to integrate my knowledge of the law and
legal processes into my description of my own experiences of sexual
violence and seeking justice, because I believed that would make
them more useful for others. But my public-facing writing and
publications (which have been such an important and rewarding
part of my life) have historically been in the somewhat impersonal,
analytical style of an academic. Even my writing for the National
Self-Represented Litigants Project, from 2013 on, which has been
directed to a wider public rather than an exclusively legal audience,
was still about law, legal policy, and processes. I could let my hair
down a little in my blogs, but the primary style of all this output was
still expository and analytical. This book would require me to find a
new and different "voice" in which to write.

But at the same time, I felt that there was a continuity between
the stories I had collected as a researcher of peoples' experiences
and the story I wanted to tell in this book. I had learned over years
of interviewing subjects for my research projects that to engage with
people and encourage them to tell me what was really going on for

them—to be truly authentic and disclosing—that I needed to be authentic in my role too. This has meant respecting every story and trying to accurately and honestly convey that experience. In all of my research on different topics, it has also meant connecting personal experience to access to justice, and interrogating the legal edifices that frequently retraumatize them in the process. Now I had to apply the same commitment to myself and my own story.

I had no idea how long this project might take me, and I was very afraid that my life would end before I could complete it. When I began to write this book in 2018, I had already had metastatic ovarian cancer for two years and knew that my illness was chronic and incurable. I had no idea how long I had. And once I had decided I wanted to write this book, it became extremely important to me to complete the project.

When I first began to send my overview and chapter outline around to publishers, my anxiety grew. Accustomed to finding a publisher with reasonable ease, I was now being turned down by each one I approached. This included imprints who had published my work in the past, and with whom I thought I might have some "credit." They were confused and, in many ways, understandably. This law professor who usually wrote about other people's stories and used these narratives to make reasoned arguments about changes in legal practice and services and law reform, now proposed writing about her own rape and sexual assault. As the number of rejections grew, I started to wonder if I would ever find a publisher and, of course, this raised even more doubts in my mind that I could write this book.

Lots of people encouraged me to keep going. Paradoxically, I found strength in the realization that this book represented continuity not only in terms of my method and approach to storytelling, but in its potential to once again make me feel like an outlier. Yet again I was having what I thought was an excellent idea, but others were less than convinced. This was a familiar feeling.

With the help of my brilliant research assistant Rebecca Flynn, I started to identify trade publishers who published books on sexual violence and social justice topics more generally. I was looking for a publisher who believed in the book, as well as my ability to write it. A publisher who accepted that our personal stories can be illuminated by deep analysis, and that deep analysis can be brought to life by personal stories. When I found Amanda Crocker at Between the Lines, I felt like I had come home.

So I had a publisher, but I still needed to find my voice. This was a long and often difficult process of trying to figure out how much of "me" to put into the book (my instinct was as little as possible). Friends who read initial drafts told me I had to get over this, that my story would be the heartbeat of the book. I agonized and wrote and rewrote the initial chapters, but theirs (and that of my editor, Mary Newberry) was the right advice. I had to accept that my story was important not just as a vehicle for my analysis and arguments for change, but simply as my story.

Once I did accept this, it was incredibly empowering. Like everything that involves personal trauma, figuring out and committing to an intention is very important. It has taken me years to be able to talk openly about this history. The more practice I get, the easier talking about my past abuse has become. However some of the other consequences of committing to confronting the scourge of sexual violence and advocating both with and for other survivors have been unexpectedly painful.

THE LONELINESS OF THE SURVIVOR

Deciding to move forward with a lawsuit against the Anglican Church for historic sexual abuse, and making my public disclosures in 2014 at Sexual Assault Awareness Day, set me on a path that has changed my life. I have no regrets about these decisions, and remain so grateful to those who supported and encouraged me to take these steps. The outpouring from other survivors who contacted me following my disclosures took me somewhat by surprise, but I realized at once that this was part of my new reality.

More difficult to adjust to was the loneliness and isolation and the resulting fight for recognition and safety that is often a consequence of speaking up about sexual violence. While I am familiar with feeling something of an outlier in my academic world, I was not prepared for the intensity with which my efforts to call out tolerance of sexual misconduct and the protection of predators would be resisted by my own university and other institutions. I naïvely assumed that once people understood what had happened to me, or to someone on whose behalf I was advocating—whether sexual abuse, harassment, assault, or even rape—they would prioritize the wellbeing and safety of girls and women. I assumed, wrongly, that the hardest part of my journey would be the embarrassment and lingering shame of coming forward and saying "me too," not the institutional reactions to my calling out sexual violence.

What I did not expect was what I now know as the second assault; the resistant and sometimes judgmental response of the responsible institution or law enforcement agency, along with some individuals within it. The tendency of institutions to minimize, deny, and suppress complaints about sexual violence is described by Jennifer Freyd and others as "institutional betrayal,"[1] but in practice it is often difficult to separate the institution—whether a school, university, church, or social club—from the individuals who make and enforce decisions on its behalf. Of course, it's not really possible to compare an actual assault with participating in an institutional or legal process, but living through these consequences of stepping forward definitely feels like a second layer of trauma. I was not psychologically prepared for the loneliness and isolation that has been a continuous part of my experience since my public disclosures, the consequence of our collective discomfort and silence when faced with the reality of sexual violence and its impact.[2]

I had felt very alone with my terrifying, shameful secret when I was abused by the minister. I felt alone again in my shame and panic when I was date-raped. When I drove home from work in Ireland to the home I shared with my violent domestic partner, I felt incredibly isolated and afraid. Other parts of this story came with a different kind of loneliness; when I stepped into the witness box to give my testimony in the criminal trial in 2019, I was being cheered on by many people, but still in that moment I felt alone. When I was told that the jury had been unable to reach a verdict and had been discharged, I was surrounded by many angry and outraged people, but only I could really feel the weariness and resignation that I am sure many survivors experience upon having their (worst) instincts confirmed. I have come to realize that this kind of lonely feeling is inevitable for survivors, however much we are supported. Only we stand in our own shoes, and only we can stand up and speak about what happened to us.

Other parts of my public disclosure felt tremendously personally empowering; for example, when the British news media picked up my piece in the *Church Times*[3] and opened up the discussion about the morality of the Anglican Church in aggressively litigating sexual abuse complaints, and the support I felt from friends and many colleagues when I spoke at Sexual Assault Awareness Day. But almost immediately after I made my disclosures that day, as female students started to come forward to the administration with their own stories of sexual harassment and assault, I realized that while my speech was widely applauded, some of its consequences were not welcomed. I began to be told to "shut it down." I felt increasingly isolated as I urged the university to disclose the formal investigation of my faculty colleague to the law school community, but found that my colleagues supported secrecy. I kept being told not to talk about it. I found myself alone in advocating for protections for students participating in the investigation. These were all issues that I assumed there would be widespread consensus on, but I was increasingly feeling like an outlier. Most of all, I felt very alone when I acted on my belief that my university should not be able to secretively "pass-the-trash" to another law school by giving my now former colleague a non-disclosure agreement. I told the truth when prospective employers contacted me to ask why had he left the law school, but it slowly began to dawn on me that I was the only faculty member who would do this. I was not going to be supported by either my employer of twenty-five years or my faculty association, who had both signed on to the NDA. When the university refused to defend me in the defamation suit, I was taken aback at the silence and the obvious discomfort and fearfulness of my colleagues, many of whom had significant status and solid job security.

The defamation suit created a force field around me in my workplace. While support flooded in from colleagues and students in other universities and from other survivors and advocates, in my own school I found myself shunned by former allies for going "too far" and bringing shame to the university. There was a sense of fear or danger in associating with me, and perhaps drawing to them the persecution everyone knew I was suffering from our former colleague. I recognize that we all naturally try to avoid the messy and uncertain parts of life. But I still struggle with this. And the isolation made me all the more vulnerable to the defamation suit he brought against me; if the plaintiff had believed for a second that my university would have defended me, he would not have sued me (he was right, they did not defend me until compelled to do so by a court; see chapter 6).

By the fall of 2019, as the silence around me continued, I began to experience increasingly acute PTSD symptoms of nausea and stomach cramps each time I went into the law school. I was forced to accept that I could no longer go into the building without being triggered. I felt foolish, but I had to ask for accommodation to teach outside the law school, and could no longer go into my own office. Of course, this only increased my isolation. PTSD is still an unfamiliar concept to many and I found it difficult and embarrassing to explain this to colleagues.

I am emphasizing this loneliness for two reasons. First, because I think it is crucial to anticipate that speaking up about sexual violence and our flawed ways of dealing with it can be a painfully isolating experience. I never considered giving up—by agreeing to the secrecy surrounding the university investigation, for example, or "apologizing" for the "defamation" and promising never to do it again—but it is important for me to acknowledge how heartbreaking it has been to feel let down by some whom I hoped for more from, but who were just too freaked out to stand beside me publicly. Second, my experience underscores the depth of isolation—as well as fear—experienced by those with far less power and privilege than I who step forward to report sexual misconduct or to advocate for victims. Think of a student reporting on a teacher, an employee reporting on a co-worker or manager, a congregant reporting on a minister, or an articling student who is a woman of colour reporting on a white male partner in the law firm. I have never regretted my decision to come out, or to stand up for other survivors—but the price is high.

Neither do I have anything other than unambiguous pride and clarity about my decision to sue the Anglican Church, to use my insider knowledge of the civil legal process to call out the shameful litigation practices of the church and its insurer, and ultimately to push the insurer to a new claims process. Finally, taking the step of participating in the criminal process to hold the minister who abused me to personal account was the right thing to do, but it hasn't been easy. All my reservations about working in this system—lack of empathy, lack of trauma training among professionals, the distortions of an adversarial system, the problem with juries who are exposed to rape myth all the time in the public culture—have been realized. But the decision I made was the right one.

Clarity over our decisions in the face of choices is a wonderful source of strength and peace. I have that, and am very grateful for it.

THE WRITING PROCESS

Most of the writing of this book was done during one of the most difficult years of my life, as I lay in bed following surgery, then chemotherapy, then radiation, and tried to deal with legal proceedings in another country and the refusal of my university employer to help me. Those were dark and scary months, as I contemplated personal bankruptcy and we continued to try to stay optimistic in the face of my progressive illness. There were days when I thought that the stress inside my head might explode.

I found that writing about what had happened to me, and my experiences with my own and other cases, was in many ways a calming and reassuring experience. Throughout my life I have used writing as a way of working out what I think and feel about everything, beginning with my childhood diaries, progressing through my "conversations" with God when I was a young Christian, and continuing into many volumes of adult reflection. While I am writing I am always absorbed in that process, a strategy learned very young and a way of coping for me always.

But this writing project and its subject-matter came with some additional challenges. Typically, after a couple—or more—hours of working intensively on this book, I would raise my head, take a pause, and realize I was feeling really jittery and on-edge, my nerves buzzing. This is my chronic PTSD kicking in. Of course, burying myself for hours in thinking and writing about both the personal material and even the more detached critique and analysis in this book was an inevitable trigger for that. But I became accustomed to this, and with PTSD anticipation is a huge part of the battle; it really helps. It was unavoidable that I would feel "PTSD-ish" (as my family are accustomed to me describing this) after hours of working on the manuscript. After all, I was literally burying myself, cognitively and emotionally, in the detail of extremely upsetting events and recollections. What does this feel like? I have never done this, but my best metaphor is still that it is the emotional equivalent of sticking your fingers into an electric socket.

THE MINISTER: THE FINAL CHAPTER

Despite this, strange though it might sound, writing this book has been empowering and ultimately deeply satisfying. Writing has been my safe place all my life, and no amount of PTSD seems to change that, thank goodness.

There are a few loose ends to tie up. The retrial of Meirion Griffiths took place in January 2020. It was held at Portsmouth Crown Court, about an hour's drive from Winchester where the first trial took place in July 2019. This time I testified by video link, having decided a few months earlier that I did not need to be physically present in the courtroom for a second time. It was a wise decision for me. I sat at my kitchen table one January morning in front of my laptop with my dog—Teddy—curled up at my feet. At Bernie's suggestion, I surrounded the laptop with framed pictures of the kids, which I had moved from other parts of the house. Bernie sat at the far end of the table. The sun shone brightly that morning on Lake Erie, which we live beside, and the water glinted and winked back at me when I looked out over the lake.

It was utterly surreal to sit in front of a blank screen (due to technical difficulties, they could see me but I could not see the judge, defence counsel, jury, or anyone in the courtroom) and testify again to the truth of the story I had been telling about the minister since 1999. Surrounded by everything familiar to me, I was participating in a bizarre ritual of question-and-answer as defence counsel cross-examined me, again.

This time felt even harder than the first, despite the comfort of my surroundings and Teddy warming my feet. Perhaps it was because I knew what was coming this time—in theory, and as a law professor, I knew the first time also, but cross-examination is not an experience that can possibly be imagined until you go through it. Perhaps it was the dissonance between sitting in my beloved home and the brutality of the attacks from defence counsel. Or maybe I was just tired of it—tired through to my innermost core.

I faced many (although not all) of the same questions, but now with the added edge that if I departed in any minor way from what exactly I said the first time I testified, I was of course pulled up by defence counsel and asked, over and over, if I was lying or making it up. To give one example: this time I was asked if I remembered anything else about what the minister did with his hands when I was told to kneel in front of him and put his penis in my mouth in his study that day. I said yes, he put his hands on the back of my head—he was pushing me on to him. "You didn't tell us this the first time!" exclaimed defence counsel. "You didn't ask me" I replied. She tried the same line a few more times before giving up. The strategy was exactly the same as the first trial; she was taking every possible chance to humiliate and demean me, and render me an unreliable witness in the eyes of the jury.

There was an effort to introduce some lines from my teenage diaries. I had made a statement about these earlier and was expecting this. I was asked over and over again if I had sexual relations with my Christian boyfriend (I did not). This was an effort to disprove my statement that before I was first assaulted by the minister, I had never seen a man's penis. I had not.

Once I was done (two and a half hours) I disconnected and it was over. I had never seen the faces of the jury and had no idea how my testimony had been received. Jo French from Sussex police, whom I had met at the first trial in Winchester, called me after I was done; this was the end of the day in the UK and the jury had been sent home. Jo was encouraging and personally supportive as always. But I felt awful. I had some sense of relief that I was done, but I felt the familiar disorienting, buzzing, PTSD energy coursing through my body. Bernie asked me what I would like to do that would make me feel better, safer, calmer. I wanted to go to the barn and see my horse, Jayden.

I didn't ride that day, but instead did something that riders call "join up" with their horses. "Join up" is a training method used to train young horses to come toward their owners (to "join up" with them) respectfully and quietly.[4] As Monty Roberts, the renowned horse trainer, writes "Join-Up methods rely on horse and trainer establishing a bond of communication and trust."[5] Jayden is already well-trained but I use join up as a way of continuing to connect deeply with him using body language alone.

There is no tack and few words. We walk together around the arena, me on the ground beside him, his nose level with my right shoulder. We weave circles and shapes on the ground, and step together over small obstacles. I just walk forward and he walks with his nose at my shoulder. When I stop, he stops. When I change direction, he does too. It's a very deep bonding experience to have a large, strong animal walking beside you "to heel" as a dog would (actually rather more obediently than Teddy would). The emotional connection is very strong. Within a minute, I started to feel calmer and my breathing slowed and steadied. By the time I left the barn an hour later, I was beginning to feel a sense of peace and calmness. The worst was over.

For the following couple of days I was exhausted. But I was done and life carried on. I started teaching in the new term. I talked to Jo each day that week about progress in the Crown Court in Portsmouth. She could not tell me about the evidence, but checked in regularly to let me know where the process was. The jury went out on Friday morning. It was hard waiting through the weekend. I rode a lot. I told myself I had done everything I could whatever the verdict. I'm not sure I convinced myself.

On Monday morning, just as I was arriving at the Cancer Centre at Victoria hospital in London, where I am treated, I got a call from Jo. The jury had reached a verdict. Four guilty and two not guilty verdicts (the not guilty verdicts were for two lesser charges, perhaps reflecting an uneasy tolerance of more ambiguous acts). He was convicted of charges citing specific and multiple occasions of sexual assault against both myself and the other complainant. We had done it. After decades of lies and cover-up, Meirion Griffiths was finally out there in the bright light of publicity, a convicted abuser. Justice was done.[6]

The same week as the verdict, the BBC showed a two-part documentary about the Anglican Church's cover-up of decades of complaints against Bishop Peter Ball. *Exposed: The Church's Dark Secret* featured two resolute campaigners for justice, both victims of Ball as children, whom I had come to know and respect, Phil Johnson and Rev Graham Sawyer. The documentary highlighted what we had discovered at the Independent Inquiry into Child Sexual Abuse in March 2018 when the inquiry focused on two case studies: the diocese of Chichester and the allegations against Ball.[7]

Exposed also described the role of Eric Kemp, bishop of Chichester from 1974 to 2001, in supressing complaints about Peter Ball, whose ministry fell under his supervision. Kemp hired a private investigator to undermine the credibility of the complainants. The investigator concluded in a 1993 report for the bishop that Peter Ball had abused "very many young men." Nonetheless, Kemp continued to denigrate Ball's accusers—one of whom, Neil Todd, committed suicide in 2012—and did not reveal the report to police. I was close friends with Kemp's daughter Alice, who was the same age as me and regularly saw and spoke to Bishop Kemp when I hung out with Alice after school. This was the same period during which I was being abused by the minster, whom Kemp had supervisory responsibility for as his bishop. Another shoe dropped.

Also that week, once the Griffiths conviction was reported in the UK press, I heard from the girl (now a woman) who grew up in the house next door to me in Chichester. A few years younger than me, she was abused by another man involved in the Anglican Church during the same time period as I was abused by Griffiths. Our abusers even shared an MO—each would come to the house by car, speak to our mothers who encouraged us to leave with them despite our excuses, and then drive us away—and abuse us. I looked at a photo of my young neighbour taken at the time I knew her that had been printed in the papers when her abuser was imprisoned in 1990.[8] Her face was so familiar and so innocent. It made me cry. Sometimes it feels like the revelations will never end.

At the Cancer Clinic the day of the verdict I also had good news; for the time being, my cancer was reasonably stable. I was making a work plan to focus on fundraising to ensure the longevity and if possible, permanence, of the National Self-Represented Litigants Project[9] which I had founded in 2013, and for which (as well as for other advocacy) I had just received the Order of Canada. The year 2020 was off to a good start.[10]

CHANGING THE LEGAL PROCESSES

In this book many of the stories I tell focus on the flaws and omissions of our current legal processes, both civil and criminal. These are to a large extent self-evident and well-documented, in more detail than I can do so here, by many others beside me.[11]

My intention is slightly different; it is to explain what needs to change from the perspective of someone who is both a survivor-participant and a legal scholar. To that end here is my list of priorities; first for both civil and criminal cases.

1. The elimination of all remaining statutes of limitations regarding both civil and criminal sexual abuse and rape cases, recognizing what we now know about the time it takes for many survivors to feel able and ready to come forward.

2. A revaluation of the legal measurement of witness "credibility" that is informed by an understanding of trauma and its effect on behaviour and memory and insulated from assumptions that tie credibility to specious, sexist, and irrelevant beliefs about how women should behave, dress, and respond to sexual violence.

3. Related to this, a realistic, fair, and trauma-informed reappraisal of "relevant" information to adjudication over a claim or allegation of sexual violence. Unfortunately the more information sought and provided, the more potential for highlighting minor and irrelevant discrepancies or inaccuracies and using these to attack the overall information of the plaintiff/complainant. We don't expect someone who ran out of a burning building twenty years ago to recall what colour socks they were wearing. And if they get it wrong they are not lying about the building being on fire. "Relevance" currently includes anything that the defence can dig up on the complainant that makes her look bad and undermines her credibility to the decision-maker(s). This practice is sustained by a rape myth: that any minor, inadvertent inconsistency in information about a traumatic event means the complainant is lying.

4. A revaluation of the legal measurement of "impact" that is trauma-informed. For example, many victims will have contact with an abuser whom they know personally in the days and weeks after an attack as they attempt to make sense of what happened and feel "normal" again. If their abuse occurred within an industry, institutional, or club context, they might be checking out if they can feel safe about still participating in that activity alongside this person. This does not mean they consented to the sexual violation they experienced. It must be assumed that impact is inevitable after a sexual attack however functional or dysfunctional the survivor's life now is (I heard in the civil process that I seemed to have "done just fine" and therefore my abuse had not harmed me). Most disgusting, I have experienced efforts by defence "experts" to distribute causality for present trauma between different life events; for example, I was told that much of my PTSD was the result of poor parenting experiences and my earlier cancer diagnosis. This is an unsustainable clinical argument and a primitive effort to minimize survivors compensation.[12]

Three of these four points are about "drawing trauma into the frame,"[13] a critical rebalancing in both criminal and civil cases involving sexual violence. As our awareness of the prevalence of sexual violence increases, the problems of the existing system—with its rigid and unrealistic notions of "credibility," "harm," and "impact," uninformed by an understanding of the trauma of sexual violence[14]—become all the more apparent.

I also propose some specific changes in the investigation and trying of sex crimes that arise directly from my experience, but are well-documented elsewhere.

5. Better training in trauma for police officers working on sexual offences cases, including ensuring that a trained person is available where an individual identifies themselves as a sexual assault victim in that first call. I worked with some very compassionate police officers but none were adequately trained to understand the impact of trauma.

6. Similarly, trauma training and education on the dynamics of sexual violence more generally for judges and lawyers working on cases of sexual violence.[15]

7. Examining the appropriateness of juries for sex crime trials, given the pervasiveness of rape myth in the public culture.[16]

8. If juries are used, enabling potential jurors to privately identify as victims of sexual violence—or perhaps affected by knowing someone personally who has been accused of sexual violence—and opt out of the jury pool.

9. Related to "relevance"(point number 3, above), prosecutors and defence counsel should exercise restraint in demanding intrusive personal information from complainants, including their personal diaries, phone data, and so on, making this the exception rather than the norm.

10. Similarly, trauma-informed practice should reject the assumption (which drives a lot of the "fishing" in complainant's personal phone records and journals) that any contact after an alleged attack between victim and accused means that the behaviour was consensual. Most victims know their assailants and continued contact is often the consequence of their trying desperately to make sense of the world they just woke up in after the attack, or even remake the world they lived in before the attack.

11. The more rigorous application of Canada's rape shield law[17] to enable the protection envisaged by this provision against the irrelevant introduction of a victim's sexual history. This is critical to prevent the exploitation of any information about prior sexual history that is embarrassing and humiliating and plays on rape myth in reducing the victim's credibility.

12. An end to witness whacking:[18] bullying, and intimidation by defence counsel and consequences for those who persist.

There are some additional changes that need to be implemented in relation to civil cases over sexual assault and abuse

13. Acknowledgement that protracted litigation is often used intentionally as a means of wearing the plaintiff out and expending all their funds, thereby forcing them to give up. This tactic can be penalized by increased costs awarded after trial, but it is widely accepted and tolerated.

14. Serious efforts to approach settlement in civil cases before inflicting intrusive and traumatizing discovery processes on plaintiffs.[19]

15. The use of neutral qualified experts (on trauma and the other long-term consequences of sexual abuse) to help judges to assess fair levels of compensation, rather than "hired guns," so-called experts retained by each side.[20]

16. The elimination of non-disclosure agreements for termination of employment or other engagement (such as team coaching or volunteer coordination) involving any form of sexual misconduct. Case law in the United States is beginning to void such agreements where there is a future danger to others.[21] Where a victim asks for anonymity, this is easily achievable in a settlement agreement without a commitment to indefinite secrecy for the perpetrator and a cover-up to other future employers.

The other arena for redress and adjudication in relation to sexual violence is workplace and institutional investigative processes. Unlike legal procedures, these presently often take place in secret with unclear procedures and outcomes. There is an urgent need for a code of best practice, ideally promoted by political and legal community leaders, that employers and institutions can be publicly pressed to adopt. As a quasi-legal, private process, workplace investigations can (and do) make up the rules as they go along, and this does not always work well, as my own experience at the University of Windsor shows. A code of best practice should ensure that every investigation has clear terms of reference and scope and that the protocols protect and support complainants as well as those who are the subject of the investigation.

Parties with information need to be able to come forward feeling protected, but they first need to know of the existence of an investigation into allegations of sexual misconduct. Parties need clarification of the nature of public communications that can be made both inside and outside the workplace/institution, and that cannot be suppressed by claims of defamation.[22] While it is certainly personally damaging to be the subject of a workplace investigation into sexual misconduct, information about an investigation that is conducted fairly attracts conditional or qualified privilege (that is, protection against defamation claims). Ultimately, while staying cognisant of the possibility of an investigation to be used as a means of discrimination, it is critical that there is careful public information about an investigation to enable individuals to come forward and ensure a thorough investigation.[23]

Another critical element in a code of best practice for workplace investigations into misconduct is that outcomes must be provided to complainants (not always the case, as I discovered) as well as reported to appropriate oversight authorities. Public reporting need not and should not include names, but should provide the numbers of complaints, investigations, and their outcomes.[24]

Where institutions have historically manifestly failed to report to police and respond to sexual violence in their midst—the Anglican and Catholic Churches come to mind, but there are others—they should be legally mandated to report all allegations of sexual abuse, assault, and harassment to outside authorities.[25] Unions need to question whether they should always support a member accused of sexual predation, especially when complainants are members of the same union. We are a long way from transparency and real institutional accountability yet, and we must take steps to change this.

THE LEGAL PROFESSION

The legal system is a patriarchal and self-invested system that has for decades protected the powerful. It has done so by establishing legal norms—of "credibility," "harm," and "impact," among others—that tolerate male misconduct and minimize the consequences of sexual violence for women and girls. Changing the formal letter of the law is critical to changing attitudes, experiences, and outcomes, but also important is understanding the investment of legal system actors, and in particular, the legal profession, in the present system.

Legal practice in relation to sexual violence, along with practice regarding other forms of discrimination and harassment, reflects the profession's inherent conservatism and preference for the status quo. This means that practice is still often uninformed by knowledge of the impact of trauma or the inherent power dynamics of sexual violence. The disconnect between legal practice and the survivor experience is made even greater by the legal profession's traditional approach to legal advice; pressing obscure, theoretical points of law to protect a client, or to caution them against acting. Orlando da Silva memorably describes this as the "negative catastrophic scenario."[26] This legal culture means that lawyers for both sides—plaintiff complainant or defendant alleged perpetrator—tend to focus on risks however small, rather than providing a more useful analysis of the potential upsides and downsides of acting.

Defence lawyers in civil cases habitually advance legally minimal and often unsustainable threats to shut down complaints[27]—threadbare or even erroneous legal arguments are widely regarded as appropriate "zealous advocacy."[28] The profession's zeal for making arguments that are aggressive yet speculative is highly effective in intimidating many would-be complainants and deterring them from coming forward to report sexual harassment and assault. Many in the profession also appear to accept the tactic of attacking the credibility of a witness by intruding into their personal life. It is an uncomfortable reality that the role played by lawyers and speculative legal threats is significant in further increasing the many disincentives to women to speak up about sexual violence.

Many plaintiffs' lawyers practise with the assumption that every victim simply wants a monetary pay-out and that a non-disclosure agreement is in their best interests. Plaintiffs often say that no other type of outcome, including systemic changes that might protect women in the future, was even contemplated by their lawyers. This is especially ironic given that many survivors come forward precisely because they want to ensure that other women do not suffer the same harassment or attacks that they have. Many more regret agreeing to be silenced by a non-disclosure agreement.

The legal profession needs to take a long, hard look at how they offer services in cases involving all forms of sexual violence. In civil cases, plaintiffs' (victims') lawyers need to listen to the motivations and goals of their clients, realistically appraising their risks without using scaremongering as a device to force them into settlement. There is no good reason why counsel for a victim of harassment or assault should feel obliged to recommend a non-disclosure agreement as part of a settlement, despite the fact that this has become the bargaining norm. They can secure the anonymity of their client without promising secrecy about the identity of the perpetrator.[29] Defence counsel (acting for an accused or alleged perpetrator) in both civil and criminal cases currently widely use aggressive and bullying behaviours, casually making threats to intimidate the other side. Attacks on the personality and lifestyle of the complainant are common, making many victims feel that it is they who are on trial (I certainly experienced this myself). Victims are routinely bullied in the witness box and subjected to widely speculative claims and threats in writing. We need to create new norms for what is "good lawyering" here. Defence counsel are responsible for ensuring that a defendant or accused has a fair trial; this does not require them to denigrate or intimidate the other side.

Lawyers on both sides, as well as judges, who work on sexual violence cases need to be far better educated on sexual abuse related trauma. This type of training is still virtually unknown inside the legal profession, despite growing numbers of available educational resources. We also need a registry of lawyers willing to work with complainants on a contingency or pro bono basis so more women are able to bring forward civil claims of sexual abuse and harassment. The legal profession, which carries both power and responsibility in relation to justice for the victims of sexual violence, needs to do much, much better.

CHANGING OUR UNDERLYING BELIEFS ABOUT SEXUAL VIOLENCE

My list of reforms to our current legal and investigative processes would go some way toward creating a system of redress that could encourage victims to come forward to report, and could change their widely miserable experience in doing so. I would like to see the legal profession understand and commit to using their power in these processes responsibly, and to being informed by knowledge of sexual violence and trauma and not just legal rules and technicalities.

Convincing policymakers and lawyers to make these changes can go some way toward creating a fairer system of redress, but what is far more difficult is changing our underlying beliefs and assumptions about sexual violence. The culture of minimization—the "it's not such a big deal, get over it" culture around male sexual misconduct—shows up everywhere. It is there when a report is first brought forward; it is there when decisions get made about appropriate next steps; and again when (and if) there is an eventual adjudication. So pervasive is this minimization that it is even in the mind of the victim when she considers whether it is "worth" complaining, or if she should have "fought back harder." To many, sexual harassment is still "just a bit of fun," "not a big deal," "just locker room talk," and "everybody does it."

How did we get here, and how do we change course?

THE THREE FAILURES

Powerful decision-makers, in workplaces, governments, and institutions, at best minimize sexual violence and its consequences and at worst (and not uncommonly) engage in the same behaviour themselves. There are well-established patterns of protection for those who persistently harass and assault women, including silencing victims and would-be complainants with intimidation and threats. If you complain you will lose your job; if you complain no one will believe you; if you complain I shall tell everyone you are a slut, or have bad credit, or once modelled risqué lingerie; if you complain your parents will be deeply distressed. Such threats are highly effective, and especially when made by someone with power over a victim.

Of course, not all decision-makers support this culture. However, I am interested in living in a world in which recognition of the dynamics of sexual violence, the protection of potential victims, and the imperative of dealing with sexual misconduct is normative: not the other way around.

For that to happen, we need to acknowledge and reverse three failures both in our public culture and in our personal lives.

Of knowledge

The first is a *failure of knowledge*. There is a chronic lack of general knowledge about the power dynamics of sexual violence, the patterns of predator behaviour, the traumatic impact of sexual assault and its endemic nature in workplaces, schools and universities, faith groups, and social settings, as well as the disproportionate impact of all of this on women who are already marginalized. I am constantly astonished in conversations at how little people know about these issues, and how reluctant and embarrassed they are to talk about it.

We need more education, offered much earlier (well before the orientation session in freshers week at university). We need news media to take some responsibility for providing relevant, accurate information that offers some context when it reports on particular "newsworthy" cases. Otherwise the media becomes part of the reinforcement of existing norms without expanding knowledge or understanding. But above all, we all have personal responsibility for educating and informing ourselves. I often hear people say that they only took this step of making themselves more aware when they had a daughter or, even, when their daughter experienced sexual assault or harassment. That's great, but imagine a world in which we strove to educate ourselves—by reading, or talking to survivors, or taking responsibility for a new workplace complaints process—outside the need to protect our own child?

Of courage

The second failure is a *failure of courage*. Time and again I listen to or read stories of people who recognized that sexual harassment or assault had occurred, perhaps to someone in their workplace or church or club, but did not do anything about it. They looked away and got on with their lives. I understand it is still counter-culture to step up and speak out and, as this chapter has taken pains to state honestly, there are many personal costs—but there is no escaping the fact that this is what we must do. I know that speaking up for victims is a dangerous path, especially given the status quo of tolerance and minimization. I have been called crazy, over-emotional (a common smear of anyone with personal experience of sexual abuse), reckless, strident, and much worse. But I would far rather be called any number of names than fail in my courage to speak up when I believe that there is danger to women and girls. Preventing this happening to even one person would make it worthwhile.

Of morality

The third failure flows from these first two. We may be reluctant to name this, but our unwillingness to confront the pervasive nature of sexual male-on-female violence is also a *failure of morality*. I realize that claiming moral rightness for any stance is fraught in a complex, diverse world; but I cannot understand the condemnation of sexual violence and a recognition of the patterns of power that protect predators as anything other than a choice between right and wrong.

Despite the culture of minimization, sexual violence is almost always much, much worse than we can possibly imagine, both in how it happens and in its traumatic consequences. It is morally wrong to look away, or say we are too busy with other things, or that it's someone else's responsibility not our own, or that it's just a rumour and best left alone. Rumours are often all that victims have to convey what is happening to them, so afraid are they of speaking out explicitly. This does not mean immediately accepting every account, but we must be there to listen, support, and understand what has happened. We are all responsible for one another here, and our moral commitment to one another—as workplace colleague, manager, or friend—should be clear.

* * *

We all have lessons to learn and new understandings to reach that will inform and shape our personal agency in relation to sexual violence, whether as a survivor, an advocate, or simply a listener. We can start with simple acceptance of the trauma of sexual violence and a recognition of the immense obstacles faced by those who speak up.

I may not live long enough to see this cultural change happen. But I stubbornly believe that not only must change happen, but that it will. I hope that my story can be a small contribution to that.

ACKNOWLEDGEMENTS

Thank you from the bottom of my heart to the women whose stories are told in this book. I hope I have done you justice, and I honour your courage.

To my fellow survivors, and to everyone, too numerous to list here, who supports, comforts and cheers us on – you are part of the change we need, thank you.

Thanks to my amazingly dedicated research assistant Rebecca Flynn, who also brought me to Between the Lines and Amanda Crocker. Mary Newberry, my editor, is the best person I have ever worked with in this role; thank you for making this a great experience. The remarkable Ali Tejani helped me to develop my Medium blog in which I first wrote some of the stories that are part of this book. Thanks also to Sahar El-Kotob for her excellent research and editing skills as the book first took shape.

Many dear friends read earlier drafts for me and I am grateful to each of you for your invaluable input – especially Mary Woolsey, Brady Donohue, Phil Hart, Pete Conway, Bill Bogart, and Dayna Cornwall.

I am so lucky to have met David Greenwood, who is a model of best practice and compassion for lawyers everywhere. My other lawyer hero in this story is Natalie MacDonald, whose dedication to holding my institution to account has sustained me on many difficult days.

And then there is the home team. Sibyl Macfarlane and Mark Mayer patiently reviewed my early ideas and drafts and gave me crucial advice and input. Hope Moon always expanded my sensibility about who I was writing for and about, and both the similarities and differences in our experiences. Along with Ashley Colley and Jagjit Choda, the collective love and support of my kids and their partners kept me going when I first wondered if anyone would publish this book, and then on the days when the writing was really hard to do. I love you all very much.

Finally, I want to acknowledge the person who walks every step along life's path with me, my husband Bernie Mayer. It's never easy to live with someone in the throes of writing a book, and this book was more challenging than anything I have ever tried to write before. There were plenty of moments when someone who understood me less deeply, or who cared less about the need for women to step forward and speak out about sexual violence, or was less resilient in living with my vulnerabilities and trauma, might have been sorely tempted to suggest that this endeavour was a bridge too far.

Of course you never ever did that Bernie, or probably even considered it. Because you know more than anyone how important this project has been for me, and so you gave me everything—encouragement, ideas, editorial, and endless patience and love—that has made it possible. Thank you.

Julie Macfarlane
Kingsville
April 2020

Notes

PREFACE

1   Men and boys are also the victims of sexual violence. Much of this book
    is just as relevant, I believe, to their experiences, but it is written from the
    perspective of a girl and a woman.

CHAPTER 1: PRIVATE GRIEF

1   Research suggests that two of three individuals who are sexually victimized
    will be revictimized. Catherine Classen, Nigel Field, Clare Pain, and Patricia
    Woods, "Posttraumatic Personality Disorder: A Reformulation of Complex
    Posttraumatic Stress Disorder and Borderline Personality Disorder,"
    Psychiatric Clinics of North America, 29,1 (April 2006), viii-ix.
2   N. N. Sarkar and Rina Sarkar, "Sexual Assault on Woman: Its Impact
    on Her Life and Living in Society," *Sexual & Relationship Therapy*, 20,4
    (November 2005).
3   Tom Mendelsohn, "Law Professor Wins Damages from the Church of
    England Over Historic Abuse," *International Business Times*, March 19, 2016,
    www.bishop-accountability.org/news2016/03_04/2016_03_19_Tom_Times_
    Law_over.htm.
4   STOPP was formed in 1968 to campaign for the abolition of corporal
    punishment, widespread in UK public and private schools at this time. I
    worked for STOPP from 1985–87, when it was wound up after the law
    (for public schools) was changed in 1986 (*Education No. 2 Act*). See Mark
    Gould, "Sparing the Rod," *The Guardian*, January 9, 2007.
5   *Education (No. 2) Act 1986* (UK), 1986, c 61.
6   *The School Standards and Framework Act 1998*, 1998, c 13.
7   *Roberts-Costello v UK*, [1994] 1 FCR 65, [1994] ELR 1. I worked on this
    case (and got to know the remarkable mother of the child whose case we
    brought) along with others while I was at STOPP.
8   Karyn Freedman, *One Hour in Paris: A True Story of Rape and Recovery*
    (Calgary: Freehand Books, 2014), 108-109.
9   *R v R*, [1991] 3 WLR 767, [1991] UKHL 12.
10 An avoidance response, described by Karen Weiss, "'You Just Don't Report
    That Kind of Stuff': Investigating Teens' Ambivalence Toward Peer-
    Perpetrated, Unwanted Sexual Incidents," *Violence and Victims*, 28, 2 (April
    2013).

CHAPTER 2: PUBLIC DENIAL

1   See for example, "SACHA," Sexual Assault Centre, accessed September 19, 2019. http://sacha.ca/resources/statistics.

2   Carly Parnitzke Smith and Jennifer Freyd, "Institutional Betrayal," *American Psychologist*, 69,6 (September 2014). See also Cathy Humphreys and Stephen Joseph, "Domestic Violence and the Politics of Trauma," *Women's Studies International Forum*, 27, 5 (November 2004).

3   Shana Conroy and Adam Cotter, "Self-reported Sexual Assault in Canada, 2014" *Statistics Canada*, (July 2017).

4   Christine Rotenberg, "From Arrest to Conviction: Court Outcomes of Police-reported Sexual Assaults in Canada, 2009 to 2014," *Statistics Canada*, (October 2017).

5   Ninety per cent men on women, and 93 per cent of men on men. Reported in National Center for Injury Prevention and Control of the Centers for Disease Control and Prevention, "National Intimate Partner and Sexual Violence Survey," Centre for Disease Control and Prevention, 2010.

6   Patricia Weaver Francisco, *Telling: A Memoir of Rape and Recovery* (New York: Harper Perennial, 2000), 19.

7   Sarah Henstra, *The Red Word* (New York: Grove Atlantic, 2018), 14.

8   Feminist Next Door (@emrazz), "Can you name all 59 women who came forward against Cosby? Can you name half of them? Can you name 5? Would you recognize them out of context? Do you want an autograph? Cool, so we agree that women don't make rape accusations to become famous," Twitter, April 27, 2018.

9   Karen Weiss, "Too Ashamed to Report: Deconstructing the Shame of Sexual Victimization," *Feminist Criminology*, 5, 3 (July 2010): 286.

10 Melissa Lindsay, "A Survey of Survivors of Sexual Violence from Three Canadian Cities," Department of Justice Canada, 2014.

11 Lindsay, "Survey of Survivors," 3.2-3.3.

12 "Silent No More," *Pantyhose & The Penal Code,* March 15, 2015, https://pantyhoseandthepenalcode.wordpress.com/2015/11/26/why-law-students-wont-report-sexual-assault/.

13 Weiss, "Too Ashamed to Report," 286.

14 Lesley Campbell, "Why Law Students Won't Report Sexual Assault," Pantyhose & The Penal Code, November 26, 2015.

15 Laura Wilson and Katherine Miller, "Meta-Analysis of the Prevalence of Unacknowledged Rape," *Trauma, Violence & Abuse*, 17, 2 (April 2016): 149-159. Heather Littleton, Carmen Radecki Breitkopf, and Abbey Berenson, "Beyond the Campus: Unacknowledged Rape Among Low-Income Women," *Violence Against Women*, 14, 3 (March 2008).

16 See for example Heather Littleton, Carmen Radecki Breitkopf, and Abbey Berenson, "Beyond the Campus: Unacknowledged Rape Among Low-Income Women," *Violence Against Women*, 14, 3 (March 2008).

17 Daisy Whitney, *The Mockingbirds* (New York: Little Brown & Company, 2010).

18 The results of the survey are reported in Brady Donohue, Hannah Bahmanpour, and Carolina Patterson, *An Analysis of the Silence Surrounding Sexual Assault in Ontario Law Schools* (April 2014), 27.

19 "Lindsay, "Survey of Survivors.""

20 Tricia Nadolny, "'Who Would have Believed Me?' 83-year-old victim says of sexual abuse by a priest," *Pittsburgh Post-Gazette*, August 14, 2018. "Pope Francis Accuses Chilean Church Sexual Abuse Victims of Slander" *The Guardian*, January 18, 2018.

21 *Jane Lm Doe v Dr. Larry Nassar*, 2017 WL 7688293 (Cal Sup Ct); NPR, "Believed," National Public Radio, podcast audio.

22 Alyshah Hasham, Kevin Donovan, and Katrina Clarke, "Students were Warned Away from Q Internships: Professor," *Toronto Star*, November 3, 2014.

23 See the further discussion in chapter 7.

24 There are more than twenty cases of this nature currently in Canada, and they are the subject of a doctoral thesis in progress (Mandi Gray, "Cease/Desist or Cease/Resist? Civil Suits and Sexual Violence" (PhD diss. [in progress], York University). See also, Andrea Janus, "Judgment in Mandi Gray sexual assault case 'glorious,' but change to legal system will be slow: advocates," *CBC News*, July 23, 2016.

25 This myth is reinforced by classic stories such as Harper Lee, *To Kill a Mockingbird* (New York: Warner Books Inc., 1960). In a recent Pulitzer Prize-winning book, Ken Armstrong and T. Christian Miller tell the story of Marie, whose (true) report of rape led to police charging her with lying. Marie had not lied, and her attacker went on to rape several more women: T. Christian Miller and Ken Armstrong, *A False Report: A True Story of Rape in America* (New York: Crown Publishing Group, 2018).

26 St. Albertus Magnus, c 1200-80.

27 See, for example, *Calumny of Apelles* by Sandro Botticelli. Then-defence counsel (now judge) Kirk Munroe tried to show this painting to the jury in a 2013 criminal trial to argue that the deception of women has a long history. He was denied by Justice Renee Pomerance: Sean Fine, "New Judge Once Used Controversial Tactic in Sex-assault Case," *Globe and Mail*, February 11, 2015.

28 Sara Crosby, *Poisonous Muse: The Female Poisoner and the Framing of Popular Authorship in Jacksonian America* (Iowa City: University of Iowa Press, 2016).

29 Ellen Friedichs, "8 Societal Barriers that Make it Hard to Report Sexual Assault," *Everyday Feminism*, November 3, 2014.

30 Paul Elam, "Rape liar Christine Blasey Ford and the #MeToo Shuffle," *A Voice for Men*, September 21, 2018.

31 Meredith Mandell, "Bill Cosby's Conviction was Hailed as a #MeToo

victory. But Advocates say More Needs to be Done," *NBC News*, May 3, 2018.

32 Ken Armstrong and T Christian Miller, "When Sexual Assault Victims are Charged with Lying," *The New York Times*, November 24, 2017.

33 See example, NSVRC, "False Reporting," US Department of Justice, 2012.

34 Robyn Doolittle, "Why Police Dismiss 1 in 5 Sexual Assault Claims as Baseless," *Globe and Mail*, February 3, 2017.

35 Doolittle, "Why Police Dismiss 1 in 5 Sexual Assault Claims as Baseless," 65.

36 "The Second Assault," Jumping Off the Ivory Tower, podcast audio, April 23, 2019, https://soundcloud.com/user-69965354/the-second-assault.

37 Thames Valley Police, "Tea and Consent," YouTube, video, November 2015.

38 Hattie Williams, "Abuse Survivor Julie Macfarlane tells IICSA of her Battle for Justice," *Church Times*, March 13, 2018.

39 Elaine Craig, *Putting Trials on Trial: Sexual Assault and the Failure of the Legal Profession* (Montreal: McGill-Queen's University Press, 2018).

40 See, for example, Marisa Kwiatkowski, Mark Alesia and Tim Evans, "A Blind Eye to Sex Abuse: How USA Gymnastics Failed to Report Cases," *Indy Star*, August 4, 2016.

41 Chana Joffe-Walt, "LaDonna," This American Life, podcast audio, May 25, 2018.

42 Jody Kantor and Megan Twohey, "Harvey Weinstein Paid off Sexual Harassment Accusers for Decades," *The New York Times*, October 5, 2017.

43 This story is told in chapter 6.

44 Ronan Farrow, *Catch and Kill: Lies, Spies, and a Conspiracy to Protect Predators* (Boston: Little, Brown and Company, 2019).

45 Kimberly Crenshaw, "Demarginalizing the Intersection of Race and Sex: A Black Feminist Critique of Antidiscrimination Doctrine, Feminist Theory and Antiracist Politics," *University of Chicago Legal Forum*, 1, 8 (1989).

46 Errin Haines Whack, "Why Few Women of Color in Wave of Accusers? 'Stakes Higher'," *Associated Press News*, November 18, 2017.

47 Deborah Gray White, *Ar'n't I a Woman?: Female Slaves in the Plantation South* (New York City: W. W. Norton & Company, 1999).

48 See for example Debra Merskin, "Three Faces of Eva: Perpetuation of The Hot-Latina Stereotype in *Desperate Housewives*," *Howard Journal of Communications*, 18, 2 (April 2007): 133–151.

49 See Constance Backhouse, *Colour-Coded: A Legal History of Racism in Canada 1900-1950* (Toronto: University of Toronto Press, Scholarly Publishing Division, 1999).

50 Trina Jones and Kimberly Jade Norwood "Aggressive Encounters and White Fragility: Deconstructing the Trope of the Angry Black Woman," *Iowa Law Review*, 102 (2017).

51 Sometimes described as an "emotional tax." See for example Dnika Travis and Jennifer Thorpe-Moscon, "Report: Day-to-day Experiences

of Emotional Tax Among Women and Men of Color in the Workplace," *Catalyst*, February 15, 2018.

52 Travis and Thorpe-Moscon, "Day-to-day Experiences of Emotional Tax," 2.

53 See Mark Savage, "R. Kelly: The History of Allegations Against Him" *BBC News*, August 6, 2019.

54 Hayley Miller, "Time's Up Takes Aim at McDonald's, Walmart Over Sexual Harassment Complaints," *HuffPost*, May 22, 2018.

55 The teacher was eventually dismissed by the school board in June 2017, and is still in the process of facing disciplinary action by the Ontario College of Teachers, which could remove his licence to teach. See http://www.cbc.ca/news/canada/windsor/fired-windsor-high-school-teacher-s-license-now-suspended-1.4646390?cmp=rss

56 Elspeth Maynard, a teacher at the school from 1990–2014.

57 This is described in chapter 6.

58 This expression has become widely used to describe the hiding of sexual and other misconduct in settlements with abusers (commonly in non-disclosure agreements), who then can be hired by other employers with no knowledge of this background. See Sandy Wurtele, "Preventing the Sexual Exploitation of Minors in Youth-Serving Organizations," *Children and Youth Services Review*, 34,12 (December 2012).

59 Amber Tamblyn, "Amber Tamblyn: I'm Done with Not Being Believed," *The New York Times*, September 16, 2017.

60 In conflict theory, "lumping it" means having a genuine grievance but deciding to do nothing and to keep quiet about it. See for example Deborah Kolb and Linda Putnam, "The Multiple Faces of Organizational Conflict," *Journal of Organizational Behaviour*, 13, 3 (May 1992).

61 Graham Bowley and Jon Hurdle, "Bill Cosby is Found Guilty of Sexual Assault," *The New York Times*, April 26, 2018.

62 Anthony A Bliss, "1979 Metropolitan Opera Letter on Accusations About James Levine," *The New York Times*, December 3, 2017.

63 Aja Romano, "The Sexual Assault Allegations Against Kevin Spacey Spans Decades. Here's What We Know," *Vox*, December 24, 2018.

64 "Harvey Weinstein Timeline: How the Scandal Unfolded," *BBC News*, January 10, 2019.

65 Freedman, *One Hour in Paris*, 73.

66 There has been a lot of debate over a default to "believing" complainants, often drawing criticism. See for example the Start Believing campaign: "About Start by Believing," www.startbybelieving.org; and Marcia Sirota, "It's Time To Start Believing Victims Of Sexual Assault," *Huffpost*, March 21, 2019.

67 Rebecca Solnit, *Men Explain Things to Me* (Chicago: Haymarket Books, 2014).

CHAPTER 3: FIGHTING BACK

1   Michelle Black et al, "The National Intimate Partner and Sexual Violence Survey: 2010 Summary Report," Centers for Disease Control and Prevention, 2011.

2   Carole Petersen "Sexual Harassment in the Workplace" (Occasional Paper no 4), Centre for Comparative and Public Law, Faculty of Law, University of Hong Kong, June 1, 2002.

3   "Free Legal Advice Clinic," Hong Kong Federation of Women's Centres, www.womencentre.org.hk/En/Services/counselling/lac/.

4   Joe Chidley, "Bernardo the Untold Story," *Maclean's*, September 11, 1995.

5   This debate was reignited by the release of the trial transcripts in 2000; Kirk Makin, "Homolka Transcripts Tell a Chilling Tale," *Globe and Mail*, March 27, 2018.

6   Canon law is the system of laws and legal principles made and enforced by certain authorities of the Catholic Church in order to regulate its external organization and government and to order and direct the activities of Catholics toward the mission of the Church. See: Fernando Della Rocca, *Manual of Canon Law* (Milwaukee: Bruce Publishing Company, 1959), 3.

7   Christabel Chamarette is now retired from academia but maintains a private practice and is still an activist for child sex abuse victims.

8   Clemens Ley, Maria Rato Barrio and Andreas Koch, "'In the Sport I Am Here': Therapeutic Processes and Health Effects of Sport and Exercise on PTSD" *Qualitative Health Research*, 28, 3 (2017): 506.

9   Recent research has focused on developmental changes in the amygdala and hippocampal, especially as a result of early childhood trauma. Studies suggest a link between how the brain processes fear and memory, and ways in which "exposure to adversity could become biologically embedded": Nim Tottenham and Margaret Sheridan, "A Review of Adversity, The Amygdala and the Hippocampus: A Consideration of Developmental Timing," *Frontiers in Human Neuroscience*, 8, 3 (2010).

10 Freedman, *One Hour in Paris*, 152.

11 Freedman, *One Hour in Paris*, ix–x.

12 "Historic Cases Review of Roy Cotton and Colin Pritchard," Diocese of Chichester, The Church of England, 2017, www.safeguarding.chichester. anglican.org/documents/butler-sloss-report-addendum/, 39.

13 "Stop Church Child Abuse," Stop Church Child Abuse, accessed September 19, 2019, http://stopchurchchildabuse.co.uk/. Stop Church Child Abuse was originally founded by a group of survivors and their lawyers to call for a public inquiry into cover-ups of abuse in the Anglican Church.

14 The Independent Inquiry into Child Sexual Abuse (IICSA) was established by the UK government in 2014 and opened in 2015. It had a rocky beginning, with three chairs resigning before the business of the Inquiry was taken

forward by the current chair, Professor Alex Jay. The Inquiry has a wide remit, investigating historical suppression of complaints of abuse inside not only the Anglican Church, but also the Catholic Church, and another 11 institutions). See also "About Us," Independent Inquiry Child Sex Abuse, www.iicsa.org.uk.

CHAPTER 4: GOING PUBLIC

1   The first story associated with #MeToo was the New York Times report of 05/10/17: Jodi Kantor and Megan Twohey, "Harvey Weinstein Paid Off Sexual Harassment Accusers for Decades," *The New York Times*, October 5, 2017.

2   "Support for Same-Sex Marriage at Record High, but Key Segments Remain Opposed," Pew Research Center, June 8, 2015, www.people-press. org/2015/06/08/section-2-knowing-gays-and-lesbians-religious-conflicts-beliefs-about-homosexuality/, 4.

3   Sarah Henstra, *The Red Word* (New York: Grove Atlantic, 2018).

4   Brady Donohue, "On Pantyhose," Pantyhose & The Penal Code, January 26, 2014, pantyhoseandthepenalcode.wordpress.com.

5   Freedman, *One Hour in Paris*, 182. We had counsellors in the room.

6   Julie Macfarlane, "Featuring Professor Macfarlane," Speech presented at Windsor Law's Sexual Assault Awareness Day, March 5, 2014 (Speech on file with the author).

7   Julie Macfarlane, "Featuring Professor Macfarlane."

8   Julie Macfarlane, "Featuring Professor Macfarlane."

9   Julie Macfarlane, "Featuring Professor Macfarlane."

10 Sean O'Neill, "Sex Claim Woman 'Ripped to Shreds' by Church Lawyers," *The Times*.

11 Others attest to the liberation of going public on other issues that we might otherwise hide and feel shame about. See for example Beth Beattie, "Shaking off Mental Health Stigma," Jumping Off the Ivory Tower, podcast audio, March 26, 2019, representingyourselfcanada.com/shaking-off-the-mental-health-stigma/.

CHAPTER 5: FROM LAW PROFESSOR TO LITIGANT

1   See for example Julie Macfarlane, "The Evolution of the New Lawyer: How Lawyers are Reshaping the Practice of Law," *Journal of Dispute Resolution*, 25 (2008): 61; Julie Macfarlane, "Will Changing the Process Change the Outcome? The Relationship between Procedural and Systemic Change," *Louisiana Law Review*, 65,4 (2005); Julie Macfarlane, "Culture Change? A Tale of Two Cities and Mandatory Court-Connected Mediation," *Journal of Dispute Resolution*, 2 (2002); "Experiences of Collaborative Law: Preliminary Results from the Collaborative Lawyering Research Project," *Journal of Dispute Resolution*, 21 (2004).

2   See for example Julie Macfarlane *The New Lawyer: How Clients are Transforming the Practice of Law* (2nd edition 2018 UBC Press, Vancouver) and especially chapter 3.

3   See *Limitation Act 1980* (UK),1980, ss 11,14.

4   In *A v Hoare*, [2008] UKHL 6, the House of Lords accepted for the first time that a sexual assault case could fall within s33 of the Limitations Act, which allows the court to use its discretion to extend the limitation period where it would be "equitable" to do so. However the discretion is still applied narrowly; in *CD v The Catholic Child Welfare Society & Others* [2018], EWCA Civ 2342, the claim was barred on appeal because of concerns about access to evidence and witnesses in an historic case and emphasises that if a defendant can show a real possibility of significant prejudice, this will defeat the claim.

5   For US states that have abolished limitations for civil claims of rape and sex abuse, see: Catalina Sugayan and Peter Horst, "Statutes of Limitations for Civil Actions Based on Childhood Sexual Abuse," Sedgwick LLP, waldorfrisksolutions.com/wp-content/uploads/2017/01/Childhood-Sexual-Abuse-Statutes-of-Limitations-2017.pdf.

6   See the review of US criminal statutes of limitation: Brittany Ericksen and Ilse Knecht, "Statutes of Limitations for Sexual Assault: A State-by-State Comparison," Victims of Crime, 2013, https://victimsofcrime.org/docs/DNA%20Resource%20Center/sol-for-sexual-assault-check-chart---final---copy.pdf.

7   Graham Bowley and Jon Hurdle, "Bill Cosby is Found Guilty of Sexual Assault," *The New York Times*, April 26, 2018.

8   US, SB 813, *An act to amend Sections 799, 801.1, and 803 of the Penal Code, relating to crimes*, 2015–16, Reg Sess, Cal, 2016. For a chart showing US states that have repealed the statute of limitation in criminal cases see Ericksen & Knecht, "Statutes of Limitations for Sexual Assault: A State-by-State Comparison."

9   Some of these (Florida, for example) make an exception where there is DNA evidence. For states that have abolished limitations for civil claims of rape and sex abuse, see: Catalina Sugayan and Peter Horst, "Statutes of Limitations for Civil Actions Based on Childhood Sexual Abuse," Sedgwick LLP, 2017, waldorfrisksolutions.com/wp-content/uploads/2017/01/Childhood-Sexual-Abuse-Statutes-of-Limitations-2017.pdf.

10 In Sweden, the time limitation on bringing criminal proceedings for rape is 10 years: *Limitations Act (Sweden)*. Prosecutors dropped the rape investigation in May 2017, unable to get access to Assange. When Assange was removed from the Ecuadorean Embassy in April 2019, the investigation was reopened but subsequently closed, referencing difficulties with the impact of the time lapse on the victim.

11 George Joseph, "US Catholic Church Has Spent Millions Fighting Clergy Sex Abuse Accountability," *The Guardian*, May 12, 2016; Laurie Goodstein

and Erik Eckholm, "Church Battles Efforts to Ease Sex Abuse Suits," *The New York Times*, June 14, 2012.

12 *Leaving Neverland*. Directed by Dan Reed. HBO, 2019.

13 "Victorian Government Response to the Report of the Family and Community Development Committee Inquiry into the Handling of child Abuse by Religious and Other Non-Government Organisations '*Betrayal of Trust*'," Parliament of Victoria, 2014, www.parliament.vic.gov.au/images/stories/committees/fcdc/inquiries/57th/Child_Abuse_Inquiry/Government_Response_to_the_FCDC_Inquiry_into_the_Handling_of_Child_Abuse_by_Religious_and_Other_Non-Government_Organisations.pdf.

14 A phenomenon so well-established that it even has a name: "witness whacking": David Tanovich, "'Whack' No More: Infusing Equality into the Ethics of Defence Lawyering in Sexual Assault Cases," *Ottawa Law Review*, 45, 3 (2014).

15 Statement of Defence, *Macfarlane v The Rector*, Churchwardens and PCC of St Pancras Church, Chichester claim number B23YX976, paragraph viii. In fact, the legislation explicitly excludes knowledge of the law as a factor.

16 Julie Macfarlane, "Reasons Why I Didn't File a lawsuit against the Anglican Church until now: a 10-step chronology," Memo, November 2015.

17 Macfarlane, "Reasons Why I Didn't."

18 Macfarlane, "Reasons Why I Didn't."

19 Hattie Williams, "Abuse Survivor Julie Macfarlane tells IICSA of her Battle for Justice," *Church Times*, March 13, 2018, https://www.churchtimes.co.uk/articles/2018/16-march/news/uk/abuse-survivor-tells-iicsa-of-her-battle-for-justice.

20 Judith Lewis Herman, *Trauma and Recovery: The Aftermath of Violence – From Domestic Abuse to Political Terror* (New York: Basic Books, 1997), 8.

21 For an overview see: David Lisak et al, "False Allegations of Sexual Assault: An Analysis of Ten Years of Reported Cases," *Violence Against Women*, 16, 12 (2010): 1318. See also the discussion in chapter 1.

22 Elaine Craig, *Putting Trials on Trial: Sexual Assault and the Failure of the Legal Profession* (McGill-Queen's University Press, 2018), 41–42 and 120–23.

23 This was in response to the widely ridiculed campaign at Antioch College that year to raise awareness of the need for consent by creating a Sexual Offense Prevention Policy. See "Is It Date Rape," SNL Transcripts Tonight, October 8, 2018, snltranscripts.jt.org/93/93bdaterape.phtml.

24 Michael Buchhandler-Raphael, "The Failure of Consent: Re-Conceptualizing Rape as Sexual Abuse of Power," *Michigan Journal of Gender and Law*, 18, 1 (2011).

25 Julie Macfarlane, *The New Lawyer: How Settlement is Transforming the Practice of Law* (Vancouver: University of British Columbia Press, 2008).

26 Ecclesiastical is owned by the All Churches Trust, which was founded by the Church of England; two of its founding members were the archbishops of Canterbury and the archbishop of York. Ian Elliott, "Opening Comment

from Ian Elliott," Sea of Complicity: Reflections of CofE Abuse Survivor, June 25, 2017, seaofcomplicity.blog.

27 Rachel Boulding was a journalist of high principles and integrity. Sadly, she died of breast cancer in May 2017.

28 Described in chapter 7.

29 See chapter 7.

30 See for example: "Social Justice: Expert Witnesses and Access to Justice," *Law Times News*, February 8, 2016.

31 Julie Macfarlane, "An Abuse Survivor's Tale," *Church Times*, December 11, 2015.

32 Macfarlane, "An Abuse Survivor's Tale."

33 Macfarlane, "An Abuse Survivor's Tale."

34 "C of E and Insurance Affiliation," Sea of Complicity: Reflections of CofE Abuse Survivor, June 25, 2017, seaofcomplicity.blog.

35 Martin Bashir and Callum May, "Church of England 'Withdrew Emotional Support for Abused'," *BBC News*, July 21, 2017. The Elliot report, an independent report commissioned by the church and written by Ian Elliot, also reached the conclusion that there was a conflict between the pastoral responsibilities of the church and the aggressively adversarial approach taken by its insurer. See Harriet Sherwood, "Damning Report Reveals Church of England's Failure to Act on Abuse," *The Guardian*, March 15, 2016.

36 Sherwood, "Damning Report."

37 Email from an Anglican priest who prefers to remain anonymous

38 As the class reminded me, I needed one too: see Julie Macfarlane & Bernie Mayer, "When Mediators Sue," in *More Justice, More Peace: When Peacemakers are Advocates*, ed. Susanne Terry (Roman and Littlefield, London 2020)

39 My thanks to all those who helped me to write this statement, including my students, David, and my former student Kadey Schultz, now a partner at Shultz Frost.

40 "Quantum" is the amount of damages in a civil case.

41 Julie Macfarlane, "MAH00012," YouTube, video, February 28, 2016, youtube.com/watch?v=AJQFEB-_fh0.

42 Julie Macfarlane, "Statement," Independent Inquiry into Child Sexual Abuse: Anglican Investigation, August 7, 2017; Julie Macfarlane, "Opening Statement," Mandate Now, audio, https://soundcloud.com/user-346264450/iicsa-13318-prof-julie-macfarlanes-evidence-during-the-c_of_e-chichester-hearing.

43 *Brown v Board of Education of Topeka* (1954), 347 US 483 (US SCC).

44 *Egan v Canada* [1995] 2 SCR 513, 124 DLR (4th) 609.

45 The Independent Child Sexual Abuse Inquiry is the largest ever public inquiry in the UK and is investigating the suppression of complaints about child sex abuse in a number of institutions, including the Anglican Church. For further discussion of the IICSA process and my role as a core partici-

pant, see Elam, "Rape liar."

46 See for example "Hopes of Female Archbishop as Sentamu Retires," *Daily Telegraph*, October 2, 2018; Ann Fontaine, "Church of England Sexuality 'Fudge' Makes Everyone Gag," *Episcopal Café*, February 28, 2014.

47 Julie Macfarlane, "The Insurers Have Listened," *Church Times*, July 15, 2016.

48 "Our Guiding Principles for the Handling of Civil Claims Involving Allegations of Sexual and Physical Abuse," Ecclesiastical, September 2018.

49 "Our Guiding Principles," 3: "limitation should be pleaded as a defence to a claim sparingly in relation to physical and sexual abuse claims. Ecclesiastical has an internal escalation procedure, which requires the pleading of a limitation defence to be considered and approved only at a senior level before it is pleaded in any individual case."

50 "Our Guiding Principles," 3: "Ecclesiastical recognises that requiring claimants to undergo multiple medical evaluations may cause further distress. Ecclesiastical will always consider the appropriateness of agreeing with the claimant the instruction of a joint expert."

51 "Our Guiding Principles," 3: "Ecclesiastical will be mindful of the power imbalance that is often presented in such cases even where the claimant was over the age of 16 at the date of the abuse."

52 Our Guiding Principles," 3: "Ecclesiastical will not insist or include a confidentiality requirement in a settlement agreement unless specifically requested by the claimant."

53 See the discussion in chapter 7.

54 The government inquiry into child sexual abuse in a range of institutions, including the Anglican Church. See "About Us," Independent Inquiry Child Sex Abuse.

55 Julie Macfarlane, "Minister and Clergy Sexual Abuse Survivors Information Sheet - August 2016," MACSAS, 2016, http://www.macsas.org.uk/ Claims%20Factsheet.pdf.

56 See Ecclesiastical, ecclesiastical.ca/services/claims/ abuse-claims-guiding-principles/.

57 For a detailed description of the dynamics of this negotiation, from both my own perspective and that of my husband, an internationally known mediator, see Julie Macfarlane & Bernie Mayer, "When Mediators Sue," in *More Justice, More Peace: When Peacemakers are Advocates*, ed. Susanne Terry (Roman and Littlefield, London 2020), 225–47.

58 As this book goes to press, I was finally able to make contact with the other complainant. This has already become an extraordinarily cathartic and meaningful connection. When I asked her (by email) what it was that prompted her to finally come forward, like me so many decades later, she wrote this: "A number of cases of sexual abuse by clergy and high profile celebrities such as Jimmy Savile had begun to be reported in the national press, prompting a greater confidence that the culture and behaviour of

society and the Church was beginning to change ... [it seemed] that I might now be believed and that he might be brought to justice at last—and I couldn't hold back any longer."(March 19, 2020, email)

59   My thanks to Detective Sergeant Alan Fenn of the Chichester police, whose professionalism and kindness I have come to appreciate. Thanks also to DC Jo French for her compassion and dedication.

60   Released in early 2016, *Spotlight* won Best Picture at the Academy Awards in 2016. *Spotlight*. Directed by Tom McCarthy. Open Road Films, 2015.

CHAPTER 6: HOLDING MY INSTITUTION TO ACCOUNT

1   Examples of child (and adult) sexual abuse by church officials are widespread. So much so that in the UK (see "About Us," Independent Inquiry Child Sex Abuse) and Australia (see "Australia Abuse Inquiry: Catholic Church Rejects Call to Overhaul Confession," *BBC News*, August 31, 2018) have been established to determine the extent of culpability and how so many abusers were protected by their churches for so long.

2   Among numerous examples, UK football clubs which sheltered sexual predators later convicted include Crewe F.C., Newcastle United F.C. Chelsea F.C. and Southampton F.C. See Mark Townsend, "Football abuse scandal grows with 55 clubs now involved," *The Guardian*, December 3, 2016. In gymnastics, the Larry Nassar case at Michigan State University is perhaps the most notorious. See *Jane Lm Doe v Dr. Larry Nassar*. More examples of sexual abuse associated with sports coaches (who often have an especially powerful influence on young athletes) are emerging all the time.

3   See Jody Kantor and Megan Twohey, "Harvey Weinstein Paid off Sexual Harassment Accusers."

4   For example, the fourteen hospitals where serial predator Jimmy Savile abused children in the UK. See Sandra Laville and Josh Halliday, "Jimmy Savile abused children at 14 hospitals across six decades – report," *The Guardian*, January 11, 2013. See also Andrew Kendrick and Julie Taylor, "Hidden on the Ward: The Abuse of Children in Hospitals," *Journal of Advanced* Nursing, 31, 3 (March 2000).

5   For example, see Marina Hyde, "R Kelly, Michael Jackson and Bryan Singer. Who knew? Everyone," *The Guardian*, January 31, 2019.

6   Jon Krakauer, *Missoula: Rape and the Justice System in a College Town* (New York: Anchor Books, 2015). 152–54.

7   See chapter 5.

8   *MacFarlane (sic) v Canadian Universities Reciprocal Insurance Exchange*, 2019 ONSC 4631, Tab D of the Application Record of July 8, 2019, affidavit of March 22, 2019, paragraph 9.

9   *MacFarlane (sic) v Canadian Universities Reciprocal Insurance Exchange*, paragraph 11.

10   As well as providing critical letters of reference for prospective employers,

law professors are commonly asked to write letters of good character to law societies for student admission.

11 See Julie Macfarlane,"How a Good Idea Became a Bad Idea: Universities and the Use of Non-Disclosure Agreements in Terminations for Sexual Misconduct" (forthcoming) *Cardoza Law Review*, 21 (2020).

12 Anthony Giddens, *The Constitution of Society* (Berkeley: University of California Press, 1984), 24.

13 Some commercial organizations share some of the qualities of an institution; for example, a network of franchisees, or a generational family-owned business.

14 Jeff Coolidge, "Raising Spirit in Institutional and Public Life," *New England Journal of Public Policy*, 17, 118–20.

15 See chapter 2.

16 Some of the first athletes to raise concerns about lack of protocols around sexual abuse at USA Gymnastics have stories of being banned from their training facility and left off the team. See "Believed," *National Public Radio*.

17 This is why a clause prohibiting this exclusion was part of my settlement with the Anglican Church, described in chapter 5.

18 See Agnes Grant, *No End of Grief: Indian Residential Schools in Canada* (Winnipeg: Pemmican Publications, 1996); Paulette Regan, Unsettling the Settler Within: Indian Residential Schools, Truth Telling and Reconciliation in Canada (Vancouver: UBC Press, 2010).

19 See Jennifer J Freyd and Karrieela Birrell, *Blind to Betrayal: Why We Fool Ourselves We Aren't Being Fooled* (Hoboken: Wiley, 2013); and Carly Parnitzke Smith and Jennifer Freyd, "Institutional Betrayal," *American Psychologist*, 69,6 (September 2014): 575.

20 Julie Macfarlane, "Betrayed by my University (church/sports club/workplace/police/the legal system)," Medium, April 15, 2019, https://medium.com/@ProfJulieMac/betrayed-by-my-university-church-sports-club-workplace-police-the-legal-system-9c84d1fc31aa.

21 See also the discussion about reporting to police in chapter 7.

22 Melissa Platt, *Feelings of Shame and Dissociation in Survivors of High and Low Betrayal Traumas* (University of Oregon: ProQuest Dissertations and Theses, 2014).

23 Jennifer J Freyd, *Betrayal Trauma: The Logic of Forgetting Childhood Abuse.* (Cambridge: Harvard University Press, 2006).

24 Taking on the Church," November 27, 2017, Jumping off the Ivory Tower, podcast audio, representingyourselfcanada.com/taking-on-the-church/, 9:10–9:30.

25 For a classic exposition, see John Henry (Cardinal) Newman, "What is a University?" in Rise and *Progress of Universities and Benedictine Essays*, Mary Katherine Tillman, eds. (Herefordshire: Gracewing Publishing, 2001), 16. As Newman eloquently describes it, the university is "the place where the professor becomes eloquent, and is a missionary and a preacher, displaying

his science in its most complete and most winning form, pouring it forth with the zeal of enthusiasm, and lighting up his own love of it in the breasts of his hearers. It is the place where the catechist makes good his ground as he goes, treading in the truth day by day into the ready memory, and wedging and tightening it into the expanding reason."

26 In the US, see "Statistics about Sexual Violence," National Sexual Violence Resource Center, 2018.

27 See "Responding to Transgender Victims of Sexual Assault," Office for Victims of Crime, June 2014; "Sexual Assault and the LGBTQ Community," Human Rights Campaign, accessed November 3, 2019, www. hrc.org; Cate Carey et al, "Incapacitated and Forcible Rape of College Women: Prevalence Across the First Year," *Journal of Adolescent Health*, 56, 6 (June 2015).

28 Carey et al, "Incapacitated and Forcible Rape," 678.

29 Jennifer Freyd, "Official Campus Statistics for Sexual Violence Mislead," Aljazeera America, July 14, 2014, america.aljazeera.com/opinions/2014/7/college-campus-sexualassaultsafetydatawhitehousegender.html.

30 First written about here, Lori Ward and Mark Gollum, "Universities Should Protect Students, Not Reputation: Professors Call for Elimination of Confidentiality Deals," *CBC News*, May 7, 2018. See also Samantha Beattie, "Universities 'Acting Like Church Did Decades Ago' On Sexual Misconduct Secrecy," *Huffpost*, April 11, 2019; and Jane Gerster, "Should Canada Restrict the Use of Gag Orders In Sexual Abuse Cases?," *Global News*, March 25, 2019.

31 Concern about liability for failing to provide "due process" for the alleged perpetrator swamps more likely legal consequences such as a suit by students against the university for failing to protect them. See for example the Dartmouth class action: Amanda Arnold, "Surviving the 'Predators' Club'," *The Cut*, November 19, 2018.

32 This story is told in chapter 2.

33 Also described as "deceptive trust development." See Loreen Olson et al, "Entrapping the Innocent: Toward a Theory of Child Sexual Predators' Luring Communication" *Communication Theory*, 17, 3. Accounts of grooming by Michael Jackson of both young boys and their families are explicit and chillingly manipulative. See also *Leaving Neverland*, Dan Reed.

34 According to Dame Janet Smith's report for the BBC, Savile began abusing girls in the 1940s and continued until his death in 2009. He is believed to have sexually abused at least seventy-two young girls. See Dame Janet Smith, "The Jimmy Savile Investigation Report," BBC, February 25, 2016.

35 Jimmy Savile, *Love is an Uphill Thing* (London: Coronet Books, 1976).

36 "Six Years Later, Penn State Remains Torn over the Sandusky Scandal," *Washington Post*, December 28, 2017.

37 See *Jane Lm Doe v Dr. Larry Nassar*.

38 *R v Ghomeshi*, 2016 ONCJ 155.

39 George Pell was an Australian cardinal in the Catholic Church convicted of sexual assault against young boys in 2018 and sentenced to six years in prison in 2019. On appeal, the High Court of Australia quashed his conviction ruling that the jury "had not properly considered the evidence." *See* BBC News, April 7, 2020: "George Pell: Court quashes cardinal's sexual abuse conviction."

40 "The Anglican Church Case Studies: 1. The Diocese of Chichester 2. The response to allegations against Peter Ball; Investigation Report, Independent Inquiry Child Sex Abuse, May 2019, www.iicsa.org.uk/key-documents/11301/view/anglican-church-case-studies-chichester-peter-ball-investigation-report-may-2019.pdf.

41 The former bishop of Lewes in the Diocese of Chichester pled guilty to indecent assault and misconduct in public office, relating to the sexual abuse of sixteen young men over a period of fifteen years, in 2015. He died in 2019. See Sandra Laville, "Former Bishop Admits Sexually Abusing Young Men" *The Guardian*, September 8, 2015.

42 From the December 18, 2013, letter.

43 It is frequently asserted that transparency over the existence of an investigation and its subject might result in a defamation suit. While this is a theoretical possibility (the single case on point, *Elgert v Home Hardware Stores Limited*, 2011 ABCA 112, is described as "somewhat of an anomaly"). See Kelly J Harbridge, "Workplace Investigations: A Management Perspective," Canadian Bar Association (conference), November 25–26, 2011. The defence of qualified privilege protects any assertions made without malice (see *Korach v Moore and Board of Education for the City of Windsor* (1991), 1 OR (3d) 275. See also the further discussion later in this chapter.

44 For example, "Our Mission" *Students for Consent Culture*, accessed November 3, 2019, sfcccanada.org/. The organization is "dedicated to supporting anti-sexual violence advocacy and activism on campuses" across the country.

45 *MacFarlane v Canadian Universities Reciprocal Insurance Exchange*, 2019 ONSC 4631, Tab D of the Application Record of July 8, 2019, affidavit of March 22, 2019, paragraph 35.

46 Defamation suits are being weaponized against more vulnerable individuals, including students, who raise the alarm about a potential sexual predator. For example, Stephen Galloway has sued twenty-five individuals personally for defamation after a UBC investigation by retired judge Mary Ellen Boyd found that "on a balance of probabilities," he had not committed sexual assault. See Marsha Lederman, "Steven Galloway Sues Woman who Accused him of Sexual Assault," *Globe and Mail*, October 30, 2018. Gray, "Cease/Desist or Cease/Resist? Civil Suits and Sexual Violence."

47 Anonymous email to Julie Macfarlane.

48 Julie Macfarlane, Email to Provost and VP Student Affairs (University of Windsor), March 8, 2014.

49 VP Student Affairs (University of Windsor), Email to Julie Macfarlane, March 15, 2014.

50 Nonetheless, the rights of witnesses are often overlooked in a system by discounting their testimony or requiring them to participate in a system which is too traumatic to allow them to provide a full account of their experiences. The 2002 Report concerning vulnerable and intimidated witnesses undertaken by the Scottish Executive suggests that they may not always be aware of their rights, informed of any potential violation to their rights, nor able to defend them. Victim protections are even more precarious in private workplace investigations which set their own rules. See Reid Howie Associates, "Vulnerable and Intimidated Witnesses: Review of Provisions in Other Jurisdictions," Scottish Executive Central Research Unit, 2002, www. webarchive.org.uk/wayback/archive/20180517063954/http://www.gov.scot/Publications/2002/07/14989/7997.

51 See the discussion in chapter 2.

52 Julie Macfarlane, Email to President (University of Windsor), September 14, 2014.

53 President (University of Windsor), email to Julie Macfarlane, September 17, 2014.

54 Julie Macfarlane, Email to President (University of Windsor), September 18, 2014.

55 The Windsor University Faculty Association (WUFA) collective agreement is silent on the issue of confidentiality of external investigations.

56 Employers have both direct and vicarious liability for sexual and other harassment under provincial human rights legislation. For an overview see Neena Gupta, *Sexual Harassment: A Guide to Conducting Investigations* (New York: LexisNexis Butterworths, 2004), 44–47.

57 That is, a defence to defamation. See *Kanak v Riggin*, 2018 ONCA 345

58 Gupta, *Sexual Harassment*, 55.

59 "Taking on the Church," Jumping Off the Ivory Tower, 8:45–9:10.

60 Macfarlane, "An Abuse Survivor's Tale."

61 "Access to Justice, A Step at a Time," *National Self-Represented Litigants Project*, April 4, 2018, representingyourselfcanada.com/access-to-justice-a-step-at-a-time/.

62 "Collective Agreement between the Faculty Association and the Board of Governors of the University of Windsor," University of Windsor, July 1, 2017– June 30 2012, Article 29-07.

63 Orly Lobel, "Trump's Extreme NDAs," *The Atlantic*, March 4, 2019.

64 In England and Wales, the Solicitors Regulation Authority has now issued first a recommendation, and not advice instructing solicitors not to sign on to NDAs that cover up misconduct or a criminal offence. Solicitors Regulation Authority, "Warning Notice: Use of non-disclosure agreements

(NDAs)," March 12, 2018, https://www.sra.org.uk/solicitors/guidance/warning-notices/use-of-non-disclosure-agreements-ndas--warning-notice/.

65 For an overview of the development and use of NDAs, see Norman Bishara, Kenneth Martin, and Randall Thomas "An Empirical Analysis of Noncompetition Clauses and Other Restrictive Postemployment Covenants," *Vanderbilt Law Review*, 68,1 (2015).

66 Elana Schor, Congress' Sexual Harassment System, Decoded," Politico, November 21, 2017.

67 See Sandy Wurtele, "Preventing the Sexual Exploitation of Minors in Youth-Serving Organizations" *Children and Youth Services* Review, 34,12 (December 2012).

68 Simon Murphy, "UK universities pay out £90m on staff 'gagging orders' in past two years," *The Guardian*, April 17, 2019.

69 See for example *Bowman v Parma Board of Education* 44 (3d) 169 (Ohio App Ct 1988) and *Doe-3 v McLean County Unit District No. 5 Board of Directors* 973 NE (2d) 880 (Ill 2012).

70 For a useful review of Ontario law, see: "Just Cause for Dismissal," KCY at Law, June 22, 2017.

71 Beattie, "Universities 'Acting Like Church Did Decades Ago.'"

72 CURIE is the insurer for all Canadian universities.

73 CURIE, Email to Julie Macfarlane, April 2019.

74 "Our Mission" *Students for Consent Culture.*

75 Founding partner of MacDonald and Associates and author of: Natalie MacDonald, *Extraordinary Damages in Canadian Employment Law* (Toronto: Carswell, 2010).

76 For example the leading case on extraordinary damages in employment law, *Galea v Wal-Mart Canada Corp*, 2017 ONSC 245.

77 Slightly over $10,000 was raised by a Go Fund Me page (organized by another supporter, Windsor alum Khalil Jessa) towards a modest but appreciated fraction of Natalie's eventual costs.

78 More than fifty 50 per cent of family litigants now come to court without a lawyer, and 30 to 40 per cent of civil litigants. See "Self-Represented Litigants in the Courts: How They Are Shaping the Jurisprudence," National Self-represented Litigants Project, December 13, 2018, representingyourselfcanada.com/self-represented-litigants-in-the-courts-how-they-are-shaping-the-jurisprudence/.

79 *MacFarlane v Canadian Universities Reciprocal Insurance Exchange, 2019,* 2019 ONSC 4631.

80 *MacFarlane v Canadian Universities Reciprocal Insurance Exchange,* paragraph 44.

81 *MacFarlane v Canadian Universities Reciprocal Insurance Exchange,* paragraph 39.

82 *MacFarlane v Canadian Universities Reciprocal Insurance Exchange,* paragraph 45.

83 *MacFarlane v Canadian Universities Reciprocal Insurance Exchange,* paragraph 46.

84 Dartmouth: see Emanuella Grinberg, "Lawsuit: 'Predatory' Dartmouth Professors Plied Students with Alcohol and Raped Them," *CNN*, November

16, 2018; Mary Washington: see Scott Jaschik, "Redefining the Obligation to Protect Students," *Inside Higher Ed*, December 20, 2018; Lawrence: Bruce Vielmetti, "Lawrence University sued over sexual misconduct procedures," Millwaukee Journal Sentinel, July 13, 2018; Dillard: see Danielle Drellinger, "Dillard Rape Lawsuit says University Failed to Protect Students" New Orleans Advocate, March 29, 2017.

85 Madeleine Thompson, "Dartmouth Settles Sexual Harassment lawsuit for $14 million," *CNN*, August 6, 2019.

86 See the discussion in Julie Macfarlane,"How a Good Idea Became a Bad Idea: Universities and the Use of Non-Disclosure Agreements in Terminations for Sexual Misconduct" (forthcoming) *Cardoza Law Review*, 21 (2020).

87 Natalie Macdonald, Email to Julie Macfarlane

88 "Believed," *National Public Radio*, 6:22–6.54.

CHAPTER 7: ON THE STAND

1 A Catholic priest Laurence Soper was previously extradited: "Priest extradited to UK on historic sex charges," *Church Times*, January 21, 2019.

2 See discussion in chapter 2.

3 See for example Caelinn Barr, "Thousands of Rape Reports Inaccurately Recorded by Police," *The Guardian*, September 19, 2019. See also this phenomenon in the US: Ashley Fantz and Sonam Vashi, "How Rape Cases Went Wrong," *CNN*, November 29, 2018. Flawed investigations, including the inaccurate recording of rape complaints by police, have led to mass injustices for victims of sexual assault. According to Barr, "Thousands of Rape Reports": "The inaccuracies in recording can range from incomplete paperwork to not recording a report of rape as a crime but noting it as an incident. This can lead to no investigation being carried out and the accused going on to reoffend."

4 Holly Johnson, "Limits of a Criminal Justice Response: Trends in Police and Court Processing of Sexual Assault" in Elizabeth Sheehy, eds., *Sexual Assault in Canada* (Ottawa: University of Ottawa Press, 2017).

5 "The Second Assault," Jumping Off the Ivory Tower.

6 "The Second Assault," Jumping Off the Ivory Tower (Cherlene is Asian-Canadian).

7 "Tackling Campus Rape Culture," Jumping Off the Ivory Tower, podcast audio, November 20, 2017, https://soundcloud.com/user-69965354/tackling-campus-rape-culture, 00:04:21.

8 Tackling Campus Rape Culture," Jumping Off the Ivory Tower.

9 See discussion from earlier in this chapter.

10 A civil restraining order generally only applies in family law situations and, generally speaking, has the same effect as a peace bond. To obtain a restraining order under the *Family Law Act*, a complainant will have to file paperwork in a municipal court. Normally, one will not be able to appear in

front of a Family judge for weeks but can bring an urgent motion in emergency situations. See: "Restraining Order," *Ministry of the Attorney General*, 2009 ; "Protection Orders," *Victims Info*, www.victimsinfo.ca/en/services/protection-orders; "What is the Difference between a Restraining Order and a Peace Bond?" *Steps to Justice*, stepstojustice.ca/questions/abuse-and-family-violence/what-difference-between-restraining-order-and-peace. In the context of criminal harassment, the Department of Justice Website offers the following information in regard to Peace Bonds, Civil Protection Orders, and Civil Restraining Orders (See "A Handbook for Police and Crown Prosecutors on Criminal Harassment," *Department of Justice*, July 31, 2017, www.justice.gc.ca/eng/rp-pr/cj-jp/fv-vf/har/part2.html#sec2.11.3:

This level of intervention should be considered when the complainant fears for his or her safety and the suspect poses a risk of injury or of an offence resulting in physical violence, or other conduct such as the infliction of severe psychological damage. There is often insufficient evidence to support a charge. Peace bonds and civil protection orders are not substitutes for criminal charges. Charges should be laid where there is evidence to support them.

An application for an order under section 810 of the Criminal Code should be considered where there is fear that the suspect will cause personal injury to an individual or the individual's spouse or child, or under section 810.2 where there is fear that the suspect will commit a "serious personal injury offence," which by definition also includes psychological damage. Peace bonds are also available under section 810.01 where the complainant is within a subsection 423.1(1) category, such as a justice system participant or journalist, and there is a fear for that person's safety; or under section 810.1 when the suspect's conduct involves prohibited sexual conduct against persons under age 16.

11 Described in chapter 5.

12 Julie Macfarlane, "There can finally be justice," Medium, January 31, 2019, https://medium.com/@ProfJulieMac/there-can-finally-be-justice-626ee0f3d750.

13 In Canada, the defendant would be asked to elect either a jury trial or a judge-only trial. See *Criminal Code*, RSC, 1985, c C-46, section 536.

14 See for example, Jennifer Temkin and Barbara Krahe, *Sexual Assault and the Justice Gap: A Question of Attitude* (New York: Bloomsbury Publishing, 2008), 75–97, 99–176.

15 Martha Burt, "Cultural Myths and Support for Rape," *Journal of Personality and Social Psychology*, 38,2 (1980).

16 Burt, "Cultural Myths and Support for Rape".

17 Michelle Sleed et al, "The Effectiveness of the Vignette Methodology: A Comparison of Written and Video Vignettes in Eliciting Responses about Date Rape," *South African Journal of Psychology*, 32, 3 (December 2002).

18 See for example, Theodore McDonald and Linda Kline, "Perceptions

of Appropriate Punishment for Committing Date Rape: Male College
Students Recommend Lenient Punishment," *College Student Journal*, 38,1
(March 2004); Anna Wakelin and Karen Long, "Effects of Victim Gender
and Sexuality on Attributions of Blame to Rape Victims," *Sex Roles*, 49,9
(2003) (also showing impact of homophobia towards gay male victims).

19 For example, Claire Gravelin et al, "Blaming the Victim of Acquaintance
Rape: Individual, Situational, and Sociocultural Factors," *Frontiers in
Psychology*, 9 (2018); Temkin and Krahe, *Sexual Assault and the Justice Gap*,
108–109.

20 See Heather Littleton, Amie Grills-Taquechel, and Danny Axsom,
"Impaired and Incapacitated Rape Victims: Assault Characteristics and
Post-Assault Experiences," *Violence and Victims* 24,4 (February 2009).

21 Daisy Whitney, *The Mockingbirds* (New York: Little Brown & Company,
2010).

22 For two widely used examples of scales used to structure such studies, see
the "Perceived Causes of Rape Scale (PCR)" in Gloria Cowan and Wendy
Quinton, "Cognitive Style and Attitudinal Correlates of the Perceived
Causes of Rape Scale," *Psychology of Women Quarterly*, 21,2 (1997):
228–232; and the "Acceptance of Modern Myths about Sexual Aggression
(AMMSA)" in Heike Gerger et al., "The Acceptance of Modern Myths
about Sexual Aggression Scale: Development and Validation in German and
English," *Aggressive Behavior*, 33,5 (September 2007): 425–26.

23 Temkin and Krahe, *Sexual Assault & the Justice Gap*, 75–97.

24 Temkin and Krahe, *Sexual Assault & the Justice Gap*, 99–109

25 Peremptory challenges (where a potential juror can be dismissed without
reason) have been abolished in both England and Wales). England abolished
the use of these challenges in 1988. In Canada, peremptory challenges were
formerly governed by section 634 of the *Criminal Code*. However, Bill C-75
has recently eliminated the use of such challenges. Bill C-75 came into
effect September 19, 2019 so the impact of this shift remains to be seen.

26 In Canada the process is different. The accused is arraigned in front of the
entire pool of potential jurors and enters a plea. The jury pool is typically
then divided into groups of twenty. Each potential juror comes in one by
one and indicates if there is a reason that they cannot sit on the jury. In
sexual assault cases, a judge may state that if someone has been a victim of
assault themselves, this may not be an appropriate case for them to sit on as
a juror. Sometimes, people will reveal that they have been victims. However
this discussion takes place in public, which raises obvious difficulties for
someone identifying as a sexual assault victim.

27 Clare McGlynn, "Rape Trials and Sexual History Evidence: Reforming the
Law on Third-Party Evidence," *The Journal of Criminal Law*, 81,5 (2017).

28 *Criminal Code*, section 276(1). For the history behind this, see Peggy Kobly,
"Rape Shield Legislation: Relevance, Prejudice and Judicial Discretion,"
Alberta Law Review, 30,3 (1992).

29 Craig, *Trials on Trial*, 121–22.

30 See the examples in Craig, *Trials on Trial*, 46–48.

31 See for example "'Rape cases dropped' Over Police Search Demands," *BBC News*, July 23, 2019.

32 Anonymous, "My Sexual Assault Case was Dropped because I Wouldn't Hand Over my Phone," *The Guardian*, July 31, 2019.

33 *R v Ghomeshi*.

EPILOGUE

1 See for example Jennifer J Freyd, *Betrayal Trauma: The Logic of Forgetting Childhood Abuse*. (Cambridge: Harvard University Press, 2006).

2 Karyn Freedman points to the fact that unlike combat experiences that result in intense PTSD, sexual violence is experienced alone. This makes speaking up publicly all the more powerful, and frightening. Freedman, *One Hour in Paris*, 129.

3 Julie Macfarlane, "An Abuse Survivor's Tale," *Church Times*, December 11, 2015.

4 "Join-up" is an equestrian training method promoted by, among others, Monty Roberts. See Monty Roberts, *From My Hands to Yours: Lessons from a lifetime of training championship horses* (California: Monty and Pat Roberts Inc., 2002).

5 "Monty Roberts," montyroberts.com/about-monty-roberts/.

6 See for example, Lila Randall, "Woman waives anonymity to condemn evil vicar who told victims 'this is what God wants,'" *The Daily Mirror*, January 15, 2020; and Dave Battagello, "Local university professor grateful to see minister convicted of 1970s sex offences," *Windsor Star*, January 16, 2020.

7 Available on the IICSA website at: "Anglican Church Case Studies: Chichester/Peter Ball Investigation Report," *Independent Inquiry Child Sexual Abuse*, May 2019.

8 Michael Walsh received a custodial sentence for abusing a number of children, but released after two years and returned to his position in the church. Chichester church abuser 'allowed back into choir,'" *BBC*, June 27, 2017.

9 See "About Us," National Self-Represented Litigants Project, Representingyourselfcanada.com: "The National Self-Represented Litigants Project (NSRLP) builds on the National Self-Represented Litigants (SRL's) Research Study conducted by Dr Julie Macfarlane from 2011–13. The Project takes its mandate from the Final Recommendations of the Research Report: 10 Actions Steps for the SRL Phenomenon. Since 2013, the NSRLP has continued to generate energy and motivation towards serious contemplation of system change, reflecting the findings of the Research Study. The core of our work is to advocate for better and deeper understanding of the needs, motivations and challenges of self-represented litigants."

10 Griffiths was sentenced almost a month later, on February 21, 2020. I
    read my victim impact statement (available here: https://medium.com/@
    ProfJulieMac/before-the-abuse-began-i-was-a-different-person-my-victim-
    impact-statement-888b1588d983) over videolink at 6 am (given the time
    difference) from San Francisco. He was sentenced to eight years, the
    maximum possible under the law at the time of the offences.

11 See for example, Elaine Craig, "Putting Trials on Trial: Sexual Assault
    and the Failure of the Legal Profession" McGill-Queen's University Press
    2018; Elizabeth Sheehy *"Defending Battered Women on Trial: Lessons from the
    transcripts* "(Vancouver: UBC Press, 2014); and Elizabeth Sheehy, Jennie
    Abell, and Natasha Bakht *"Criminal Law and Procedure: Proof, Defences and
    Beyond* , 5th Ed (Toronto: Captus Press, 2014).

12 The assignment of percentages to different factors considered to be caus-
    ative in trauma is a common practice among some described as "experts,"
    for example Dr Tony Maden, a frequent witness for the Anglican church in
    sexual abuse cases.

13 Louise Ellison and Vanessa E. Munro, "Taking Trauma Seriously: Critical
    Reflections on the Criminal Justice Process," *International Journal of
    Evidence and Proof*, 21, 3 (2017): 184.

14 For a seminal work, see Judith Herman, *Trauma and Recovery: The Aftermath
    of Violence*, 3rd Edition (New York, Basic Books, 2015).

15 "Judicial Training in Sexual Assault Law and Social Context," Department
    of Justice, last modified February 4, 2020, www.justice.gc.ca/eng/csj-sjc/pl/
    jt-fj/index.html.

16 See Jennifer Temkin & Barbara, *Sexual Assault and the Credibility Gap: A
    Question of Attitude*, (Oregon: Hart Publishing, 2008), 53–71.

17 *Criminal* Code, section 276(1).

18 David M Tanovich, "Whack No More: Infusing Equality Into the Ethics
    of Defence Lawyering in Sexual Assault Cases," *Ottawa Law Review*, 45,3
    (2015) 495–525.

19 Ecclesiastical Insurance is the Anglican Church's insurer, with offices in
    both the UK and Canada. The "Guiding Principles" for sexual and physical
    abuse claims adopted by Ecclesiastical UK, that were negotiated in my
    civil case settlement against the church included a provision committing
    to speedy resolution where possible and the use of a JSM or joint settle-
    ment meeting. "Our Guiding Principles for the Handling of Civil Claims
    Involving Allegations of Sexual and Physical Abuse," "An Overview of the
    Claims Process," Ecclesiastical, September 2018. Ecclesiastical Canada has
    published its own "Guiding Principles" and these include a provision that
    reads: "where liability has been established . . . , Ecclesiastical will usually
    make an offer to settle the claim. Ecclesiastical may propose mediation
    with the claimant": "Abuse Claims," *Ecclesiastical*, ecclesiastical.ca/services/
    claims/abuse-claims-guiding-principles/. There is obviously a great deal

more to do in order to limit the use of discovery processes and drawn-out negotiations that re-traumatize victims.

20 Ecclesiastical Insurance (UK) provides the following guiding principles: "Our commitment to appointing joint medical experts where appropriate: Ecclesiastical recognises that requiring claimants to undergo multiple medical evaluations may cause further distress. Ecclesiastical will always consider the appropriateness of agreeing with the claimant and their advisers the instruction of a joint expert.": "Our guiding principles for the handling of civil claims involving allegations of sexual and physical abuse," *Ecclesiastical*, September 2018, www.ecclesiastical.com/documents/guiding-principles.pdf.

21 See for example US case law: *Giannecchini v Hospital of St. Raphael*, 47 Conn Supp 148, 154–61 (Sup Ct 2000), *Doe-3 v McLean City*, Unit Dist No 5 Bd of Dirs, 973 N.E.2d 880 (Ill. Sup Ct 2012). See also a discussion of the legal arguments in Julie Macfarlane, "How a Good Idea Became a Bad Idea" (forthcoming) *Cardoza Law Review*, 21 (2020).

22 See Neena Gupta, *Sexual Harassment: A Guide to Conducting Investigations* (New York: LexisNexis Butterworths, 2004), 55.

23 This needs to be recognized in negotiating collective agreement provisions between employers and employees in relation to the conduct of investigations. Collective agreements should not promote secretive investigations of sexual misconduct.

24 For example, Ontario universities and colleges are now required to report— Sexual Violence and Harassment Action Plan Act (Supporting Survivors and Challenging Sexual Violence and Harassment, 2016)—to the minister the number of times sexual violence services are accessed by students.

25 In Canada, the *Child, Youth and Family Services Act, 2017*, SO 2017, c 14, Schedule 1, section 125, requires every member of the public and professional to report any reasonable suspicion of child abuse or harm. In the UK there is no such mandatory reporting and the Independent Inquiry into Child Sexual Abuse in the UK (IICSA) is presently considering the question of mandating the Anglican Church to pass on reports of sexual abuse to police. See "Mandatory reporting of child sexual abuse—A survey of the Victims and Survivors Forum," Independent Inquiry Child Sex Abuse, April 2019.

26 "We're Only Human," Jumping Off the Ivory Tower, podcast audio, February 18, 2020 https://representingyourselfcanada.com/were-only-human/

27 For example, cautioning that any public information about sexual misconduct investigation may result in a defamation action or that talking to a victim who has signed a non-disclosure agreement about stepping forward constitutes an actionable tort. For many examples of legal over-reach in order to suppress sexual violence cases, see Farrow and Ronan, *Catch and Kill*.

28 A term widely used in professional codes of conduct for lawyers to describe the lawyer's duty to their client; see for example "Rules of Professional Conduct," Law Society of Ontario.

29 See Macfarlane, "How a Good Idea Became a Bad Idea," (forthcoming) *Cardoza Law Review*, 21 (2020).

INDEX